A MAN OF GOD is *Still* A MAN

Understanding the natural side of a spiritual man in a marital or dating relationship

By
Philemon

PHILEMON

Philio Publishing

www.philiopublishing.com

Copyright © 2014 by Philemon

All Rights Reserved. Printed in the United States of America. No part of this book may be used or reproduced in any manner whatsoever without written permission except in the case of brief quotations embodied in critical articles and reviews.

978-0-9622996-8-1

Library of Congress Control Number: 2014908840

FIRST EDITION Published 2014

Editing by Karla Joy McMechan

Cover design by Exodus Design Studios

Translations of the Holy Bible used in this book for the glory of God

NLT: Scripture quotations marked NLT are taken from the *Holy Bible, New Living Translation*, copyright ©1996, 2004, 2007, 2013 by Tyndale House Foundation. Used by permission of Tyndale House Publishers, Inc., Carol Stream, Illinois 60188. All Rights Reserved. www.tyndale.com

KJV: Scripture quotations marked KJV are taken from the *Holy Bible, King James Version* (Public Domain).

NIV: Scripture quotations marked NIV are taken from the *Holy Bible, New International Version*®, NIV®. Copyright ©1973, 1978, 1984, 2011 by Biblica, Inc.™ Used by permission of Zondervan. All rights reserved worldwide. The "NIV" and "New International Version" are trademarks registered in the United States Patent and Trademark Office by Biblica, Inc.™ www.zondervan.com

ESV: Scripture quotations marked ESV are from *The Holy Bible, English Standard Version*® (ESV®), Copyright ©2001 by Crossway Bibles, a publishing ministry of Good News Publishers. Used by permission. All rights reserved. www.crossway.org

A MAN OF GOD *is Still* A MAN

Table of Contents

Why This Book? 7
Practical vs Spiritual Advice 15
About Me 18

INTRODUCTION:
Relationship Challenges in Today's Church 25

Church Hurt 26
Renewing Your Mind? 29
Changing Times? 35
Happily Single? 38
Church Divorce 41

CHAPTER ONE: *Getting Started* 43

Attraction: the Core 44
The Powerful Force of Fears 46
Want a Godly Man? 48
Learn His Rules of Love 52
Your Past 56

CHAPTER TWO: *He's Still a Man* 59

A Secret about Men 60
Do Men Know What They Want? 64
He May See You Differently 70
Meeting His Needs 71
Divorced Man with Children 75
His Life Stage 78
Guy Brands 81
Is He Ready? 98

His Mental Operating System 102
His Global Beliefs 104
When He Leaves 106
Can He Be Honest? 111
Who's Correcting Men? 113
He Just Thinks Like a Man! 119

CHAPTER THREE: Examining Yourself 123

Are You Really Ready? 124
Good Person, Bad Mate 127
Your "Just-in-Case" Man 131
Relationship Vita 134
Honestly Sharing Too Much? 136
Traditional Mental Boxes 138
Uncertainty 141
Runaway Mind 143
Negative Thinking 146
He Can't Read Your Mind 149
Show Interest 151
Is He Enough? 153
Socially Incompatible? 155
Are You a Plus-Size Woman? 157
Strong and Independent? 160
Disrespecting-Ex Dilemma 161
Your World View 164
This Man Is So Immature! 166
Exposing a Man of God? 169

CHAPTER FOUR: Relationship Destroyers 173

Compromising and Dysfunctional Needs 174
The Love Exam 177
Shifting Communications 181
The "Not Me Too!" Syndrome? 184
Your Husband vs Your Pastor? 187
When Things Go Bad 189

No Calls Yet? 193
Teasing a Man 195
How Do You Respond? 197
Challenging His Manhood 201
He Won't Lead 204
Giving Unsolicited Advice 209
Fussy 212
Do Not Describe Your Ex 213
Your Projections 215
Your Characterizations 217
Expectations and Disappointments 218
Relationship Habits 220
Over-the-Top Behavior 222
He Is NOT Your Girlfriend 223
Mind Games 226
Vague Explanations 229
Moochers 232
Freeloading Friends 234
Meddling 236
Why He Stopped Calling 239
Cheating 244

CHAPTER FIVE: *The Bed Undefiled* 249

Let's Be Clear about Sex 250
Sexless Marriages 253
Sex Always on His Mind 255
Sexual Appetite 258
His Sexual Performance 261
It's Just Biology! 262
Godly Men Cheating? 264
Power in the Blood 269
It Hardened But Falls 272
It's Fatigue 275
Premature Ejaculation 277
Oral Sex? 280
It Doesn't Fit 282

CHAPTER SIX: Love Hints..................................285

The Truth about Love 286
The Commitment: Is He Ready?...288
Testing the Commitment..290
Find, Attract, a Man of God 292
Shifting into a Full Relationship 299
Integrating into His Life...304
So, You Really Want to Be a Pastor's Wife?...........................312
Infatuation Guilt 315
First-Date Attire..318
First-Date Environment...324
A New Normal: Women Breadwinners 329
Financial Struggles..331
Grown Son Living at Home 333
Moms with Young Children..335
Girlfriend Peer Pressure 339
Jealous Friends 341
Jesus Is Not Your Boyfriend...344
Dating and Waiting?...346
Another Perspective on Fornication.......................................350

FINAL REMARKS...................................355

Where Now?..356
Intimate Relationships: How to Evaluate? 360
Evaluation Forms: 363
My Relationship Needs? 364
Is He the Right Match for Me? 366
List of Tips 368

Why This Book?

> Genesis 2:18 NLT: *Then the LORD God said, "It is not good for the man to be alone. I will make a helper who is just right for him.*

Why this book? Why now? This book provides reasons as to why men of God behave in a certain manner, why they don't marry one woman, and why they leave or divorce another. Many of these topics are often **not addressed** in other Christian relationship books. Actually, most only cover marriages and do not assist **unmarried women** of God in understanding how to attract and keep a man of God and lead the relationship to marriage; while also learning how to keep the marriage in a blissful state. It was written and designed to be a complete source of strategies and techniques for **all** women of God seeking to learn how men of God think when they are in an intimate relationship.

One of God's first statements in Scripture was about relationships: ***It is not good for the man to be alone*** (Genesis 2:18 NLT). As important as relationships are in our lives, love skills are not taught in schools. How, where, do people learn them?

I believe that God's approach to life and relationships is the way. God's love is reflected in the image of marriage. The merging of two souls to become one flesh is just remarkable; it is designed by God. Then sexual intimacy, only allowed in God's will, places the seal of the covenant of marriage on their bond. Again, it is something special and unique. Everyone is not called to this type of relationship, but those who are should find it amazing in Christ.

Marriage in Christ should also lead to character enrichment. Our goal is to conform to the ways of Christ, but merging two lives can lead to conflict and unpleasant moments. These moments give those of us who are living for Christ a way to learn what God is refining in our character. This allows us to work through difficult issues for the evolution of our souls.

Nevertheless, and quite sadly, this is not happening, and failed marriages are as common in the church today as anywhere. Even ministers are divorcing, and many other people of faith, especially women, who are struggling to find a suitable mate.

Pastors are extremely concerned about the divorce rates in their churches, often offering marriage workshops and seminars, and even counseling. They are also providing retreats for couples to attend. This approach has helped slow down the spiraling rate of divorces within the church, but it is still very high.

It is because men and women of God are still making lots of mistakes in their relationships. Attitudes and gestures that may not be considered Christ-like behavior can still be found among members of every congregation. We all have flaws. Most will argue, some get jealous and play mind games. There are always disagreements or habits that require assessing for improvement.

So many are not clear or do not understand that **God never chooses your mate for you**. He gives you complete responsibility, but He helps you. He has given you a powerful brain to make decisions, His word to regulate those decisions, the Holy Spirit to guide you, and His anointing for discernment.

Yes, God will place you in the company of the right man or send him in your presence. However, here is a stipulation, a condition you will have to meet: **you must be fully prepared and ready**. It seems simple but so many women of faith are not, although they think that they are. God will never send a man to you in that condition. Why? Because he loves that man so much and doesn't want **YOU to hurt him** in your ill-prepared state. Men may come to you, but not the right one, until you are fully prepared and ready.

A MAN OF GOD *is Still* A MAN

Being fully prepared for marriage and having a successful marriage are simply the result of applying knowledge. Notice I said "applying." Knowledge can empower you, but only becomes powerful when it is applied.

In writing this book for women of God, my goal is edification. Isaiah 1:17 says **Learn to do well** (KJV) Also Hosea 4:6 states **My people are destroyed for lack of knowledge** (KJV). This is why, as a teacher, I want to assist women in gaining wisdom and knowledge that they can apply on how to understand the **natural side of the spiritual man** in a relationship.

I heard Dr. Mike Murdock of Wisdom Center Ministry once say, "Wisdom is the ability to recognize differences," and I totally agree, especially within relationships. This book will help women of God to recognize differences. It covers relevant topics and provides practical tips for resolving relationship issues with men of God, before and after marriage.

In this book both married and unmarried women will learn how to **speak the language of the natural side of men of God,** receiving more wisdom and clarity regarding a man's actions in a marriage or dating relationship. After all, he is still a man—not perfect, **but he wants to be understood as a man.**

You know, Paul said something that I love to use as a reason why you need this book. He said, **Not that I was ever in need, for I have learned how to be content with whatever I have** (Philippians 4:11 NLT). This scripture reminds us to look for and identify the presence of discontent in our lives, acknowledge it as sin, and seek God's grace to overcome it.

I like to pull out the word "learned" from Paul's statement. Where did he learn to be content with whatever he has? He learned it, acquired it, from experience and other resources. This is what I'm providing in this book—a resource to guide you through your own experiences, including how-to skills and knowledge to explain why some men of God have discontentment in a relationship **or built-up resentments** in their marriage, and why they may sin (e.g. **cheat),** among other things.

You may ask, "**Why this book for me, a woman of God? Why focus on women instead of men?**" As you will notice throughout this book, I truly believe in my core that women have the power to single-handedly change their marital and dating relationships.

Women often ask me, "Why are you, a man, writing about what women should do? Why don't you write a book telling men what they should do?" I really get this, but here is a fact: for 99.9% of men who call me, it is more about how to fix an issue. It surprises me that most are not interested in learning about it. They'll say, for example, "Philemon, I've tried everything. Maybe you can shed some light on how to fix it." If my response is detailed, most lose focus or interest quickly.

I love it when women call me. For them, it's all about learning why. "Why is this happening? What is he trying to say? What should I do about it?" I can send them a three-page response and every single word will get read, and then they will ask follow-up questions.

This doesn't mean that men are less interested in their relationship than women; it is just how they are wired. They are not into details on this subject and compartmentalize their lives. This is why I choose to write for women. It's an effective way to help both men and women.

Women of God who have made a good choice in selecting the right man have changed their relationship by themselves through implementing some great techniques. I will be sharing them with you, along with stories of women of God who continually make poor choices in their relationships.

This is why I am a coach and why I am writing this book. Together we can make a difference by improving dating and marital relationships in today's church.

Unmarried women of God, this book will help you wherever you are in the premarital process—dating or not, in a committed relationship or not. It will help you to understand the selection process and how to prepare yourselves for marriage. Many relationships end abruptly, just when a woman is sure "He is the one!" I will give you insights to why this happens and tools to avoid it.

Be sure to read the parts for married women, too. The seeds of issues in marriages are present in dating relationships. Learn ways to recognize these issues now and avoid planting the seeds.

Married women of God, this book will help you to increase your understanding of the man of God you married. Learn ways to smooth out any kinks within your marriage.

Be sure to read the parts for unmarried women, too, because the roots of issues in marriages are present in dating relationships. Many of the tips and techniques for them will help you to understand your man, yourself, and your relationship and how you got to where you are now.

If you are still wondering why you should read this book, just know that some how-to knowledge is missing or not clear in most Christian-based books on relationships. Also, changing societal dynamics are not addressed in them. Why? I believe for various reasons.

First, the Bible shares great romantic stories of couples facing many of the same issues seen in relationships today. We can see how couples like Jacob and Rachel, Abraham and Sarah, just to name a few, have issues with commitment, communication, anger, jealousy, among others. However, we often have to speculate on specific details, on how these biblical couples resolved their problems, and on what skill sets they used that may be helpful for you today.

Second, most of these books are addressing issues based solely on **divine order** when it comes to marriage, saying this is what we should do. However, there are things actually occurring in relationships and marriages of people in the church today that are

NOT addressed in these other books. Too many households are operating outside of divine order, e.g., households in which men are NOT actually serving as the head as such. Are we to ignore these occurrences?

Lastly, some Christian writers simply avoid writing about the sexual improprieties that are going on in the church.

I won't hold back here. The world today promotes a self-centered, pleasure-seeking perspective on morality and sex: "If it feels good, do it. If it makes you happy, go for it." One can preach until blue in the face, and it won't stop sexual weakness in the church. You hear the rumors about some, while others hide it very well—but it is still happening. I will not get off into what you ought to or ought not to be doing. You already know right from wrong. I will address how things are actively operating in the lives and relationships of some people of faith nowadays and provide proven, effective, ways to resolve the issues.

The final reason for my writing this book is that women in the church **get hurt** often in marriages and while dating. I hate seeing this and want to assist in protecting hearts. Therefore, this book provides proven strategies women can use to protect themselves and avoid being hurt.

Some of you Christian women may find some of these strategies difficult to understand when you first read about them. If you bear with me, I will explain how they can help you find and maintain a loving, Christian, marital or dating relationship in these changing times. I will also make it clear how simple men are to understand and why I believe that women have the power to get what they want if they harness their power. I will teach you how in this book.

A man of God is still a man. He wants the woman who wins his heart to understand his natural side. Men have just as many difficulties meeting that special woman of God as women have finding men of God. Just for the record, men also get hurt just as often as women and have difficulties getting over broken relationships, too. A man is also left picking up the pieces of his heart. He will submerge himself in Scripture and prayer hoping to feel better. Some men also do other (sometimes stupid) things to deal with relationship hurt.

I would say that, yes, it is easier for most men to get over a past hurt than it is for women. This is only because a pool of more prepared women of God is readily available for him to date and marry in the church today. This is not the case for women of God in the Church. I know it's hard to accept this, but it is the truth.

I've heard so many women say, "He says he is a man of God, but he was a jerk with me. Yet, he married sister so-n-so right after our break-up. Why couldn't he marry me?"

My response: "Was he actually a jerk, or did you expect him to be flawless? Maybe you called mistakes or habits 'bad behavior.'"

You see, some women tolerate flaws because they understand that a man's flaws have nothing to do with how he actually treats her in the relationship. Such a woman will understand that there are some things she may not like about him, just as there are things he may not like about her. This will not stop her from being loving towards him. She will know how he wants to be treated because she took the time to learn. He, in turn, will find her to be the woman he has prayed for and cannot live without. If he is in the right stage, he will marry her.

I believe strongly that, when a woman uses her power—such as the classic "dropping-the-handkerchief" effect, along with solid wisdom, she can become the woman he cannot live without. She will understand that everything most men do can be considered positioning just to impress a woman and become her super hero. By learning to have an approving spirit towards all men, a woman becomes her personal best and lays the foundation for finding the godly man just right for her.

While reading this book, just think in terms of possibilities. Clear your mind of your past views and experiences and of what you have seen from maybe your parents, friends, other church members, in social media posts (Facebook) or other books. There is no way around what must be done for a successful relationship:

applying God's principles within your relationship, learning research-based skills, and having the right attitude of focusing on giving instead of receiving. You also need to know how to navigate through bad situations in your marriage and relationship leading to marriage because things will go wrong from time to time.

Women of God who capture the attention of men have a few things in common:

- They are not confused by the meaning of Proverbs 18:22 and understand and implement the law of proximity, something I teach in my coaching practice.
- They take full responsibility for their own feelings.
- They truly apply Mark 12:31, **Love your neighbor as yourself.** This translates into having a "love-all-men" attitude.
- They are not negative about men in general and always find what is good in every man they meet, regardless of physical attraction.
- These women's airspace commands respect while still alerting men of God that it is safe for landing.

Guess what? You can be that woman from this point on. You can be the one "he findeth." By reading this book, developing new skills, and using the tools offered, you will have the confidence and capability of knowing men. You will be able to find and attract the one who is right for you because you will know what really goes on in his head.

Practical vs Spiritual Advice

Is some of the advice provided in this book spiritual in nature? Yes. Is some of it practical? Yes. Are both the practical and spiritual sides aligned with Scripture? Yes!

I offer this book to you as a bridge that will help you in understanding the natural side of a spiritual man in a marital relationship or in a dating relationship leading to marriage. I believe this is the best way to achieve lasting, loving, spiritually based marriages in Christian communities today. It will take an acceptance and understanding of our human, practical side, that it may be aligned with our spiritual side and with Scripture.

As a Relationship Coach and a Christian, I am often faced with a few challenges in dealing with believers who make a distinction between being spiritual and being practical. They deem the "practical" as something "unspiritual and man-made;" something that should not be followed. This includes information from research models that I find useful for assisting in understanding their relationship issues.

Actually, these research models are based on solid findings and not on someone's opinion. They have been proven as reliable after careful studies and peer reviews, including, for example, information about different attachment styles, how our behavior changes at different stages of our life (e.g. when a couple has a child), how our needs affect our psychology, and more.

I do understand believers' concerns for not allowing anything to disconnect them from God. I always assure them that anything I accept as true and useful is also godly. That is, I make sure that the practical sources I use are aligned with Scripture, the spiritual side.

For example, the Book of Colossians, especially 2:20-23, is often given as a guide for evaluating the practical vs the spiritual and rejecting non-biblical sources. However, after discussing this with pastors and Bible scholars, I find it serves as an excellent source on how to evaluate any teaching in order to make sure it is aligned with Scripture.

Let's take a look at Colossians 2, verses 21-22, reading from the King James Version:

(Touch not; taste not; handle not; Which all are to perish with the using;) after the commandments and doctrines of men?

Operating from the principles of Isaiah: **learn to do well**, we must know that words have meaning. The word **perish** in this verse means "to destroy." The word **using** has to do with the "misuse of something," and **doctrines** means "what is taught." If research models regarding marital and dating relationships provide intrinsic value, it will not be applying or using information that will destroy, because what's being taught will enhance one's life and relationship. It will not promote sin or disconnect them from the Word of God.

When applying this to clients' relationships, often I show them how their behavior affects them spiritually, and how the practical information from a particular research model can help them to improve their life spiritually. Together we take a look at Colossians 3:12-14 (NIV) which states the following:

Therefore, as God's chosen people, holy and dearly loved, clothe yourselves with compassion, kindness, humility, gentleness and patience. Bear with each other and forgive one another if any of you has a grievance against someone. Forgive as the Lord forgave you. And over all these virtues put on love, which binds them all together in perfect unity.

When behavior is presented as being unkind or without humility or gentleness or a display of not being patient, the imbalances within their practical knowledge of how to resolve this directly affects their spiritual life. We simply need to balance our practical and spiritual knowledge, accepting that which brings value and not fighting to separate the two. We need both the practical and the spiritual in order to "do well" in accord with Scripture. As you read the practical information I am including in this book, just know this is designed to balance out your spiritual knowledge.

When a believer approaches me, saying, "I need some spiritual advice about my relationship and a scripture that will fix my problems," I listen carefully. Most of the time, I find that their issues involve a lack of knowledge or skills that resulted in the undesired behavior that is manifesting itself in their life. Something practical and measurable is affecting their marital or dating relationship. Whereas I do believe that we should search God's Word for insights on dealing with all matters in our life, I also follow the scripture **Learn to do well** and accept wisdom that has value to our spiritual and natural life, even if it comes from more practical, research-based models. As said earlier, I always make sure that the sources I use are aligned with Scripture.

About Me

I am certified as a strategic interventionist, marriage educator, and relationship and strategy coach and mentor with a strong Christian foundation. My work involves taking my clients from where they are to where they want to be in their marriage or relationship, their life, or their business.

As a constant student in this area, I have spent the last fifteen years of my life devoted to relationship-improvement methods. I've coached many women of God, providing love lessons and assisting them in understanding men. Even though the study of relationships has been my passion, I've received my degrees in the area of Business. While this background has certainly helped me in running my own businesses and in coaching people about business, more importantly, it gives me a deeper understanding of what it takes to be a breadwinner in today's world.

My training as a coach includes certifications in Christian Relationship Coaching, providing strategies for helping people of faith. However, the most useful tools for helping people improve their relationships have come from my training as a Strategic Interventionist with a focus on marriage education and divorce prevention from the Robbins Madanes Training Center for Strategic Intervention (RMT). This powerful school of coaching with Anthony (Tony) Robbins and Dr. Cloé Madanes offers groundbreaking strategies that incorporate human-needs psychology and other high-quality disciplines, including Ericksonian therapy, strategic family-therapy, organizational psychology, neuro-linguistics, psychology of influence, strategic studies, traditions of diplomacy and negotiation, and much more.

I have also completed training in other useful areas: "Bridging the Couple Chasm, Gottman Couples Therapy: A New Research-Based Approach," a workshop for clinicians from The Gottman Institute; Neuro-Linguistic Programming, a great tool for changing or eliminating undesired behaviors; Transactional Analysis, Spiral Dynamics, Archetypes Coaching, and Matrix Therapies and have completed training from many other coaching or "change agent" and relationship programs. Again, it has been critical for me to ensure that all of my training aligns perfectly with Scripture, with the goal in improving others, and with my walk in Christ.

My research into men and their relationships began informally in the year of 2000. I began writing about relationships in late 2001-2002 for a promotional, online, email newsletter distributed monthly to over one hundred thousand members. The feedback from those articles was simply amazing. I have continued this research throughout the years and am using many of the findings in this book.

I am married to a wonderful woman who loves and supports my work.

Why I Can Help You, a Woman of God?

I am a Christian and a pastor's son (PK=Preacher Kid) who believes in the biblical approach to marriage and relationships. Educated at a Christian university, I have remained a constant student in the area of relationships and human development.

On the light side, it may also help to have been given the biblical name "Philemon" by my parents, which was hard to spell and pronounce growing up.

My father was a faithful member and teacher in the Baptist church until I was around twelve years old and then served as pastor (Bishop) in a Pentecostal non-denominational church. My mother served as pastor's wife (first-lady), missionary, and church counselor.

Our parents raised me and my sisters and brother in the ministry, nurturing us and teaching us how to be productive citizens who serve God. My father set an amazing example as a husband and in manhood, ensuring that his two sons know what it means to be a man and the head of a household.

I lost my mother to breast cancer two days after Christmas in 2005. She was my best friend and I think of her every day. She taught me how to love people for who they are and always sought to help the helpless. I simply just miss her.

As we were growing up, dad would make my siblings and I write weekly reports on the book of Proverbs. I have to admit that I dreaded doing this and talking with him about what I learned—I wanted to play outside. However, I can see now that Proverbs has been a guiding source of principles for me ever since. Whenever seeking proven knowledge for clarity, if Scripture is somewhat silent on a subject, I will default to Proverbs 18:15 (NLT), *Intelligent people are always ready to learn. Their ears are open for knowledge.*

As a pastor's son, I saw inside hundreds of church marriages and relationships that were supposedly based on biblical principles. I grew up with these burning questions inside me, troubling me:

- Why, I wondered, would a particular pastor or minister date his secretary, pick up prostitutes, and even spread deadly diseases to women in the church?
- Why would others do drugs, steal from the family, or even molest a child?
- How could a man of God force his family to live in such low standards that the entire family died from carbon monoxide poisoning due to his belief that God did not want him to have a job, but to be a full-time preacher?

I truly believe God has given me answers to these burning questions and helped me to understand the system of thinking that leads men of God to such behaviors. Yes, they sinned (showed ignorance of scripture), but I've learned why such men go against their own rules and beliefs and those in Scripture. I will share this with you in this book.

Additionally, Why I Can Help You?

I have made my own mistakes in relationships. Divorced after thirteen years of marriage, I totally understand what my shortcomings were as a man and am using the knowledge gained through this experience to help others. I remained divorced for six years and know firsthand what it is like to be out in this new, Christian, dating climate. Therefore, I understand very well the challenges of the Christian dating scene right now.

And finally, I have come to understand men of God through my research. In the last few years I've interviewed, questioned, and interacted with hundreds of them in a "What Men Really Want" social media research group. From this I can provide you with a perspective that maybe you have not considered.

There are a lot of relationship do's and don'ts circulating these days. There are hundreds of blogs and Christian dating sites online, many reality shows on match-making on TV, and books (seemingly being published every month) on understanding men, saving your marriage, and online dating. All of this available relationship information can be overwhelming and is often contradictory.

What I do know is that there are exceptions to every theory or concept written. Some unconventional methods may work even if they are not supposed to. But look at it this way: A broken clock is always right at least twice a day. Yes, "the exceptions" have worked before; but I still believe it is best to stick with sound principles while being flexible.

Just know that every strategy you read about may not work on your husband or person of interest, whereas sometimes a non-traditional approach will. This is why I say to be flexible. This is true for all of the tips in this book: Being flexible will serve you well. Keep your mind open and spiritual.

So, What Does Work?

I'll share a little right now. Well, for certain, the ability to be vulnerable works, along with cultivating relationship skills and being

authentic. Are you this way? If so, then these statements are true about you:
- You are an individual who understands your core gifts. Not talents, but what you believe deeply in and are passionate about. (Although, you may be afraid to speak about them or allow them to show up in your life.)
- You know what your needs are, that they will change based on where you are in life, and that these requirements are based on something deeper than just attraction.
- You are clear on your values and know your rules.
- You understand that it is not about finding the right man to marry, but being the right woman.

In other words, you must have a clear picture of who you are and what is currently motivating or influencing your choices. This is more easily said than done. But if you pray and put in the necessary personal work, your chances of meeting and settling down with that great guy is one hundred times better and can happen. On top of this, you will simply have a great life.

This is why I believe that everyone needs a coach or mentor to help them discover their hidden needs, relationship readiness level, and values. These love-lesson skills are not easily attainable, because they are not taught in school, although they are necessary.

Relationships have become a hot and booming industry even in the church, especially the how-to-attract-and-keep-a-man segment. It seems that everyone is writing books and speaking on relationships—from ministers and college professors to engineers and anyone who believes that their title places them in a position to speak about relationships.

It seems that everyone is an expert or guru now, and I will never be negative about anyone's relationship advice. It is so encouraging that many are focusing on relationship improvement methods. My only concern is that I noticed that several gurus usually provide only one-size-fits-all type of advice. I like to call this "retail-relationship advice." This approach often does not get to the core of a particular relationship problem. Why? Because all of the facts are not being collected. This concerns me and can be hazardous when it sends a person away with a flawed action plan.

How Am I Different?

What makes me different from some relationship coaches or gurus in this relationship industry? I'm not sure, but I do know that we all have our approaches; I can only share my perspective. However I do listen to lots of TV and radio shows with relationship gurus as guests. Some of the responses and answers to viewers and listeners are often quite incomplete, maybe due to time constraints. I say this because I've received calls from clients watching or listening who are confused regarding what steps to take in their personal situation based on what they heard. Therefore when I think about how I'm different, three things come to mind.

First, I know that I am a devoted student of marital-and dating-relationship dynamics and have taken advantage of a broad spectrum of the training available in this field.

Second, I do not believe in giving quick one-size-fits-all relationship advice. To be really effective in a person's life regarding their relationship, I have to truly understand their world and history before evaluating issues and suggesting solutions. Therefore, I am big on assessments to collect information and like to begin by asking probing questions.

Third, unlike coaches who act as if they are perfect in their relationships, I am willing to put on the table that, although I am a man of God, have relationship skills, and have coached others; I make relationship mistakes just like other men. For example, not always recognizing my conversation tones, being easily distracted and not listening at times, being a little messy around the house, and not following through as I should. I can sometimes become angry or raise my voice and see my relationship skills go out the window for a brief moment.

This is human nature and no one is perfect in their relational skills one hundred percent of the time. But, because of my skills, what I do have is **awareness**, a very important relationship skill. This is why my outbursts are few and far between and **extremely brief**. You see, it always kicks in, alerting me to re-evaluate the situation.

That said; just know that experts do not always have it together. Many are not in a relationship, have been divorced so many times that it's hard to count, or have been married so long that they have forgotten what it is like to date. It doesn't mean that you shouldn't listen or learn from them. Just be alert to their strengths and weaknesses and recognize that this thing called "relationship" is just not easy. A happy, life-long, relationship requires constant work and daily practice to ensure life-long success.

Before tagging a subject as "how men think" or "from a male perspective," I look for synchronicity between myself and other men who have faced some of the same experiences and issues. I like hearing them make the same observation that I have, before using it as a generalization.

Through my research I have discovered not only the similarities between men and the concepts they agree on, but also the differences between them. It shows how differently men think depending upon their current life stage, relationship pattern, and personal experiences. Women who can get a basic understanding of men can learn how to handle them. In other words, they learn how to speak men.

Reading and applying the lessons and techniques in this book will help you understand the natural side of the spiritual man in a marital or dating relationship. And it will become clear to you why that special man of God in your life becomes detached or even steps away, what you can do to avoid this from happening, and how to become the woman he cannot live without. Let's lay a little foundation regarding some challenges in the next few topics.

INTRODUCTION:

Relationship Challenges in Today's Church

TIP There are men out there who are living holy and faithful to God's word. They are NOT to be placed on a pedestal, because they do make mistakes, although often unknowingly. It will not be where these men of God live at their core.

They just want to do God's will and purpose in their lives. They love God and the life of living holy.

I honor these men.

Just know that these men are still men, too. They react to the same issues in their marriages and relationships that face any other man in society.

Church Hurt

> 2 Corinthians 12:9 NLT: *Each time he said, "My grace is all you need. My power works best in weakness." So now I am glad to boast about my weaknesses, so that the power of Christ can work through me.*

The quality of our lives is directly tied to the quality of our relationships. With this in mind, there is nothing like church hurt. People are more vulnerable in church because they have such high expectations of being treated a certain way, a better way.

Church hurt can come from many directions, but the primary source is in our relationships with others in the church, our lack of getting along. It can come from dating, or disagreements, or terrible issues occurring within families or marriages.

Can I be honest? I've been hurt in the church myself and have seen lots of other people hurt, too. Some lose their moral compass using the story of being hurt in the church, as if this hurt is a license to allow dark emotions to take over their life. Some lose their love for others, destroy their bodies with substance abuse, or become resentful, angry, or sexually promiscuous. It baffles me because this approach is like drinking poison yourself, then waiting for church folks to die for hurting you.

A relationship with God is personal. A church is a building for public worship and social gatherings with the purpose of giving encouragement to believers. Scripture didn't make it any more than that, we did. As the Lord said to Paul, **My grace is all you need.**

My power works best in weakness (2 Corinthians 12:9 NLT).

How do we deal with being hurt on the job, at school, beauty or barbershop, or at the grocery store? We either find a replacement or report it to someone we believe will be better. Church hurt is VERY real, but just like any other hurt, we must learn to move on while never losing our spiritual character or relationship with God.

Don't get me wrong, moving on doesn't always mean leaving a church. You can just move away from the situation or from the people causing the pain. Sometimes staying to navigate the issues is a way to grow because God is enlarging you to have more confidence and/or to enhance you spiritually.

I often hear in the church the expression "**enlarge my territory**." Many have equated this to mean personal success, e.g. opportunities, money, more things; but I believe one should want their spirit and knowledge to be enlarged, since these are more fulfilling. Most of the time when we use a phrase like this (and I will also add the phrase "**highly favored**") it is to meet our basic human need for worthiness or significance. It is saying, "Look at what God is doing for me," sending a subtle message, "but NOT for you."

Sometimes you will hear people say or insinuate, "Maybe if you give God more time, or give more offering, he will do the same for you. Or this: "His/her life is not blessed, because he/she disobeyed God." Some in the church never know how this can cause hurt.

Even if a church member is truly sincere when standing up to give testimony about a blessing they received, some in the church could wrongly perceive them as bragging or subtly degrading them. People are sensitive to such things when their life is not going as desired. They often believe others are throwing low blows at them.

You may be approached by one of these hurt individuals. If you are sincere, then respond to them in love and not by rising up against them for confronting you. I know the Bible says in Ephesians 4:26 that you can be angry, but sin not. However, if you rise up at your brother or sister because they approached you, it is violating Galatians 6:1 which says . . . ***you who are godly should gently and humbly help that person back onto the right path.***

And be careful not to fall into the same temptation yourself
(NLT). Getting upset yourself is matching fire with fire. This scripture also helps in any relationship.

Yes, church hurt is real. But it can be as simple as making a choice. We can choose to embrace the hurt, become a victim of "Why me?" or treat the wounds and set boundaries if necessary, so that the hurt doesn't become spiritually life threatening.

While on this subject, I feel it is imperative to discuss next how our thinking and suppressed emotions affect our relationships in and out of the church.

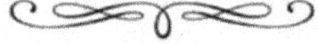

Renewing Your Mind?

> Romans 12:2 NLT: *Don't copy the behavior and customs of this world, but let God transform you into a new person by changing the way you think. Then you will learn to know God's will for you, which is good and pleasing and perfect.*

We are often told via sermons or reading the Bible that we must renew our minds. Although I'm using mostly the New Living Translation in this book, I grew up reading the King James version, and this passage has been indelibly impressed on my mind,

> **I beseech you therefore, brethren, by the mercies of God, that ye present your bodies a living sacrifice, holy, acceptable unto God, which is your reasonable service.**
>
> **And be not conformed to this world: but be ye transformed by the renewing of your mind, that ye may prove what is that good, and acceptable, and perfect, will of God.** (Romans 12: 1-2)

I've heard many explanations about what this means exactly and how to do it. In addition, I've noticed how much this interpretation has affected the lives of godly people in their relationships and walk with Christ. Many preachers and teachers will have their own unique perspective.

I won't tell you how to interpret this scripture, but will share what has resonated with me. After studying the Bible, it became extremely clear to me what God's original intent for mankind was before the great fall in Eden. The first words of Jesus reinforce God's intent, when he said, **Repent**, [i.e., change your mind or thinking] *for the kingdom of heaven is at hand.* (Matthew 4:17 KJV) The original translation for "at hand" was "arrived or is here." I can go a lot deeper because this can be a book within itself.

From my studies I've learned that "renewing our minds" means to have a shift in consciousness and returning to the original mindset that we had before the fall from grace by Adam and Eve. This was a mind that loved and honored God with a clear understanding of man's rightful place: a proxy on this earthly domain under God's sovereign Kingdom rule. Not to just buy fire insurance by getting saved and waiting for this great bye and bye in heaven. Salvation is part of the message and paramount since the great fall of Eden, but He also wants his children to rule this earth under HIS governance.

All the miracles performed by Jesus, such as healing the sick, raising the dead, feeding a multitude with so little, walking on water, and calming a storm with these words, **Peace, be still**—this was Jesus demonstrating the truth that God's Kingdom had come to earth. He preached the Good News of the Kingdom and taught about life within it and, when people simply responded to him in faith, He demonstrated the impact, power, and authority of God's Kingdom on not just the spirit, but human life and the environment. This is such a powerful message.

In addition, I've learned that becoming a living sacrifice is NOT conforming to a worldview perspective that rejects God and His revelation, in essence taking an unbeliever's approach to His Word. In this scripture the word "world" refers to the spirit of the age, i.e., current social norms and values. God's kingdom is NOT a democracy. If the spirit of the age goes against God's Word, we are to reject these norms.

When living in this world, there is some adjusting we must do, whether we think so or not. I believe this is why so many of God's people are confused and conflicted. Morality changes over time. Because of new information, it is not constant. But **the Bible does**

not change. Sometimes we adjust to social norms. For example, we are not killing people for adultery, as in John 8:3-11; we are not killing our children by stoning them to death if they talk back, as in Deuteronomy 21:18-21; and we do NOT believe in slavery, as in Ephesians 6:5 or 1 Timothy 6:1-4.

It is argued that believers often pick and choose what they will adjust to. However, I'm not sure if this argument is solid as such. As a believer, if the Bible teaches something directly, most look at it as binding authority. Some Bible commands and examples are clear, easy to understand and apply. Some are more difficult to understand; they may not be as clear and not as easy to apply. The key is to take your rightful place in the kingdom to find God's perfect will for your life. You must learn to take rule of your life and dominate in your domain here on earth, as God originally intended under his governance. He wants you to stop letting things on this earth dominate you i.e., food, money, ignorance, drugs, sex… because you are a King's child and should act in that manner. Take a look at Psalms 115:16 and Genesis 1:26 that state: *God gave the earth to man to rule*.

But some still find this difficult because of some preacher's and teacher's interpretation of God's word. If Bible commands are difficult or not understood, this sometimes creates more problems. This is because believers who **read the Bible with understanding** can see some changes from the past, and it may bring about a question, "If we changed for this, why not change for that?" This, too, can be another book within itself. Many have become frustrated because they can see the state and condition of the church nowadays due to sin and weakness and because of a lack of knowledge.

As we deal with renewing the mind, I like to take this a little further based on my experience and training. If one is to adjust their mind, it is also just as important for one to understand how the mind works. If we learn how to balance light and dark emotions in order to get the lessons they have to teach, this will be paramount in our spiritual development instead of causing frustrations and conflicts.

You see, the mind is a biological network that recognizes and identifies patterns of events in one's life and reacts. Signals are sent triggering emotions that instantly decide your state and adjust your behavior accordingly. Understanding this can assist in acquiring godly emotional fitness. I don't want to go any deeper because this could also be another book, but understanding the way the mind works can explain patterns of behavior.

I can only share my experiences. When coaching those who love God, I've noticed that there is often a lot of guilt and fear associated with their religious beliefs. It is a fear of being punished by God and a feeling of guilt for not living up to their religious, cultural, principles. I would hear things like: "I'm sick or not doing well because I'm out of God's will especially in my thoughts.

When digging deeper, I notice that there is a pattern of scary, dark, emotions such as guilt, grief, fear, resentment, confusion and despair that show up in the lives of these God-fearing people. It's like this internal emotional war between their overall well-being and the strong need to suppress these emotions because of the importance of abiding by their religious faith. I believe this is why so many faithful lack fulfillment in their lives and why some are suffering with all types of conditions in their body, including weight gain from stress and feeling tired all the time among other things.

For one, I've learned that definitions must be examined closely because many struggle with issues that come to mind suddenly and cause them to suffer. For example, many people of faith are troubled, feeling guilty or confused about the meaning of "lust" in the scripture Matthew 5:28 (NLT), **But I say, anyone who even looks at a woman with lust has already committed adultery with her in his heart.**

It's not a look, but "a look with lust" that constitutes lust. The dictionary defines lust as "an intense or unrestrained sexual craving," or "an overwhelming desire or craving." Lust is not just one thought, as some believe. Thoughts of attraction, appreciating a good-looking woman, can occur and can be dismissed quickly without sinning. But if one has an intense or overwhelming craving thought, this can constitute lust. Therefore, feeling guilty about a single thought is unwarranted in my opinion.

In many church environments there is this tendency by peers and some leaders to suggest that members avoid distasteful emotions. The faithful are encouraged to escape the dark ones, rather than to pay attention to them. There is this need to tell them to pray away or get into the Word in order to renew their mind, as if this will be a quick fix. I've learned that doing so can change the state of a person in that moment, and they will have words to challenge those thoughts. However, as a coach helping others to get where they want to be in their lives and relationships while serving God, I understand that the issues will still not be resolved until they have faced the lessons.

How does this affect relationships, one's ability to find a suitable mate, and the marriages of people of faith? It can have a drastic effect! It can explain things ranging from why someone is NOT married to sexual sins.

We all have an instinctive, unconscious mind—a sacred gift from God. We also have a conscious mind—a faithful servant. Often the church culture honors the servant and has forgotten the gift.

Emotions are part of the unconscious mind. They are an essential part of the body's wisdom that God has given us. Because it is not encouraged, most of us seldom experience our negative emotions completely when in tune with what we are feeling. If we learn how to listen to them, the dark emotions can be our greatest spiritual teachers. They will serve us by creating more passion for our mates and by helping us to get other things done in life, serving God to the fullest.

During troubled times, peace of mind is the best protection. We have to learn what the dark emotions are trying to teach us. Only then can we be graced with the peace we seek in life. Doing so will help us to grow in our love and compassion for ourselves and others. There is no shortcut to a totally fulfilled life. There are great lessons to be learned to help us get there and have better relationships. I believe that we have to embrace what is there and to learn about our mind in order to renew it, rather than suppressing emotions because we feel that they disconnect us from God. When, in essence, they are there trying to teach us something so we can get closer to Him.

The key is learning how to develop your emotions to become fit to a point that they serve you instead of frightening you.

Here is a strategy for you to use right now: Search within to see if there are any particular emotions that you resist or avoid feeling. Choose one emotion at a time. Next, write a letter to that feeling. Simply express why you are struggling to accept it. Then you will have a specific prayer to ask God for guidance.

Changing Times?

> Ephesians 5:23 NLT: *For a husband is the head of his wife as Christ is the head of the church. He is the Savior of his body, the church.*

Times are changing; this is troubling to some believers. One big issue for them is the husband's role as **the head of his wife**. In the Bible Paul says this quite clearly to both the Ephesians and the Corinthians. But nowadays, there is a lot of resistance to this order. Women often say that this scripture refers only to domestic issues, things related to the home. It has a lot to do with women's relationship with money now that they are earning more.

This spirit-of-the-age concept must be acknowledged because many women are rejecting this authority, stating that women are equal to men. A man can get into a lot of trouble if he disagrees publicly; women's groups will have his head. As I stated in the last section, we believers have adjusted to some social norms. If we are honest, we admit that we pick and choose which orders to adjust to. However, this particular biblical statement, **For a husband is the head of his wife as Christ is the head of the church** . . . (Ephesians 5:23 NLT) is deemed binding authority by traditionalists who are NOT willing to adjust to it.

Why are some women uncomfortable saying that men have authority over them? Well, men used to be the primary earners, but not anymore and probably NEVER again. Many women feel that a true leader, the true head of a family, will be earning more money than other family members. Many families are in this situation. As a result, they are adjusting their perceptions for these changing times and this troubles traditionalists.

This new social-statistical dilemma is affecting marriages. Although many feel that adjusting to it is going directly against binding authority; and yet, it is happening. Why? Well women now make up forty percent of the breadwinners in society and in some communities, e.g. among African Americans, it is even greater. This is because the barriers to success for women have dropped; women are being hired at a faster rate than men and are making more money. This is affecting the stability of marriages.

The man of the house is no longer the person bringing home all of the money to support his family. His wife now shares in that responsibility. Therefore, a man serving as the sole provider of a family is becoming virtually obsolete. It is the reason why some megachurches specifically target their ministries to these high-earning women.

It is true that statistics show that men still make more than women. What it does not factor in is their take-home pay. A large percentage of men are divorced with children and making child support payments and some, alimony. In these cases, a man may bring home much less than his spouse. In addition, many women have kids and receive child support payments, therefore earning even more money.

What has this done to the psyche of men? A lot, but it is more difficult for men who think in terms of tradition. Many older ministers believe that men of today are weak and don't operate under divine order. They don't like what they are seeing today. They don't believe that their wives should work and earn more money, and some preach on this subject. However, many in their congregation who fit this category are not in the financial position to make this happen.

Let's be honest. Although some men in the church do not desire to have a stay-at-home spouse, most do desire this, but it is really not practical anymore, unless they are willing to lower their standard of living drastically. Sometimes it is a matter of safety, too, because your income can determine your zipcode. This makes it increasingly difficult for a man of God who believes higher earnings are tied to being the head of the house. He will feel as if it can't be the case. Why? Because his wife is making more money and he feels that his role has diminished.

This can also keep a man of God from marrying a woman if he feels there is no way she would allow him to be her head, because of her financial position. This book will address this issue too.

The Bible is solid on the role of the husband in a marital relationship. Although some women believers are adjusting this to changing times and applying it to the domestic setting alone, we know that the Bible has not changed. Just as with any other attempt at communication, many people can read or hear the same words, yet there will be many different interpretations of what was said, or meant, or intended.

Apart from this, what can and what has to be adjusted is the relationship that both men and women have with money. **Divine-order marriages work. However, it must be done properly in today's climate.** A man in a divine-order marriage will make those sacrifices for his family and be a true provider and protector.

Times have changed most of all for women of God who are unmarried but no longer under the care and supervision of their father. Most are living independently, supporting themselves, making all of their own decisions, while waiting and watching for that special man of God. No wonder it is so difficult for women these days to submit in the same way as women in biblical times who had never worked outside the home.

Let's look at their situation next, in "Happily Single?"

Happily Single?

Do you consider yourself "single" just because you are unmarried? **I don't!** I dislike using "single" in this way, especially for women of God. I understand that this word is ingrained in our culture to describe unmarried people and I'm not nitpicking. I just believe that we should reconsider because of the power this word has on one emotionally. For one, it connotes something negative to most and creates self-hatred, a feeling of hurt and rejection, in those not understanding its true meaning. To be "single" actually means that you are unique, the only one. In fact, we are all single individuals. We are each unique. Many confuse being single with being alone or unattached, i.e. "mateless."

I believe that, even if we are married, we are still unique. The essence of many problems in relationships today is that most people don't see themselves as worthy or unique, thereby creating deeper issues. It is important for each of us to lose this negative perspective regarding singleness and put all of our efforts into becoming the best, single, individual we can be. Married or not, celebrate your singleness!

But I don't deny the pain you feel when yearning for a marital partner to love. Consider this:

Your sister in Christ shares with you, or stands up in church and testifies that God has blessed her with the man of her dreams. She is soon to be married. You rejoice with her, giving praises to God. However, if you are honest, in a silent moment, there is a feeling or pressing question that you ponder: *What about me? When is my time, God?*

Maybe you will wonder, *Will I ever meet the man God has for me?* Sometimes, you may think *I know I'm before God just as much as any other person and even more than her, but she is getting married and not me.*

Some may become frustrated because they allowed doubt to enter their hearts; and some put on a good face, pretending to be happy—the cycle continues.

Philippians 4:6-7 NLT assures us

> ***Don't worry about anything; instead, pray about everything. Tell God what you need, and thank him for all he has done. Then you will experience God's peace, which exceeds anything we can understand. His peace will guard your hearts and minds as you live in Christ Jesus.***

Therefore, the key out of your frustration is to have peace about your current status—in essence, be happy in Christ. Happy-though-unattached women of God are visible, not so much verbal. **While waiting, prepare yourself!**

The first thing to do is to seek God to discover the vision and purpose he has for your life. What are you supposed to be doing? Your natural-born strengths will be a starting point and easily discoverable via aptitude tests for strengths and weaknesses (available online). I've learned that your purpose is always aligned with your natural strengths, but many people have never thought of this.

Once you discover your purpose and vision, **God will place you on the path of finding the mate whose vision complements yours and aligns with it.** However, you must first develop the skills to know how to navigate this process when relating to a potential husband. This book will teach you how.

Lack of preparation is the greatest plague I observe among the women-in-waiting who come to me for relationship coaching. I believe that God works for His children to the capacity of their understanding and skills, meaning if they have the wisdom to notice differences. Therefore, if you are not clear about your requirements or vision, or do not understand how attraction works or about men in general, how can God bless you with a spouse? You are NOT ready! In biblical times **marriages were arranged**; today, it requires **preparation** and acquiring how-to **skills**.

Precious women-in-waiting, again, men of God are still men and the attraction process works the same. They respond to confidence, the best you, femininity, a great attitude, and an approving spirit. Just because you love God does not mean that you know how to be a good mate or how to attract a man.

I've asked several men of God who have recently selected wives. "Why did you pick her?" After stating how much these women loved God, everything else was about qualities that attract men in general, period.

Therefore, I urge you women of God to have peace about your unmarried status while you are making preparations. A godly man seeks a quality woman who is godly. Let your qualities shine visibly in your walk. Lay off the verbal rah-rah things you say or do to gain support from other poorly prepared women-in-waiting. This kind of preparation is the key.

Discrimination is also a key. How to know when the attraction, the chemistry you feel is lasting? Attraction is emotional, not rational, so be alert and take it slowly. When you feel "carried away," "swept off your feet," "blown away" by the chemistry between you, read the section "Infatuation Guilt" (Chapter Six) and see if you can answer the questions on the forms at the end of this book.

 Requirements and deal breakers often go out the window when there is chemistry in a relationship. This is why attraction is emotional and not rational.

Infatuation taken as the real thing leads to something no one wants: A bad relationship or Church Divorce.

Church Divorce

Malachi 2:16 NLT: *For I hate divorce!" says the* LORD, *the God of Israel. "To divorce your wife is to overwhelm her with cruelty," says the* LORD *of Heaven's Armies. "So guard your heart; do not be unfaithful to your wife."*

Is the divorce rate in the church about the same as in the world? Yes, it is—with a caveat: It depends on whether couples are seriously and faithfully following religious behaviors and attitudes. If they understand that love means sacrifice, then divorce among these faithful units is extremely low compared to national statistics.

Notice I said lower and **not** non-existent. Why do couples divorce? Why do women who are faithful to God have difficulties finding mates? It all has to do with the dynamics of life: taking actions without thinking, or thinking without taking actions. I believe it can be attributed to changing times, lack of skills, and having the right mindset to cope in today's relationships.

Couples willing to make sacrifices within their relationship were found to be more effective in solving their problems. Therefore, men of God are encouraged to make sacrifices and to maintain restraint and discipline, regardless of what is going on in their homes. Even if unhappy or developing a spirit of discontent, a man should be a stabilizing post for his marriage and family; he should make sacrifices because it shows that he can withhold storms, including emotional storms within the family dynamic. However, because of changing times, **men of God** are fighting **a new breed** of obstacles regarding being the leader of the home. They are facing issues when encouraging women to submit as Scripture indicates. You see, women are requiring more out of a man before being willing to submit.

How do I know? Well, in my coaching practice I often hear the following, "Philemon, he has to give me something to submit to. I'll submit to God," or "He doesn't submit to God as he should, and I'm not following him."

I've learned that in most cases this is more about their relationship with money and how this directly affects the way they see a man. Therefore, he is often challenged at home in every area of his life and his natural competitive instinct comes forward when dealing with his marriage.

As you learn in this book, men are naturally and unconsciously calculating whether they are winning or losing within everything they are doing. If he feels he is always losing when making those sacrifices, it has been my experience that he will either leave the church or stay while being filled with anger, and he will often look for new ways to meet his needs. In this state, it can affect his spiritual life and could cause natural weakness.

Again, **I won't always address issues from a spiritual perspective; you already get this at church**. I will provide you with practical applications to help you understand that, yes, he loves God, but he is **STILL A MAN!** Let's get started with this book.

CHAPTER ONE:
Getting Started

A "perfect marriage" is just two imperfect people who refuse to give up on each other.

 Most people repeat or react to or escape from the relationship patterns of their parents. All of their reactions to a relationship are actually still coming from a parental influence, more so than from their true self.

Attraction: the Core

Regardless of what you have heard or read, think or even believe, attraction is at the core of every marriage and every relationship leading to marriage.

Do not be deceived. Every relationship begins and ends with attraction, with either high levels of attraction or with the loss of attraction. Once attraction is lost, a man or woman loses interest in that marital partner or person-of-interest. The marriage or relationship is virtually over. Only a shell remains.

This is the reason a man or woman will stop calling, not return calls, marry someone else, leave, or—perhaps worse—just be going through the motions, perhaps keeping it together "for the children" or for the "love of God."

Attraction is not a choice and cannot be forced or turned on/off with the flick of a switch. Attraction is something that occurs naturally. Think of how magnets are drawn together and how difficult it is to pry them apart.

Attraction does NOT mean lust, although physical attraction can lead to lust, which is simply sexual chemistry devoid of anything else. Whereas sexual chemistry is certainly essential in a long-term marital relationship, it is not the only essential ingredient.

Feeling "chemistry"—i.e. sexual chemistry—in an intimate relationship does NOT mean that he is the right person for you. In fact, quite the opposite.

Beware when you find someone who is "Sooooo cute" that you tell your friends, "We have chemistry and I just know he's the one." All of the requirements you've established will go out the window. This is called "infatuation" and is usually short-lived. Or, if you rushed into marriage when infatuated, you are now waking up to the reality of a marriage without substance. What happened? Chemistry took over your judgment.

And yet, yes, attraction is what draws you to your husband or future one. There are qualities that make up attraction, even though it is emotional and happens on an unconscious level. You do want to build attraction and chemistry into your relationship, but not let it take over.

Being a godly woman with an exceptional personality can draw a man of God to you. You can develop qualities that can make you more attractive to a man of God.

Men of God are attracted by many of the same qualities as other men, and that includes sexual chemistry, of course, but also by spiritual qualities, and these balance the sexual. This book will teach you how to become more attractive from both points of view.

Women of God must also feel attraction to the one they find —both spiritually and otherwise. Often a woman doesn't realize that someone she rejects as not attractive is actually a good choice for her. Something he does destroys the attraction, simply because she doesn't understand enough about men in general. This book will help you with that, too.

When you combine attraction with meeting his needs (the secret sauce to maintaining attraction), you will find an amazingly deep spiritual connection, extreme passion, and oneness with him.

The Powerful Force of Fears

2 Timothy 1:7 NLT: *For God has not given us a spirit of fear and timidity, but of power, love, and self-discipline.*

In this section I will provide a direct cause for what usually drives a man and woman of God to behave in a negative manner during marital and dating relationship situations. It is the powerful force of fears.

Even though you may understand this concept and have the knowledge of what to do, I am aware that this is easier said than done. This is simply because **your fears can often get in the way of your applying what you know**. It can also affect your emotional healing and the source of why you are not able to overcome past hurt. I actually have a workshop on this very subject. Here is something to understand: Fear is actually an illusion because we invent it based on beliefs.

There is only one way a fear can gain power and take over—when you listen to it. Therefore, when it comes to relationships, one must identify and truly understand the fears underlying any negative reaction or action in the relationship dynamic.

Throughout this book there are examples of how a woman's actions can tap into a man of God's fears and how to avoid this. Since you will have your own fears, and since you are the creator of these fears, you will have the ability to destroy them. How? It is really simple. **Don't listen to them!**

A MAN OF GOD *is* *Still* A MAN

To discover your own fears, take a look at "The Love Exam," (Chapter Four). When you get to that part, ask yourself an additional question, "If this is how I feel loved, what is the underlying fear if I don't get it? What needs of mine am I NOT fulfilling?"

This book is also full of concepts and information regarding specific issues that affect men of God. But the most powerful forces driving both of you are direct fears. I feel that you should know this up front before reading any further.

Although often hidden, fear can destroy a relationship. It may be a fear of rejection, abandonment, not being acknowledged, or a fear of feeling disconnected or devalued, or a fear of not being taken seriously, or another.

Yes, fear is usually the source of all negative reactions in a relationship because one **often fears that their needs and wants won't get met.** Such a strong fear can drive one to abandon Christ-like behavior. It can cause one to do sinful things. One of the major results of fear is that it can bring into fruition all of your fears. In other words, one fear will cause you to act in such a manner that makes all of your fears come true.

If you believe that all men will cheat or eventually leave, you will act in such a manner that will usually produce a reaction out of him that will support this fear. He will either cheat or leave the relationship, but only because your reactions to him brought out this behavior or response to you.

As you will discover in this book, a man often fears failure, rejection, and not being honored by those he cares about. Understanding his fears, as well as yours, is simply paramount in creating the life-long connection that you seek. If you, as a woman of God, are able to ease or destroy a man of God's fears of connecting with you, there is usually nothing else that can disconnect him from you.

Want a Godly Man?

> Romans 12:1 NLT: *And so, dear brothers and sisters, I plead with you to give your bodies to God because of all he has done for you. Let them be a living and holy sacrifice—the kind he will find acceptable. This is truly the way to worship him.*

You want a godly man because you are a woman of God. However, your soul mate may be leaving because you are not clear what this means. As a coach and mentor, I'm finding that so many marriageable women of God are confused about what they want from a religious perspective. When I ask them to list their requirements and wants for a mate, they respond simply, "I want a godly man, one who seeks good, a man of prayer; we must be equally yoked, etc."

My role as a coach is to ask a client questions and explore with her who she really is as a person. My goal is to take steps to totally understand her world, to support and help her find her own answers. I encourage my clients to be extremely clear about what they desire and what vision they have for their life, or what vision they believe God has for their life. Doing this with women of God is more difficult than I ever imagined.

Why? Well, the key is to make sure that they understand how their thinking from a religious perspective affects their relationship decisions. The goal is to help them understand true character, instead of some unauthentic or mystical concepts.

During a session with a woman of God years ago, I noticed her becoming more and more frustrated coming up with answers to my questions about her relationship rules. I was pressing her because I wanted to be on her side, to advocate for her, but could not do that without her clear answers.

Finally, she shouted at me, "**I'll know by the Spirit! If you have the Holy Spirit, you'll just know.**"

Then she added, "Any person of God will know what I mean about being equally yoked, what is godly, because all you have to do is follow the Word."

This Christian woman, over forty, never married, with three children from different fathers before salvation, holding a leadership role in the church, had come to me for help finding a man of God (a godly man). She also said that she was "seasoned" and "ready for God's actions."

Here are the exact questions I asked her. Now see if you can answer them with clarity for yourself:

"So, you want a godly man?"

"What is a godly man?"

"What does 'to be godly' mean to you?"

"What would a relationship look like, feel like, or be like with this godly man?"

"How would you know that he is godly?"

"Can it be measured from your spiritual perspective?"

"Do you actually live your life according to your religious beliefs or doctrines?"

"If not, are you seeking this mate to live as you do now?"

"Are you seeking this mate to live as you believe you should live because you will correct your behavior later?"

"This is important because,

> if yes, will he accept you as you live now?
> If no, then, when you correct your behavior,
> the two of you will no longer be compatible."

> "Can you list what you believe it takes
> to be equally or unequally yoked in a relationship?"

You see I've noticed men of faith leaving a relationship leading to marriage simply because of **unclear religious perspectives** regarding relationships.

Both are believers and seeking a spouse, but they attend different churches. Now, for the record, it is not their beliefs that are different; the "home church" concept is what is keeping them apart. There are many religious cultures, but most have the same value system and beliefs on big things. It is usually only one or two minor rules that separate them.

One reason so many Christian women are still looking for Mr. Right is because they are NOT able to find a suitable mate in their own home church. They hold on to the belief that he will walk right through that door and sweep them up.

However, suitable mates are available for these women at other churches—men with the same values system on the big things. But these men are rejected all the time. Additionally, even when a woman does accept a man from another home church, the attraction between them is often lost and he leaves her eventually because she is so stuck on the very minor rules that separate them, to the point that there are arguments.

I've also found that, most of the time, these women do not practice their religious beliefs fully. Although, because of church peers, they pretend they do.

This is why I urge you to get clear about your true values based on your religious perspective. This will prevent you from rejecting a man in your proximity who has your core beliefs. It is really about matching your words with your true beliefs. Saying "God is working on me" is not a usable excuse when seeking a relationship. You must be clear where you are.

A MAN OF GOD *is* *Still* A MAN

Remember, beautiful religious expressions and talk has to be matched with an understanding of what these expressions mean to you. This allows you to know how to make the walk match the talk, especially in your relationship selection. Otherwise, the response you will get from others (e.g., praising your talk when you say things like "Jesus is my husband and companion") will be your reward and it could keep you mateless. Most of the time, such beautiful religious expressions do not translate into getting a mate just right for you.

 Get clear about what you truly believe and are actually practicing, instead of pretending in order to please church peers and family.

Learn His Rules of Love

Proverbs 1:5 NLT: *Let the wise listen to these proverbs and become even wiser. Let those with understanding receive guidance.*

There are times when a woman will rack her brain wondering what is going on with a man. He could be a man within the church, or attending another church, who has expressed interest; or a man she is actually speaking to regularly, maybe going to dinner and a movie with him, but she is not clear where this is heading, because he is behaving differently, withdrawn or has already left. This is when she needs to consider a man's attraction formula, his rules of love.

Violating his rules will explain why a man of God will lose that feeling of attraction and leave a relationship with you. Everyone has a formula or vault that holds the key to their heart; knowing the right combination will unlock massive amounts of love from them. However most never learn the right combination.

Many are following the golden rule from Luke 6:31: **Do to others as you would like them to do to you.** (NLT) However this scripture, from my perspective, is for believers. It actually means to treat people well, even if they aren't so kind to you. This is our command as Christians. However, when it comes to relationships, this command should be applied in a different way. One should **do unto others as they want to be treated**, not as you want to be treated.

A MAN OF GOD *is* *Still* A MAN

There is a huge difference between these. So many say to me, "Philemon, I gave him/her everything" and my reply is usually, "I totally understand, but it just was not what they needed. The way you need to feel love is often different than your mate."

Many are treating their spouses this way. This explains why there are so many divorces nowadays. You need to know a man of God's rules to attract and keep him, or he will consider another woman (if dating) or have a desire to leave (if married).

First, when a man leaves a woman, it is important to be clear about whether he has left to clear his head because of something he experienced and defined as disrespectful or ungodly, or whether he has completely taken himself out of your life.

In this book there are statements regarding when a man may become detached and leave. The question is why? What does this mean? And what can you do?

Keep in mind that most men will leave emotionally first; and in this case, he is noticeably detached or distant from you. However, it doesn't mean that he is out of your life completely. As I just said, you may be racking your brain wondering what happened because he is not talking.

Here is something to consider. Yes, a man must be mature enough to speak what is on his mind and to express why he is acting upset when you don't have a clue what is wrong. Here is the deal. Usually in these cases a man is not comfortable talking about the situation, because he is puzzling over how to respond. He's not sure what the right protocol is.

For example, it could be that he saw you taking a second peek at a good-looking pastor or another guy during an outing. This started his brain to wondering if he is what you want. Or, it could be something you said. Either he is unsure how to feel about it, or it has made him feel that he is not the one for you. Just keep in mind that a man does not like to be puzzled or to have the feeling that he is about to be rejected by a woman of interest.

Men of God want things simple. They are constantly calculating such things as:

Is she into me, or not?

Can I win with this woman, or not?

Does she have my back?

Does she know when to be quiet? [Are you always talking?]

Does she seek advice from other men in the church over my advice?

Does she always praise other men of God in front of me?

Is she second-guessing or competing with me?

Do I want to get into a conversation that makes me uncomfortable or makes me look weak?

A man has to process what is going on with his wife or woman of interest. While processing, he may become detached, but may still take your calls at times. He may not text until later, or may hit the reject button on the phone until he has processed a bit what ticked him off. **Here is what you should do:**

When a man starts acting angry or disconnected, this is the time to be reassuring. Start praising him about his qualities.

You must express how much you are into him (mainly his qualities.) If you do this as he processes what upset him, then the emotional calculations he makes may allow him to let it go. The reassuring method can and usually works in these cases, unless the action was a major rule breaker in his book.

If he has become detached, it doesn't mean he is gone. Do not jump all over him! (I know you want clarity, but timing is everything.) Do not ask a lot of questions. Just start reassuring him and see if this solves the problem. It allows time and a means for him to reconnect emotionally again.

Once, or if, he re-connects with you, allow a little more time to pass before trying to find out what happened. If you are married, wait until after an intimate moment; if dating, wait until after a good outing.

Then, in a quiet setting, ask him if there was something you did that "**caused him to take pause about the relationship.**" Adopt that phrase because it does not make a man feel that he must go too deeply into an explanation.

If he asks, "What are you talking about?" say, "**I noticed that you seemed preoccupied at one point, and it is my goal for us to learn each other.**"

Next, reward him and reassure him, in a very positive manner, about how much you think of him. "You are so handsome; I never want to see those eyes look sad." I think you know how to reward and what to say.

You don't have to say things that create pressure. Express positive things you like about him: his spiritual gifts, his looks, how he dresses, and his intellect, among other things. Just throw out the compliments and rewards.

However, if something you did went against a rule for him, it is possible that you may not overcome this situation with this method, especially if the relationship is very new. He will detach, become distant, and leave—usually every time.

If he has been extremely detached, and you hear him say, "I'm praying about God's directions for my life," this may be a sign that he is about to leave. I hate to say this, but men of God often hide behind "God's will" when giving excuses.

Keep reading this book to discover ways to avoid breaking his rules for love before learning them.

Your Past

Philippians 3:13 NLT: No, dear brothers and sisters, I have not achieved it, but I focus on this one thing: Forgetting the past and looking forward to what lies ahead,

Before getting started, I have a question for you. What has been your experience in past relationships—even with friends? What complaints have you been hearing about your relationships? Is there a pattern to their complaints? Consider all relationships. For each one ask yourself, *What complaints did I hear?*

On the other hand, maybe you don't get complaints, but always get the same line, something that goes like this: "You are awesome but.... Let's be friends," or "I don't think you are what God has for me," or "We're not made for each other."

Are you ever curious about the 'but'? In some cases clients I've coached brush off any suggestion of rejection, saying, "I keep attracting the wrong men," or giving some other excuse. However, other clients were lost for answers and hired me for solutions.

Through these clients I've discovered how much this lack of answers preys on every relationship that follows, thus making them more guarded. Meeting a new man, they are constantly wondering, *How are we doing? What is he thinking about me?* If a phone call or text is not returned promptly, they usually assume the worst. Do you do this, too?

Instead of silently saying to yourself, or maybe looking in the

A MAN OF GOD is Still A MAN

mirror wondering, "*What did I do wrong?*" one of the best ways to gain insights about what it is like to date you (or to be your friend, if you never dated before) is to perform a relationship performance evaluation, also known as an "exit interview."

An exit interview with a former man of interest or two may help. You may receive two or three major reasons why the relationship did not work out between the two of you. You may begin to see patterns.

I will be addressing the issues relating to why a man of God will lose that feeling of attraction and leave a relationship. Maybe you will see a mistake or two that you've been making. However, getting answers from former interests is priceless. Make sure you give them permission to be totally honest. Please remain Christ-like : -). Do not respond in anger or start arguing if you don't agree. Just listen, then thank them for the information, and move on.

You see, it may be very simple. Perhaps your breath has a foul odor even after using mints; everyone else may know this, but you will not have a clue. Maybe you kept selling yourself, or it may be something else.

"Now let's begin the next chapter by sharing a secret about men and considering a question many women ask me, "**Do men really know what they want?**"

PHILEMON

He's

Still a Man

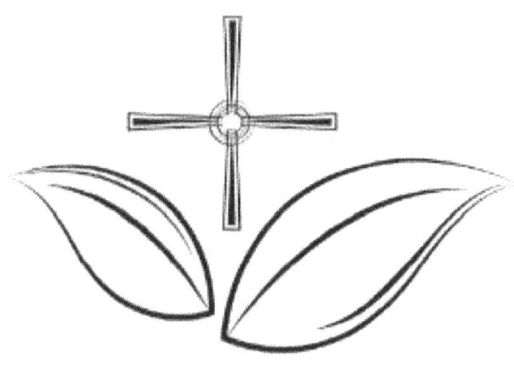

CHAPTER TWO:

He's Still a Man

Asking questions is great and necessary, but it cannot be excessive at any one time. He'll feel like it's a job interview instead of a connection.

Relax and see if you can enjoy his company first. Observe, listen and get a feel for his personality. Learn your man.

A Secret about Men

Proverbs 31:10–11 NLT: *Who can find a virtuous and capable wife? She is more precious than rubies. Her husband can trust her, and she will greatly enrich his life.*

Most men seek a loving relationship with that irreplaceable woman that God has for him. I've been telling women this for years.

Don't believe that theory about all men being these commitment-phobic creatures who are after just one thing. Yes! There are many women in the church who still believe that. Unfortunately, there are some men in every church who certainly seem to be doing that. But this does not fit with what I hear or observe in male culture today—professionally, socially, and personally.

First, understand that there is a male culture in this world that may not encourage a man to settle down until he is older. It is usually different in the church. However, let any man meet that one special woman, and he will lose it and be all over the place trying to figure out what should be his next move.

Women who understand this dynamic are the ones having success with men, and I mean Marriage. Men do NOT have any anxiety about committing to a woman like this, because they feel that they made this choice themselves. Women who make the mistake of trying to control this process and force this issue are not successful.

You see, each man has this blueprint of how his life is supposed to go, even though he may be praying for direction. This blueprint goes something like this: Get an education, make money, enjoy life, settle down, buy a house, and have kids. Whenever something goes against his blueprint, he will panic.

Women who truly understand men get this totally. So how does this type of woman handle this situation? Well, she becomes expert in changing **associations**. She knows how to create associations that being with her is a plus and can be a great addition to his plans right now at a point when he wasn't expecting to add a woman to his life. She makes him feel completely comfortable about everything in his life.

This is how a young man, who believes he is not ready, all of sudden wants to marry this amazing woman he fears he can NOT replace.

This book will help you learn how to change a man's associations. Let's begin with some observations about men that I find helpful:

- A man is always calculating the odds of a woman being "the one." He makes these **emotional calculations** based on how she makes him feel. At the same time he is creating a **mental map** of a possible future with her. Factors that play into this include the following.
- The very moment a man feels he is being controlled he will hold onto his solo life even tighter and will remain unmarried.
- Men are afraid of walking into a situation where they feel forced to commit.
- Men are even more afraid of being trapped into a relationship or marriage they never planned for.
- Another great fear is of being with a woman who may love God, but is inhibited in so many areas of life that he becomes frustrated.

How does a man combat these fears? He changes his behavior towards you. He slows down and stops calling or texting because he is actually afraid. His plan is being disrupted, and he doesn't know what to do next. Something has changed his emotional calculations of the relationship. The mental map he has been creating of your future together is no longer what he wants, what he'd hoped for.

Knowing how to navigate this process is imperative for women. Those who know how to influence by creating associations usually get their man. They stay out of the friend zone, too.

Women who don't know (including women of faith) are afraid of being played. They fear being cheated on. This is why she truly watches out for the player type of man who goes for the next great body or pretty face.

How do most women try to combat their fears? They try to rush things and gain certainty by forcing a relationship before anything else can happen. It just doesn't work and has NEVER WORKED long term. The trick is to **stop trying to make a relationship serious before it becomes serious**.

Some women in the church, even though they all KNOW it is WRONG, will throw sex at a man. This is just another way of rushing things. Please understand that this is NOT the answer either, even though, if he is weak, he may love this part, but it is more than just sex to him.

Even in this type of situation, a man will usually be wondering, either consciously or unconsciously, *Is she replaceable?*" If he believes you are, you will NOT be the one. His actions will tell you this. And the reverse is also true: If he believes you are IRREPLACEABLE, his actions will tell you.

If he has feelings for you, if he wants you, there is nothing that you have to do but say "yes" to things he suggests within your values. He probably won't declare his feelings yet, but if you are relaxed, enjoying his company and learning about him, you will see that he wants to be with you. It is just that simple.

Therefore, learn how to change a man's associations about being with YOU. Saying "yes" is one one-way to do this. This is an acquired skill that you can learn with the help of this book, along with how to assess which men are truly ready for a serious relationship. Now let's look at what men want.

Do Men Know What They Want?

2 Timothy 2:7 NLT: Think about what I am saying. The Lord will help you understand all these things.

You just read "a secret about men" and now know that, contrary to popular beliefs, every man has feelings that go beyond meeting his physical needs. At some level every man is watching for that irreplaceable woman.

As I see it, each man has a **primal, instinctual, operating system** working beneath the surface. Even he may not be aware of this system which dictates how he will respond to you. You will learn more about this in "His Mental Operating System."

He is not looking, does not feel "ready" for marriage, but suddenly, there she is! He can see just how she will fit into his life. Afraid of losing her and believing he may never meet another like her, he says to himself, *Wow, what an amazing woman! How can I live without her?* It is the classic Love at First Sight!

I can hear you now, "How can I be that woman?" I will be answering that, but first we need to find out the specific qualities that make a woman irreplaceable in a man's eyes.

Unfortunately, if you ask a man of God what he wants in a woman, he may simply say, "**a Proverbs-31 woman**." The model described in Proverbs 31 is a picture of ideal womanhood. The focus of this picture is a woman's relationship with God, not her specific abilities or marital status. A Proverbs-31 woman realizes that, regardless of her natural talents, acquired skills, and all her accomplishments, her strength comes from God. Cultures change, but this woman's God-inspired character still shines brightly across the centuries.

Although a man of God may be equally devout to his Proverbs-31 ideal woman, he is NOT looking for a carbon copy of himself. He is in search of a woman of God who complements his life.

A woman of God, however, as most of the women I coach, usually seeks the opposite. Not only do they seek a carbon copy of themselves, but they want a man who is actually better than they are. They want one who makes more money, is more intelligent, has a little more education, or a little bit more of this or that. This is why many are having difficulties finding and keeping Mr. Right.

Women want more specifics, however, asking me, "**Do men *really* know what they want?**" In my opinion, and there are always exceptions, the answer is "Maybe not!" That is, most men don't have the ability to express or explain in words what they want. (Not any more than women can give specifics on the "godly man" they want.)

But I do hear a lot of complaints from men about what they do NOT want in a woman. Unfortunately, few share this with their woman, believing she cannot accept the truth (more on this in "Can He Be Honest?").

Let me share with you what my research reveals on what men want. The thousands of men I've interviewed, questioned, and interacted with are all over the place in their explanations about what they are really looking for in a woman. The men of God among them were some of the most vocal, e.g. "a virtuous woman who serves the most-high God to the fullest." But when I asked them to explain, a few scriptures were quoted and things about how she should dress. When all was said and done, it boiled down to a man of God still being a man, because their answers were the same as most men's.

Since ninety-seven percent (97%) of men in my research (including men of God) have never read an entire book on relationships or sought guidance in this area, they really don't have the words or perspective to describe what they want. But their questions and stories about the women they have dated or married are quite revealing. I find that what men want is evolving. For the most part, men just know what they want when it happens, based on how they feel instinctively while in the presence of a woman.

The "irreplaceable woman" for most men has multiple, quality, phases to her personality. For example, she is sexy, smart and witty, but doesn't mind getting her hands dirty and is not overly particular or demanding. On the other hand, with too much of a good thing—too witty or too much of a brainiac—a man may be completely turned off.

Thus, in coaching I often say, "You can do everything right and your relationship can still blow up in your face." This is the risk of love.

I know how devastating it is to women when a man mysteriously ups and leaves. How do you respond? Some women are strong and get right back into the relationship hunt, confident they did everything right, saying "it is not *my* issue." Others are devastated and want to know why.

Either way, I want to dig deeper with them to uncover whether it is true that they did everything right.

"Philemon, I did everything right!" these women cry in dismay.

But when we dig deeper, we can always punch holes in their assessment. It is extremely hard for anyone to really see themselves, how they are perceived, and what it's like to date them.

In your eagerness for a relationship, you may not have noticed that your needs and his vary. What you are seeking in a relationship and what he seeks may be at odds. How would you know? This is why I encourage coaching as a tool to shine the light on those hidden factors that affect relationships.

It is important to understand that men and women are often seeking different things in a serious, long-term relationship.

Women seek

    Companionship: to connect with someone she can share her life with

    Attention: to be noticed

    Affection/Intimacy: to be accepted, share feelings, and be safe when her defense is down

    Commitment: to feel safe in the relationship and know, without a doubt, that he can be trusted with all of her heart

Men seek

    Companionship: to connect with someone he can share his life with;

    Praise: to be acknowledged and to be a woman's hero [She must provide a "That-a-boy!" type of campaign.]

    Loyalty: to know that his woman has his back and is loyal to him

    Sex: Yes, men of God need sex, too. They need frequent sex to feel emotionally connected. Men connect through physical contact.

The key to having a quality marriage is to understand, appreciate, and embrace these differences. However, the true key to a man's heart is as follows: **Plenty of Sex, Praise, Food, Fun, and no nagging. In other words, he wants to be left alone at times**. Yes, men want a woman of prayer and grace, but if you lack any of these five, you may have trouble in your relationship.

To be honest, I've never heard of a man leaving a woman when all of those things are in play from his perspective. NOTE: I say his perspective, not yours.

What does a woman of faith do to keep a man committed to their marriage? And if not married, how does a woman of faith get a man to commit? Just know again, that some things on this list should not happen before marriage, but HE has to believe that, besides being godly, you are this person prior to marriage:

- She is praised by others for her great character and good works.
- She is not obsessed about their relationship future.
- She is not jealous, worrying about past women he did not pick. [Just know that he could have had someone else if he wanted, but picked you.]
- She is not pressing hard for marriage, but it falls into her lap.
- She is having fun; she is funny with a love-all-men attitude.
- She is not needy or clingy!
- She gives him space. [Most men need their freedom or the illusion of it.]
- She understands that there is only Full Trust or No Trust and nothing in the middle. [He needs you to bring out the best in him.]
- She makes him feel good in her presence, totally comfortable being himself around her.
- She does not play games with men.
- She is nurturing, smart, and a woman of substance who complements his life.
- She knows how to keep him hunting by changing her appearance: dressed up one-day, wearing sweats the next, hair up and down and changing it often, having a life and friends outside of his, and not being too available.
- She is not required to have the perfect body and is comfortable in her skin.

- She is not sexually inhibited in the bedroom when married.
- She does not make her husband feel bad about his sexual urges.
- She is not pressuring or interrogating him.
- She does not have right or wrong answers to questions.
- She does not create ultimatums.
- She doesn't have "Am-I-wasting-my-time?" types of questions.
- She has the courage to speak about where she is in life—her wants and desires, but without forcing a man to feel the same way.
- She is intentional and living her life in the moment.

Keep in mind that **he is still a man** and needs these things. Again, if you are unmarried and seeking the right man for you, remember he needs to believe that you can provide these things.

If you do, he will find you unique and will decide, "*Wow, what a wonderful woman of God. I want her!*"

If you are accomplished, that's a plus; nowadays you must be able to bring something to the table if you want a quality man with a plan. With these traits you are irreplaceable, a keeper, the one he wants to marry, and the woman he cannot live without.

Again, Ladies, it is okay to state where you are, but just remember not to make him feel that you have right or wrong answers. You will usually learn a lot more about him just by being with him in a relaxed environment while listening and observing. If he tells you where he is, you will believe him. Just know that men see things better than they are; so he may stretch the truth a bit.

He May See You Differently

While you may present yourself as a solid woman of faith or an "I-know-what-I-want!" accomplished, witty, very conversational type of person with ambitious ways, he can translate those characteristics as something else. You can come across as an arrogant, bossy, competitive, argumentative person who is extremely difficult to deal with. Men love accomplished women. However, they are not seeking a business partner, but a mate to complement them and fit into their life.

What a man is usually looking for in a woman, especially on a date with the potential of a marriage, is what he can't get elsewhere, e.g. from his friends, family, or at work. If you don't measure up to that in his mind, he will not marry you.

Now, this next topic will explain from a behavioral perspective the why's behind men not marrying a woman, leaving, or becoming frustrated in a marriage. Everything else you will read in this book will help you understand ways you are not meeting his needs based on your actions. You will learn to improve in this area.

Meeting His Needs

> Galatians 6:9 NLT: *So let's not get tired of doing what is good. At just the right time we will reap a harvest of blessing if we don't give up.*

When a man's needs are met, he is happy. When they are not met, he feels unhappy. This is human nature; we all have needs. We each spend all of our time attempting to satisfy our needs, either consciously or unconsciously, and either in positive or negative ways.

Attraction is lost and a man will leave a woman because his needs are not being met, or because he is attempting to meet his needs. Of course, I would encourage you to do the same. Therefore, helping you to understand how to meet his needs is a very important part of this book. And helping women to identify their own needs is one of the first things I do in coaching them.

Before I explain this, as I said before, Christian men are charged to make sacrifices for their marriage. When needs are NOT being met, some will stay in the relationship because of their faith and Scripture, even though they are NOT actually happy or connected with their wife. Even if he doesn't leave physically, often he will leave emotionally, and there will be NOTHING there but two people pretending to be happy to outsiders but really only roommates. Christian leaders often face this dilemma because their livelihood or status is attached to a certain brand. Meeting needs is extremely important.

The most effective, practical, description of human needs that I have found is the model developed by Anthony Robbins. Tony, as he is known, is a world-renowned innovator in the field of **human needs psychology**. As a relationship coach, this model allows me to apply the complex theories of human needs psychology to practical, everyday situations—like why he left, cheated or committed other sins.

The six basic human needs are

1. **Certainty/Comfort:** We all need comfort, and much of it derives from the certainty that things in our lives will happen in a certain way. The car will start in the morning, you will get your paycheck on payday, and your mate will follow through on promises.
2. **Uncertainty/Variety:** The variety, spice, and adventure in our lives derive from the events that are uncertain and unexpected. Sports, for example, may fulfill this need for a man.
3. **Significance:** Feeling worthy of praise. We all need to feel significant to our partners and to the world at large. We need to feel that our lives have meaning.
4. **Love and Connection:** We need to be cared about, loved; we need to feel a part of someone's life and to have a meaningful connection with them.
5. **Growth:** We each have a need to become better as a person, to improve our skills, to stretch and excel in our lives.
6. **Contribution:** We need to give outside ourselves, help others, make the world a better place, and contribute something of value to society.

Each person prioritizes these six needs in a unique way. For some, safety and security matter over all the other needs; for them, certainty trumps the other basic human needs. If that need isn't being met, then no matter how well the other needs are met, the person will be unsettled and unhappy, attraction will be lost, and the person will leave the relationship. This is true for many women.

As pointed out earlier (in "Do Men Know What They Want?"), men and women seek different things in a long-term relationship, so start there. In general, women seek companionship, attention, affection/intimacy, and commitment; whereas, men seek companionship, praise, loyalty, and sex. Can you see how these fit into the six basic needs?

The bottom line: It is impossible to punch a hole in these basic needs. They really explain human behavior. If you are mindful of his needs, it can make you become the woman that he can't live without. The "flaws" that men find in women and women in men grow out of unmet needs.

The key to forming a lasting relationship is to figure out how he prioritizes the six basic needs. Which are most important to him? How do they show up in his behavior?

But wait a minute. What about you? Yes, this is a book about men, but a key concept of basic needs psychology is that **each of us must understand our own needs and what it takes to meet them before trying to meet someone else's needs.** In Chapter Three I will help you to examine yourself, how your needs affect your behavior in a relationship, and how to use your new understanding of basic human needs in order to make wise relationship decisions.

If you've established an order of needs that guarantees you'll feel continually frustrated relative to how your life is at the moment, I encourage you to go through the work of consciously reorganizing your needs. This can pay off big time in your experience of how things are going in your life. Attempting this process alone can be difficult; finding a coach or mentor to work with can be helpful.

Here is my last point on this subject: **Unmet needs create the conflicts that destroy relationships** (for examples see Chapter Four: "Relationship Destroyers"). If you use these six basic human needs as a lens for viewing situations that occur in a relationship, you will be able to understand the conflicts as they happen and this can prevent a mate from leaving.

This is why coaching is extremely powerful in building a successful relationship.

One day you may wonder, *Why is he upset or not calling?* Well, if you know his needs, then you'll probably understand that the issue you are facing is connected to them not being met, and you will know how to meet them. You will have become the one he cannot live without.

There are **two exceptions** to this:

First, **attempting to meet his needs may not allow you to meet your own**. A relationship cannot function this way, so it will not last without change. Talking with someone to sort out the issues may help, especially if both are committed to the relationship.

Second, as explained in the next section, **move slowly when dating a newly divorced man with children**. He has special needs.

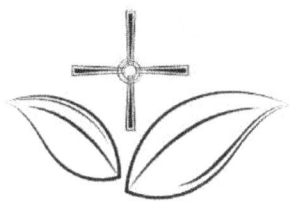

Divorced Man with Children

A divorced or divorcing man with school-aged children needs time to mourn. Ending a marriage is difficult. If you are dating a man with young children, be careful. The end of a marriage is almost like having a death in the family. There is a grieving process. I am speaking from experience here, so listen up.

While divorcing in 2003 and after the divorce in 2004, I was simply depressed, couldn't eat, and would get in the bed and lay in a fetal position at night. Yes, there were tears. I lived in an Extended Stay until I found an apartment. It felt as if my whole world had collapsed. I could no longer bathe my kids or tuck them in at night as I had before and didn't get to see my kids as much. I've found this to be the same for all of the men in my research who were divorced or divorcing with children.

If there is another man involved, it becomes even harder. There are many stages one will go through from denial, anger, and sadness to full acceptance. He could also be suffering from financial issues.

Do not get emotionally involved with a man with young kids until there is full acceptance. It's OK to be there for him; but, again, there is a process. He may simply leave and go back to his ex-wife, leaving you behind.

Here is how I coach women in my practice. I share this: **Make sure he has gone through the holidays** (e.g. Christmas, if he celebrates it with them) before you consider getting in deeper. For me and so many men in my research, once we had gone through the holidays without the family unit, acceptance was around the corner. For some men it could be the Fourth of July or another memorable holiday. Find out what was his special family holiday or event and allow it to pass before deciding to consider him a potential love interest.

The "Me, Too!" Syndrome

So many times you have to watch out for the "me too" syndrome. He will do whatever his ex-wife does, e.g. "I'm happy, too. Look at what I have!" He will act as if he is, but inside he is still resentful. If you understand this process, you'll see that maybe the relationship can't work. I am not telling you to run, but just do not get too involved emotionally.

Has He Lost Full Custody?

Here is something extremely important: **even after reaching the full-acceptance stage**, he could still feel resentment towards your children. Unless he has full custody of his own, he will probably feel the loss of daily contact with his children for the rest of his life.

If you have young kids, a man could become resentful to have kids in the house or around him that are not his own. Even if you have outings with both sets of kids, when his children go home, he will become sad and could become resentful if your kids are still around. So many women believe that it is ideal for both to have young kids, and that it could work out better—just like the Brady Bunch. **Newsflash**: Not in most cases.

I don't want to scare you, but it MUST be said. **Divorced men who are in the denial/anger stage may do physical harm to your children.** Yes, even if he is a good man. Resentment can build in him, and he will take it out on your kids. I've seen this too many times.

There are also cases where kids were abused by stepfathers and the mother never knew. Just because you can't see any abuse doesn't mean it is not happening. Before you blend a family, make sure you get coaching or counseling because the risks of not getting it can be too great.

Blending families is extremely difficult and I believe that if he has small children and you have teens, it can be better or vice versa. Don't get me wrong, because there are always exceptions.

Divorced men are often called "the best kept secret" because they are already house trained, usually not afraid of commitment and totally understand what it takes to be in a relationship. However, the key to preventing heartbreak is to make sure a divorced man has gone through all of the stages of grief before you become emotionally vested in him.

For other men under consideration, understanding his life stage will also help you in assessing and fulfilling his needs.

His Life Stage

Ecclesiastes 3:1 NLT: *For everything there is a season, a time for every activity under heaven.*

Understanding the stages of a man's life can provide clarity as to why he behaves in a certain manner. Also, being able to identify his life stage will allow you to compare where he is to where you are in your life.

Keep in mind that his life stage with respect to relationships is not determined by his age. For example, some men in their twenties will feel strongly about settling down if they see a woman with a solid, godly foundation. They will usually think, *I can build something with this woman, and we can explore or conquer the world at the same time.* In other words, the right woman can settle a young man down and, yes, he will marry her. There will be bumps and bruises on this ride, but many make it through and mature together.

My study of men in relationships at different periods in life reveals four primary stages. For simplicity, I love to express these stages using **archetypes,** personifications of the qualities of each type. Keep in mind that these men are men of faith. The four life stages are: The Explorer, The Conqueror, The Hero, and The Ruler.

The Explorer

When a man is in the Explorer stage, he may love God but has not yet figured out his place in the world. He may be lost. Often he is young, but he may also be older, starting over in his life. He does not have the ability to be on solid ground in a marriage right now. This man is simply on a quest to find himself. He is exploring what he likes or doesn't like; it is not time to rest his feet or build a foundation.

In a marriage the Explorer is usually not serious, although sometimes the Explorer will marry a woman who has the means to help him explore. For the most part, if you are interested in settling down with an established guy, he is not the one. You may have to support him financially, and he may be too preoccupied to give you the attention you need. In fact, he may simply be away from home a lot.

The Conqueror

The Conqueror has either found his place in the world or figured out what he wants to do. He has set his foot out to conquer the world. He is focusing on his target. He wants to be noticed and is telling everyone, "Look at me!" If he is older, he may be in a new career or recently divorced or widowed after many years. (Let's face it, the divorce rate is huge in the church, too, because of poor commitment and practices.) He is usually hanging out or networking a lot, maybe travelling and gathering new friends.

In a marriage this guy will require lots of praise and support. He knows what he wants; therefore you won't be able to steer him away from his desires.

The Hero

A man in the Hero stage of life has won some battle to earn his place in the world. He is enjoying the fruits of his labor and indulging himself in things he may never have experienced before. If he is older, a widower or freshly divorced after a long marriage, he may feel embarrassed, and may seek to remarry quickly. He is usually stable in his career.

In a marriage a lot of these men may change and want to

explore new things. Change can scare many women. Be open to new adventures.

The Ruler

The Ruler has indulged himself, accomplished goals, and now has a sense of discovering what is important to him in life. He is the master of his world. He is thinking of his mortality and legacy. His mind is usually at rest and not wandering all over the place seeking wins or scoring. "He's been there, done that." He is settled and will think, *It would be great to have an amazing woman to share my life with*. He wants to build a family or find someone to grow old with. He is just ready and will move fast. I like to call this the "Peace-Be-Still" stage. The wind and water is calm in his life.

Be forewarned: The Ruler is already established and does not need a woman to give him directions. So do not come into this relationship giving orders or making suggestions about the direction of his life. He will not be interested in you and, for the most part, will not get involved.

In a marriage the Ruler is simply ready and usually moves fast. A serious relationship conversation will NOT scare him away. Usually women are frightened by how fast these men move. If you ever wanted to know how a man can meet a woman and decide to get married after a few weeks, watch for a man in the Ruler stage. He rules.

Next, let's explore the relationship patterns of men in these life stages.

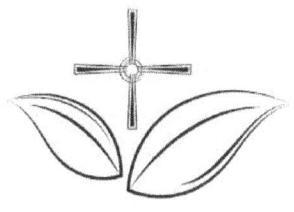

Guy Brands

Now that you understand the four life stages of men, it is also important to understand their relationship patterns. These patterns can be found in men of any life stage and will help you understand the type of man in front of you and, maybe, why he left **or whether you should leave.** Yes, you have that option, too.

Matching these patterns to life stages will allow you to make an informed decision about a man. Therefore, I've included some guidance on what you should do in general. Of course, there are always exceptions. Remember to be flexible and keep an open mind. [See the following section, "Is He Ready?" for further guidelines.]

Here are the fourteen relationship patterns I have identified through my research into men in relationships, presented as what I call **"Guy Brands."**

Mr. Fifties Reincarnated

I have to put Mr. Fifties Reincarnated on the table because this is still an active guy brand in the church. Although you may find a few who were actually raised in the 1950s, you will also find younger men who share the same attitudes and values.

Men of the 1950s usually had better manners than men today. They were also hard workers and many were strong leaders. Although, even today, many men of God believe that Scripture states the role of women clearly, the Fifties was an era that displayed a form of this belief fully. You see, the rules society placed upon women during the Fifties were repressive and restrictive in many ways.

In the Fifties high importance and expectations were placed on behavior at home, as well as in public. A woman's role was to be a caring mother; a diligent homemaker; and, especially within the Christian community, an obedient wife. A good housewife had dinner on the table precisely at the moment her husband arrived home from work, carried out his every order, and agreed with him on everything. In fact, even if she wanted to voice an opinion, it was not allowed much. A common expression was, "She doesn't know how to take care of herself."

We live in a different time now, but I still find guys in the church, guys of all ages, who believe that women should stay at home, be a housewife, and be submissive. Usually a man with this relationship pattern will have an adjusted view of women because times have changed, but at his core he is a reincarnated Mr. Fifties. He makes the decisions in his household. I also find men of God with other guy brands who also hold this view.

What should you do?

No matter what life stage he is in (*Explorer, Hero, Conqueror, Ruler*): **Look Twice/Leave.** In many cases, **if he is willing to get some love lessons**, these guys make strong husbands who can provide you with a great life. He will be family-oriented and will take really good care of you. He will always be thinking of his family.

However, **if he is not willing to get any love lessons prior to marriage, LEAVE**. These types are not caring and loving husbands in this day and time. Often they view women as second-class citizens and are looking for someone to order around.

Know the difference. Just make sure you get a clear picture of what this man expects and get some clarity prior to marriage. Not all men of God think this way, even though Scripture is clear about submission.

Mr. Looking-for-Perfection

A man looking for perfection will always find faults in you and criticize everything; he will pick on you. If you want to be with him, he can place a lot of pressure on you. Mr. Looking-for-Perfection can be a minister, a pastor's son, or any man with status in the church. He will complain about your hair, or how you dress, and will say things like "If you want to be with me, we have to follow a certain protocol, because people look at us and what we do."

This type of man can sometimes make you feel low and dirty with his negative comments, such as, "Why do you wear that stuff? You need to learn how to put on your makeup much better, too. Why are you eating that? You will put on weight. Has anyone ever said that you talk too much? Women in this town do not fit me; it is hard to find that special woman."

Every woman that Mr. Looking-for-Perfection meets has something wrong with her; he has tried everything from dating sites to friends. Run! Avoid this guy.

What should you do?

Explorer, Hero, Conqueror, Ruler: **Leave**. It will be too difficult to measure up to his expectations, no matter his stage. You will always be walking on eggshells with this guy.

Mr. Accomplished

Mr. Accomplished can be a pastor, minister, leader or what women usually think is an amazing catch. He is a man who knows all of the right words and rules of love. He knows all of the scriptures inside and out. He also knows how to romance a woman of faith. A woman is treated like a queen by Mr. Accomplished—in the beginning. But once it becomes boring, or after your first mistake, the attraction is lost and he will leave: You broke his rules!

These men can be heart-breakers, serial-daters, and extremely difficult to detect or understand. And when he leaves, Mr. Accomplished has the ability to make you feel that it was all your fault. Furthermore, he will attempt to teach you about the purpose of coming in and out of one's life.

In my opinion, Mr. Accomplished is hard to please until he becomes mentally tired of the chase. He is similar to Mr. Looking-for-Perfection, but is NOT ruthless. I'm not judging their intent, but somehow, they move from woman to woman in the church, even while teaching others about faith.

These men make great mates—once they settle on a woman. But so many hearts get broken along the way. You better have relationship skills to be with this man and bring a level of substance that complements his life.

What should you do?

Explorer, Hero, Conqueror, Ruler: **Look Twice.** This guy at any stage will have relationship skills. Just be careful. Developing your own, strong, relationship skills will help.

Mr. Dopamine

Mr. Dopamine is a guy who is in love with being in love; and yes, this type does exist in the church. He actually thrives off of this biological chemical reaction in the brain called dopamine, this great excitement that causes one to lose the desire to eat or sleep because of the newness of a relationship. He gets turned on by the excited feeling of meeting someone new, e.g. planning dates and making a woman feel special in order to be validated as a loving and caring man. But often he really wants her to desire him sexually. If she is willing, he will indulge himself by sinfully having sex.

Just like the skilled lover, Mr. Accomplished, he is a man who knows all of the right words and rules of love. He knows how to romance a woman. A woman is treated like a queen by him—until the dopamine wears off. Then the attraction also wears off; he will leave you and start looking for his next fix.

These men are also heart-breakers, serial-daters, and extremely difficult to detect or understand.

What should you do?

Explorer, Hero, Conqueror, Ruler: **Leave.** In my opinion, Mr. Dopamine is to be avoided; he will have issues at any life stage. Just as you are feeling certain of his love, he will lose interest; the thrill for him is in the chase. That's what releases the dopamine. He will weave around from woman to woman just to have that new-love feeling.

Mr. Rescuer

Mr. Rescuer will try to save you from yourself and everyone else. He is the fix-it guy and simply takes care of everything. If he is not able to help you, he sees himself as a total failure. He is a good guy, but can sometimes be controlling and can become too attached.

This is why some of them lose it if you do not need them anymore, or if you outgrow them. Also, some men in this category can become violent because their whole manhood is tied to solving problems for you. Yes, **abusive men exist in the church.** The silence around this fact hurts my ears.

The key to Mr. Rescuer is to see if he can focus on himself long enough to balance out the relationship. If not, you may need to move on because he can become very controlling.

What should you do?

Explorer and Conqueror: **Look Twice.** This guy can make modifications to his behavior with the right woman who understands his intentions.

Hero and Ruler: **Long Shot.** If he is controlling and gets angry when he is not able to fix things, beware. But if he has good intentions and can control his anger, he can be a long shot.

The Nerd/Brainiac

Nerd or "Brainiac" men are very useful, but sometimes get overlooked by women because they are socially awkward. They are very tech-savvy and will fix all of your electronics and much more. Many of them live within their heads and sometimes are not able to operate as so-called normal men socially; but most are well adjusted. They may dress funny, but many of them are very attractive. A good woman who understands them could have that touch in making them shine.

They can be an awesome catch for you because many of these men are very successful. Please do not mix up a nerd dresser with a true nerd Brainiac; nerd dressers could be dreamers who never take action in their lives and are just plain old awkward.

What should you do?

Explorer and Conqueror: **Look Twice.**

Hero and Ruler: **Promising.** This guy is just socially awkward and can make a great mate for you.

Mr. Shy

Although his shyness can come off as sweet, cute, and comforting, Mr. Shy's somewhat reserved nature can be crippling to anyone trying to date him. Mr. Shy will just NOT make a move. In some cases, a woman can try many things just to get him off the saddle, but to no avail.

The worst part: Mr. Shy can be all into you, but will have too much fear to show it! He may even ask you out, but will not show up or call. The way to handle this guy is to simply make the first move and be very direct. If this does not work, I would drop it because if he is that scared, he may never come out of his shell. When meeting a guy like this, you may have to step out of tradition and approach him to eliminate his fear of rejection.

A MAN OF GOD *is* *Still* A MAN

What should you do?

Explorer: **Long Shot.**

Conqueror: **Look Twice.**

Hero & Ruler: **Promising**. This guy is also socially awkward and can make a great mate for you. However, in some cases he will never step up and can be a long shot if you are not able to deal with this matter.

Mr. Big Kid

Mr. Big Kid is simply afraid to grow up and take on the responsibilities of a relationship and children.

Don't get me wrong, many of these men can be successful in their business or professional lives, but will never make a decision to become successful in a relationship. He may even think of himself as Mr. Big Stuff. Also, many of them can still be living at home with their parents, even though they make enough money to move out.

This guy may call you, go out, want to have fun, and may even pray with you, but marriage and family is just too much for him. Many times he will want the privilege of being married and will seek sex from you. Beware! It may not go anywhere. He simply feels that he cannot provide you with the support and emotional care you need. All you have to do is start talking about getting married and he becomes hesitant. He is actually shaking off any relationship responsibility. You should simply move on from this guy, unless he becomes aware of his actions and seeks help to change.

What should you do?

Explorer and Conqueror: **Leave.** This guy is extremely difficult to deal with in adult situations.

Hero and Ruler: **Look Twice.** Do not mix this guy up with a man who is a kid at heart, in which case he can be a great mate.

Mr. Video Gamer

First, there is nothing wrong with a guy playing video games in his spare time, especially if it relaxes him. You may have the spare time sports player or the video-player.

However, Mr. Video Gamer takes playing these games too far. He can ignore the people in his life and even find himself addicted to these games.

If this guy invites you to play with him, then this could be something special for the two of you. If not, he may not be interested in you or does not like playing video games with women.

If he is neglecting anything, e.g. the relationship, work, school, or job, then this *is* problematic.

If a man works and loves video games, then two hours per day is a reasonable amount of playing time. This is about the same amount of time as a good movie. Now, this should be the maximum amount of time he plays when you are with him. If you are not home, and he has no other responsibilities or duties to complete, then don't worry how long he plays—unless, of course, it leads him to avoid or ignore you. To be a contender for your affection, he needs to be able to balance his playing time with proper time for the relationship. Just remember, in a relationship two hours a day is a good negotiating starting point as the maximum amount of time he plays alone per day.

Just know that research shows that games are designed to be addicting. That is how they make their money.

What should you do?

Explorer and Conqueror: **Leave.** This guy is extremely difficult to handle and pulls out his video games to deal with issues.

Hero: **Long Shot.**

Ruler: **Look Twice.** He may just love video games, but can take great care of you.

Mr. Too-Nice Guy

Mr. Too-Nice can love you completely, but over time he becomes too nice to express his true feelings. He will always look to you to take charge of the relationship. He will follow your directions. He is simply afraid to be honest and direct. He would rather send you an email or text than face you about his concerns. He is actually a coward and simply too nice for his own good. Just keep in mind that his fear is more about rejection, and he avoids this like the plague. This guy should be dumped if he constantly avoids the issues and will not face you directly.

What should you do?

Explorer: **Long Shot.**

Conqueror: **Look Twice.**

Hero & Ruler: **Promising.** This guy is simply a pleaser and usually just wants to make you happy.

Mr. My-Ex-Complainer

Mr. My-Ex-Complainer spends most of his time complaining about previous relationships, e.g. his ex-wife or women he has dated in the ministry. He is bitter and blames his ex's for his not trusting women and to explain his jealous ways or actions towards you. He always says, "God is working with me on this." Therefore he may appear to be a good protector, but sometimes it is a cover to keep better track of you because of his trust issues. He must realize that the person in front of him now (you) is not the one who caused him pain. If he is not willing to work on these issues, this will be a major problem in a marriage.

What should you do?

Explorer and Conqueror: **Leave.** This guy will blame his behavior on his ex-lovers.

Hero and Ruler: **Long Shot.** Sometimes Mr. My-Ex-Complainer in these stages can find clarity that complaining about his ex is not good. He will give it up for the right woman. If you have relationship skills, you can help him see that he can win better by looking at this situation from a different perspective. He may just be a little bitter.

Mr. My-Flesh-Is-Too-Weak

Mr. My-Flesh-Is-Too-Weak is a man who states that he is godly. He could be a pastor or minister and appears to have it all together. He understands the scriptures and is eloquent in his approach to relationships by doing it "God's way." He will state publicly that he is not having sex and will speak out against those who are fornicating, as it is often put.

However, watch out for this "My-Flesh-Is-Just-Too-Weak" type of man. You see, he could really want to do the right things, and so do you, but he knows how to get sex from women and hide behind religion as to why he has to leave them. "I can't be with you because you are so sexy that my flesh becomes weak." All of this will happen after sex.

Actually, both of you can be doing exactly what you want (having sex), but seek to have it with those who are believers just in case the relationship develops further. In this case both of you are weak sexually and seek others in the Church who may be weak in that category, too. The thought process is this: "At least, we have the same religious beliefs." All of this is about meeting needs and not about truly understanding what is motivating choices and actions.

As a woman of God, please do not fall victim to this guy's approach. Be careful. Some of these men are spreading HIV and other diseases. I've found that Mr. My-Flesh-Is-Too-Weak often deceives himself and will deceive you into thinking that he is above the rest by using principles that you may actually believe. He will be so good that you may just slip up and have sex with him; and then the attraction will disappear and he will leave you. Just watch out for these Church sexual predators.

Mr. My-Flesh-Is-Too-Weak may not be malicious in his approach; however, he is still persuading women of God to have sex with him and creating environments for you to become sexually weak. He is successful because you are feeling safe with this "godly man" and your guards are down. Be careful because you may be his next victim.

What should you do?

Explorer and Conqueror: **Look Twice.**

Hero and Ruler: **Promising.** This guy may be a little confused, but once he zones in on his woman, he will ask for her hand in marriage. Just be careful at any stage.

Mr. Down Low

Mr. Down Low is bi-sexual. The term "down-low" originated within the African-American community as a slang term to identify men who say they are heterosexual, but who have sex with other men. Another way to describe this is "on the DL," i.e. being discrete.

I have to admit that you do find a lot of this type in the church, often in high-profile positions. You often find them as a choir director, musician, or a minister, but also in any profession from politicians, teachers, and university professors, to even athletic coaches.

All of these men have more to lose if they come out, so they usually attempt to hide their deeds by marrying a woman to throw others off base regarding their sexuality. This is their attempt to avoid social isolation, discrimination from peers and religious members, and being exposed. Ironically, their behavior is obvious to those watching closely.

I also know that many liars and haters in the community try to use this term against other men of faith in order to destroy their reputation out of envy or for other reasons, and it is totally false! Can you imagine how difficult it can be to have a label placed on you, against which there is NO WAY you can defend yourself? Why? Well, it is usually rooted in a secret society of men who participate in these acts, leaving others not knowing what to believe, and there is nothing one can do.

Fear of Mr. DL is common among women. As a coach, I know this first-hand. This fear is especially prevalent in the African-American community. However, there is absolutely no evidence that DL is a real phenomenon in the black community.

Here is the deal.

Most of these men have been in the prison system. Since African-Americans dominate the prison population, it is obvious that the fear will be more widespread in their community.

Studies do show that minority men are more likely NOT to disclose their sexual orientation, compared with white men but this is rapidly changing. Researchers believe that this is the reason there is an increase in HIV in the community. But if you look closely, it is not as much as you may think.

However, HIV is great among African-American women in several cities. It is unclear if it has to do with DL men or men who used drugs. Just like many rumors that run through the community that are absurd, the reality of the DL syndrome doesn't match up with all of the rhetoric. Yes, there are bisexual black men, and some even behave in an irresponsible manner. However, there has never been a widespread epidemic of such irresponsible behavior as is being described in the media. People have made lots of money off this so-called "epidemic."

The notion of DL behavior was really an attempt to explain the higher rate of HIV infection in the black community, but it has never been truly shown to be the case. The African-American community is difficult to research. It has been said that the vector that accounts for the higher rate of HIV infections is related to either the peculiar immune system of people of African descent, or to the safe sex practices (or lack thereof) in the black community. However, Intravenous Drug Users (IDU) account for 73% of the HIV cases and people having sex with them. Men having sex with men accounts for about 13% and a percentage of this is from men having sex with IDUs. This makes it difficult to measure.

A MAN OF GOD *is Still* A MAN

My advice to you

Be concerned, especially since you are a woman of God, but lose the fear! Be more mindful of men in the church who have come out of prison and those who have once used drugs than of men in general. Also STOP BELIEVING LIES. Men with hemorrhoids that can cause rectal bleeding are NOT DL! You can get these via diet and certain activities.

Stop believing this myth. Men in the church who are always talking and carrying on about gay men or using homosexual terms should concern you, too. I'm not saying that they are DL, but it should concern you.

Just know that it is easy to spot Mr. Down Low by simply paying attention. Do not get so excited in meeting a new man that you lose your ability to pick up underlying signals. Trust your inner compass or instinct that God has given you. Watch where his eyes go and listen carefully to the things he says.

Simply ask the question, "Hey, I hope this doesn't offend you, but I need to know. Have you ever had sex with another man?" Good men in the community have heard all of the rumors, and a solid one will not mind that you do a quick check to be sure.

What should you do?

Explorer, Hero, Conqueror, Ruler: **Leave.** This guy at any stage will struggle with his sexuality. He may be looking for a cover because of his position in the church, so leave!

Mr. Church Player

Mr. Church Player is simply an expert in getting women to bed. He is a pick-up artist who works on church women. He knows how to play all of the cards. His goal is only to score. Once he hits it, it is all over. A good way to describe him is like a politician who tells you what you want to hear; but when you vote him in, things never change. Players come in all shapes and sizes, but all of them are very smooth talkers.

Just know that most players do not want a serious relationship leading to marriage and some are cheap. He may lavish you in his environment, e.g. showing off his big house, but only to score. He loses interest if you know what you want and what you are looking for in a relationship.

You have to be prayed up to avoid these men because some of them are sociopaths and totally deceive you. He may also be dangerous because he may drug you on a date for sex.

What should you do?

Explorer, Hero, Conqueror, Ruler: **Leave.** This guy at any stage is out to score.

Qualifications: *Explorer, Hero, Conqueror:* Sometimes men leave this pattern and become devoted to God and then look for a woman to marry. *Ruler:* This guy will rarely seek to be with one woman; he is a church predator.

Beware of These Two!

As noted in "His Life Stage," there are men prone to violence in the church as in other parts of society. A church can become a sanctuary for them when they tell their story loudly and appear to repent. But research shows that many re-offend. This book would not be complete without acknowledging this and providing you with the early warning signs. Domestic violence can be a silent epidemic in certain cultures and I do not want to contribute to that.

Although men in any of the guy brands may abuse a woman, there are two guy brands that are particularly dangerous. I am sad to say that they exist in the Church.

Mr. Saving-Face-at-All-Costs:

Some men of God will do anything to save face just to maintain their status in the church. They will even commit murder or solicit murder-for-hire services just to keep you silent. I'm not trying to frighten you, but please take note: When dealing with a man of God with status who is doing sinful things that, if exposed, could ruin his reputation or ministry, be extremely careful. Never threaten to expose him or cause him harm or you may become a victim of a serious crime.

If he is harming the community, yes report him. But, be careful if you are angry and having a relationship quarrel. Just know that when a man has a lot to lose and his ministry is not as visible as a national one, he can be even more dangerous. He may believe that killing you will not reach any epic proportion in the media and may think it can be done easily and gotten away with. Do not threaten to expose him. (See "Exposing a Man of God").

I know this is harsh and scary but must be said. There are too many cases where men in the church who say they are "of God" are killing women, even their spouses, and molesting biological and step children. This leads to my last Guy Brand.

Mr. "I Love God," But Hits Women

Yes, he is an abuser and does it repeatedly. These men believe women should stay in a certain place and will actually hit or grab a woman to put her physically in place. Men who have abused in the past will run to the church for vindication, saying that they have changed. But beware of these men when you are seeking a relationship, even if they appear to be men of God.

You need to know that, men with anger issues and with a domestic-violence past come in all shapes, sizes, and colors. They can have a great command of the Word of God and even appear to be serious about having a relationship leading to marriage.

The National Network to End Domestic Violence (NNEDV) has identified the red flags. In a 2011 Liz Brody article at huffingtonpost.com, Cindy Southworth, VP of NNEDV, suggested that women perform this little test to determine how a man will react:

> Break a date at the beginning when he's all hot and heavy, and tell him your girlfriend needs you. If he says, "I'm disappointed, but I understand," great. But if it's, "I

can't bear to be apart," or if he makes you feel guilty, puts your friend down, or gets angry, these are not good signs!

Here are other early warning signs identified by survivors of domestic violence who reflected on the early phases of the battering relationship (circulated by NNEDV).

Beware of a man, even a man of God, who
- wants to move too quickly into the relationship
- does not honor your boundaries
- is excessively jealous and accuses you of having affairs
- wants to know where you are all of the time and calls, emails, and texts you frequently throughout the day.
- criticizes you or puts you down; most commonly tells you that you are "crazy," "stupid" and/or "fat," or that no one would ever want or love you
- says one thing and does another
- takes no responsibility for his behavior and blames others
- has a history of battering
- blames the entire failure of previous relationships on his partner, for example, "My ex was a total bitch."
- grew up in an abusive or violent home
- insists that you stop spending time with your friends and/or family
- seems "too good to be true"
- insists that you stop participating in leisure interests
- rages out of control and is impulsive

Pay attention to the "red flags "and trust your instincts. Survivors of domestic violence frequently report that their instincts told them that there was something wrong early on, but they disregarded the warning signs and didn't know that these signs were indicative of an abusive relationship.

Men of God are still men and some of them bring their violent temper to church. Don't be a victim.

How to Use These Guy Brands?

Now, how does this help you find your Mr. Right? Although a lot of men exhibit relationship patterns that are NOT promising, a quick tally shows that ten out of fourteen of these relationship patterns have at least a few men who are. Let's take a closer look at how you can use this information in finding your Mr. Right. And remember to be flexible and keep an open mind.

Is He Ready?

"Isn't anyone ready?" Women of faith ask me this often. They also ask, "How can you tell if he is ripe for a serious relationship or marriage?"

Now that you have my tips on how to deal with men based on life stages and relationship patterns, I will provide further explanations and clarity to help you recognize a man who is ripe.

For each relationship pattern described, I answered the question, **"What Should You Do?"** In most cases a relationship is either **Promising** or not. If not, then I recommend that you either **Look Twice**, consider him a **Long Shot**, or **Leave**. Let me explain how you can use these guidelines to find your Mr. Ripe.

If a man is **promising**, he is ready and he knows it. He is in the process of evaluating every woman he meets, asking himself, *Is she right for me?* You have to be able to answer that question for him. But, you will have the same question about him. Therefore, it should not become a wrestling match, but an evaluation or testing process for both of you. If he is not right for you, it doesn't mean that he is NOT ripe for a relationship. Therefore don't label him inappropriately. You must have a "love-all-men" attitude in order to find the one right for you. That means thinking well of him, even if you decide that he is not for you.

Looking twice means that you should not reject this man based on something you did not like or because he is not as together as you would like. He may be a diamond in the rough, and the right woman will make him shine. **You see, if a man feels that a woman can influence him to want to be a better man, she's a keeper.** This could be you. Evaluate this man for his potential.

Calling a man a **Long Shot** is like waving a yellow flag. It means you should be cautious. Also, it means that he is worth considering, but you should NEVER get any hopes up high with this guy. You see, a woman can come into a man's life and shake him up emotionally and mentally. He will realize that he is not as together as he believed. She can shake him into a whole new stage. In this case, your influence can make him a good prospect for a serious relationship. He will change right in front of your eyes.

The key is this: Will he be right for you? How will you see him now that he has changed? Don't make him ripe for someone else. You influenced the change, and you should be the one to accept him. Don't make him into a caricature, a stereotype of the man you found that he is not able to shake. Be flexible. Reevaluate this man. It's a long shot, but it CAN happen.

Leave really needs no explanation. There are red and yellow flags all over the place. You don't want to deal with these things. Just leave. Exit with dignity.

In looking for Mr. Ripe, understand that, in general, every man is looking for that special woman who totally fits into his life; the one he has passion for. Contrary to popular beliefs, men are not that afraid of commitment. They are afraid of what it has come to mean: loss of _____. You fill in the blank. Your job is to create an environment in which he feels he can win by committing to you, as I'll explain later in "The Commitment: Is He Ready?" in Chapter Six. Then, he will look at you from that perspective.

When a man is ripe, his conversation will reflect it. He will be saying things like "I'm tired of this or that" when it comes to relationships. "I'm looking for something deep or meaningful." He will actually tell you up front about his intentions.

If he says, "Let's just hook up and see where it goes," he is up in the air about a serious relationship or is just not ready. But don't reject him totally. He may be tired of the relationship rat race and may have had some bad experiences with women that put him in a wait-and-see mode.

But, how can you tell? Look at his life and see if he has **made preparations** for adding a woman to it. A man who is serious about a relationship usually makes preparations. You will notice more responsible actions taken about being with a woman and for the role he will play as a husband. You will be able to fit into his life as a wife. You will and should notice the preparation.

You will have to consider a few factors: The state of his finances is one major key. You see, a man is concerned about how he measures up financially. He also wants to be able to take care of a woman (be her provider). "Can I pay the bills and provide for her?" is his main question. A man who is preparing or talking preparation is speaking about his financial situation; this is usually the main point he will bring up.

Now for your consideration, how are you financially? Are you able to hold things down? This is a new time and men are evaluating your financial capabilities like never before. If you can create an environment in which he can still be the man and can fit into your life, you may be able to create that "prosperous man" you seek. You can hold things down financially until he is on his feet as he sees himself and help create this man with your influences.

This is my major point: whether or not you see this type of man in a positive manner. He can be everything that you want, except not as fit financially, but he has a plan. This man is promising, workable. You will have to consider whether he is worth the investment. Consider, especially, *Is he the type of man who will give me what I need emotionally? Does he have the character I will want for the father of my children?* This is what counts long term anyway.

If you are evaluating men based on finances, you may find one who is great and provides security, but he may not support your needs emotionally. You will still feel empty, even if you marry this man.

As I wrap up this section, the operative word is preparation. He is prepared or preparing himself. This is when you will know he is ripe.

Also, I'm not one to say that you should totally trust your gut; it is known to deceive you at times. The key is to learn how to ask better questions and gauge responses, along with using your intuition. You'll need these skills in order to make the best decisions about who to spend the rest of your life with. I'll be suggesting some good questions to ask when you are assessing this. (See especially "The Commitment: Is He Ready?" in Chapter Six.)

Let's continue with some of the other important considerations in getting to know men.

His Mental Operating System

What is a man's mental operating system? Well, it is a lot like your computer's operating system, except that each man has his own, unique, system. He uses this system to navigate in his world. The part used for operating relationships today is the programming he developed growing up. It is based on how he was socialized as a kid and on the types of relationships he grew up viewing between men and women. Whatever associations he made then about men and women and how they relate in a marriage, or in a dating relationship, are built into his mental operating system.

Current research supports the idea that a person's relationship patterns actually come more from parental influences than from who the person really is or wants to be inside. That is, most people repeat, or react to, or escape from, the relationship patterns of their parents. All of their reactions to a relationship are actually still coming from a parental influence, more so than from their true self.

Therefore, understanding a man's childhood will help you learn his take on marriage and relationships. If he had an abusive father, he could be abusive, too; or he could have made up his mind that he will never hit a woman. If he saw his mom struggle with men, he can react to these things.

The more you know about a man's childhood, the more you can learn about how he views relationships and what kind of husband he will be. Listen very carefully to determine how his mental software from childhood is aligned for or against relationships. His conversations about his upbringing and family will tell you everything you need to know. Just listen to see which direction he is taking regarding that subject.

You may discover that how he makes decisions is sometimes based on this old programming and on the "global beliefs" formed by it.

His Global Beliefs

> Proverbs 3:6 NLT: *Seek his will in all you do, and he will show you which path to take.*

Where a man is in his life stage determines a lot about his current actions in a marital or dating relationship. There is a transition between each stage, and sometimes he can become stuck or have difficulties in the movement and has no idea why. He is aware that Scripture tells him, **Seek His will in all you do** (Proverbs 3:6 NLT), and he is doing this to the best of his abilities, but he is just stuck. There may be hidden reasons for this that don't show and of which he is not aware. They may be part of the mental operating system that evolved as he grew up. Here is an example.

Naturally, a man believes he is making decisions based on current information. However, it is possible that some of the decisions he is making now are actually based on a traumatic experience that he had as a young kid. His impressionable past self may have been induced into certain beliefs or behavior by someone of influence, by his peers, or by an event relating to himself or to relationships in general.

This all comes together in the story he developed around the event(s) at that time: how his past self-interpreted whatever happened and who he blamed. Often this story becomes what I call a "**global belief**," which will have had a major effect on his life at each stage from then on.

Global beliefs can also explain how a man deals with a woman in a relationship. From the key decisions made at this pertinent emotional point in his life he created a negative identity that is affecting his relationships today—whether married or dating.

How Can This Play Out?

If a man was beaten and abused by a woman wearing red finger- and toe-nail polish when he was a child, he might have developed a story or global belief that women with red nails can hurt him. We know that this is not true, but at a traumatic point in his youth, a woman with red nails caused him extreme pain. His young self, focused on the red polish, formed a global key decision that all women wearing red nail polish are dangerous. What emotional thoughts will this negative identification trigger if your nails are red? He could feel that you can hurt him. But, how could you know? In fact, he may not be able to put this feeling into words. He just knows he doesn't like women with red nails.

What if a man was socialized to not speak up? What if he learned that when people yell it means they are extremely displeased with you—enough to cause physical or emotional pain? What type of decisions will he make in a marriage or relationship with someone who yells? How will he behave if you yell?

The key point here is to understand that a negative identification like this can limit a man's options and prevent him from having a positive relationship with a woman. It can make him feel like running. He may leave, and you will wonder why.

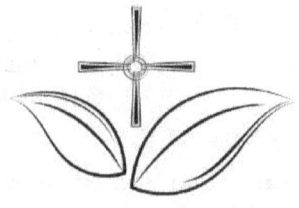

When He Leaves

Well, you have just read a whole lot about men and learned about how they make decisions, their life stages and relationship patterns, how to tell when they are ripe for a meaningful relationship, and even that, maybe, they don't know what they want. Men not knowing what they want may be a little comforting to many women because they often say that they are blamed for everything. My response to that is, "Yes, I know!" Here is something interesting: Men feel the same way.

So, why he left? The answer depends on when it happened. However, it will always be the result of lost attraction. Usually after one or two dates, something is done that turns him off, or else he could still be emotionally handicapped from his last relationship. If he left during the relationship, then it was caused by a build-up of events that assured him that you are not the one.

By now you understand that there are so many questions and a variety of answers—some may not make sense to you as a woman. Many of the answers may anger you. I am making a generalization because some women actually get it. The key is to understand that there are many reasons why a man will remove himself from your life. This book is designed to provide some clarity.

My goal for you is to make sure you do your part and focus on things you can control, not on the things you cannot. I can't help most men; they usually do not read relationship books. However, I can help you create, learn, and develop your skills to meet your relationship challenges.

REMEMBER THIS: **A man wants to be acknowledged, respected, trusted, appreciated, and to feel that he is your personal superman.** This is what makes him feel good in your presence. Allowing him a sense of freedom is powerful too. The things you do will determine his emotional calculation of these factors. If the mental math doesn't add up, he will no longer be attracted to you and will leave.

"**I trust you!**" is one of the most powerful things you can say to a man. He will want to live up to that brand. And when you add to this, "**I'm proud of you,**" it does more for a man than any accolade coming from someone else. So, say it often, "I trust you. I'm proud of you."

Other Things You Must Consider

Men are afraid of failure. If he notices issues about you early in the relationship that he cannot put his finger on, explain, or feels will hurt you, he will **leave** instead of dealing with the issues—only because he cannot be your superman in that matter.

"*How can I win?*" This is the unconscious question men ask themselves all the time, along with *Am I winning or losing this battle?* Again, this is an **emotional calculation**. Additionally, sometimes men, even of faith, may seem to embellish or exaggerate things a bit: how much money they make, how well they are doing, how tall they are, to what degree there is a problem, among other things. Here is an important fact: **Men try to see things better than they are because they are wired for victory.** Testosterone is biological fuel for winning and solving problems. If you catch him embellishing things, don't accuse him of lying, just know that he is seeing things better than they are.

Therefore, you must have skills in dealing with men in a relationship. You must understand this dynamic and learn to establish obtainable goals which allow him to take the action needed to succeed. Being critical only makes matters worse. Show him how to win while making him believe that he is extremely close to the goal, i.e. making you happy.

Men are afraid of what they are losing. Think in terms of what you are able to add to him instead of what you want to take away. One of the worst things that can happen in a relationship is if a man feels locked down when he is with you. Usually a woman's need for certainty creates this jail for men. It is a major reason why he will leave or feel trapped. The key is to allow him a sense of freedom by not constantly tripping about his whereabouts. If you are a woman of God, you should trust your husband. Yes, he has to prove that he is trustworthy, but it will never happen unless you start out with trust.

Are you draining his life's energy? Does something always come up in the relationship, some drama when he's around? Do you both have the same energy level? Or, does he feel drained in your presence, not wanting to do anything? He will leave because you sap out all of his energy. I call it negative energy when the polarity is off in the relationship.

As a relationship coach and mentor, I find these topics difficult for many of my clients to grasp. They are women who are smart and simply a great catch for any man. However, they make a constant effort to force men to connect all of the dots or make a lifetime buying decision about them within a few dates or a few short months. I'm sorry, this usually will not happen. You cannot and will not control a man.

Hint: This is another tip as to why attraction can be lost—your need to control him saps the energy right out of your relationship. A man of God will no longer be able to feel it, so will leave.

 Understand this: quality men of faith have options and are usually wondering, *Do I want to marry her or her or her?* So take the pressure off him and yourself.

If he is good-looking, educated, and makes a great living, his options will increase over tenfold. If you are a minority woman seeking a minority man, and he is good looking, educated, and has money, or is maybe a ball player, his options increase over twentyfold. Groupies will be everywhere. You must understand this concept and not take things too seriously or pressure men. Let him enjoy being with you.

Bottom Line?

Why a man won't marry you, or will leave you? **You just don't make him feel good in your presence.** It is just that simple.

You may say, "I'm a strong-minded woman. I love God and know what I want."

My response: "I'm sure this makes you feel significant, but what does this mean? How does it make a man feel good in your presence?"

You may say, "Men are out to hurt women and are looking for their next victim. Men are this or that. Men just don't...."

My response: "Saying such things creates a disapproving spirit. If this is your belief, you will find a way to make it true. He will leave, and you will constantly attract jerks. Having a negative view of men limits your dating and marriage options and doesn't work!"

I would say that in over ninety-seven percent of cases a man is not out to hurt you! This is really not his goal. Yes, you can get hurt, even if you are cautious; but it is not his intent. He hopes you are the one, but when he sees otherwise, he will lose interest and leave.

You want men to change, but have you looked in the mirror? Maybe it is you who should change or make an adjustment—primarily in your thinking or approach.

If you want a loving man, you have to realize that he DOES NOT think or see things as you do. Yes, it makes sense to you, but to him? No doubt there are things you believe strongly that he has never considered; they have never crossed his mind. What happens when you judge his intent? In most cases he will feel like a failure because he cannot make you happy. This alone will not make him feel good in your presence. As he realizes this, the attraction will drain right out of your relationship, and he will leave or become detached.

Why didn't he tell you? No doubt there are many possible reasons, but basically, it's about honesty. Can he be honest with you? Let's take a look at that next.

Can He Be Honest?

Psalm 51:6 NLT: *But you desire honesty from the womb, teaching me wisdom even there.*

His unspoken, problematic thoughts could suck the life directly out of the relationship. Actually, your unspoken thoughts can do this, too. The "I-don't-like-two-or-more-things-about-you-and-it's-killing-me" type of issue will kill a relationship.

These thoughts are unspoken because of his concern for hurting your feelings. For example, some medications, diet pills, and sinus problems might be making your breath smell extremely bad, not only in the morning, but in the evening when you and your mate may be connecting. Some women's after-sex smell can be fishy, or maybe he hates your perfume. He could love everything else about you, but these things are so offensive to him that he will simply leave. Unspoken thoughts are like a cancer in a relationship.

So here is the question on the table: Can he be honest? If he feels or believes that he cannot embrace honesty about some things with you, he will become uncomfortable and the attraction between you will be lost.

Remedy:

Create an environment where he can be totally honest about fixable things with the understanding that his intent is to improve the relationship. If you allow a man this freedom without being subject to guilt, you can have an amazing relationship.

By now you may be wondering why I am expecting you to do all of the changing, why not him?

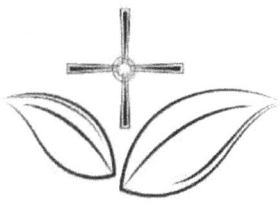

Who's Correcting Men?

Many of the complaints I get from clients, often emails from married and unmarried women, are about their frustrations with men. Yes, church men too. They shout "Who's correcting men?"

I hear your frustration, your anger, at what you see as the one-sided nature of what men really want. You tell me of the horrible experiences you've had with men and give me the impression that you do not see yourself as the problem. And maybe you are not! Let me affirm what I hear many of you saying:

> Yes, you are a good person.
>
> Yes, you do love and respect God.
>
> Yes, you are smart and independent.
>
> Yes, you are a great catch, or a wonderful wife.
>
> Yes, you have lots of love to give.
>
> Yes, you have tried your very best.

But finding and keeping Mr. Right has been out of reach for you. There are lots of jerks out there perpetrating all kinds of things, even among men of God. It's an epidemic! "What gives, Philemon?" you've asked.

Here is the truth. The information in this book may seem unfair, even difficult to swallow. I hear it all the time: "I need to know where I stand. Why do I have to change?" Or, "Sorry buddy, I'm not doing that! You must be crazy!" and, "I am not settling!" But women who understand the concepts in this book always get and keep their man! Here are some additional messages I've received.

"Philemon!"

"Why don't you tell men to stop being cheap?"

"Tell men to at least call if they are going to be late."

"Tell men to stop taking calls or texts when we are together."

"Tell men that they should stop running behind those hoochie mamas in the church, and get a real, saved woman."

"Tell men to grow up and learn some respect— including manners."

"Tell men that I'm not taking care of anyone but myself. I'm a strong, independent woman."

"Tell men to stop lying when the truth will do."

"Tell men to stop touching me without my permission."

"You need to educate men to do this or that."

These women think I ought to be out there coaching men, helping to whip them into shape.

Ladies, listen up. As I said before, I can't tell men to do anything. Even after all the sermons, relationship books or blogs you've read, TV shows and radio shows you've listen to, after all of the knowledge you think you have about relationships, please understand that men are still going to be the same today as they were yesterday. You can get all the pep talks you want from other women and from TV and radio shows, but nothing will change this fact.

So what gives? What can you do?

If You Are Not Yet Married

First, it is important to understand that, prior to selecting a man for marriage, find out his thinking surrounding relationships, and just make sure he is willing to get some love lessons. If not, **RUN** because some men of faith can have different views as to the role of women, as if they were living in the 1950s. They are easily detected by some of their comments.

Next, if he is not this way, and you want to find the love of your life, you will have to make a slight adjustment in your sensitivity and thinking to make it more accurate about men and their approach to dating. It is not my goal to make excuses for men, but to help you to understand how they do things so that you can change your approach to one that is more effective. This may not be what you want to hear, but it's true.

You must change your preconceived visual images of a relationship, be willing to try another approach, trust and follow through on some solid advice that, at times, is hard to hear. Why? Because **what you are currently doing is not working for you**. This is harsh, but it is the truth! If it were working for you, with all of your understandings and feelings, you would have a successful relationship. Why are you still available?

If You Are Married but Unhappy

On the other hand, if you are married but unhappy—either with the man or with your relationship, what can you do?

First you should determine what is unhealthy about your relationship. State it concretely and clearly. Then, you must ask yourself, *Are these thoughts and beliefs true? What makes them true?* If you are not able to pinpoint the issue, ask yourself, *What do I want that I am NOT getting?* I've learned that when all is said and done, it will boil down to **your needs are not being met**.

But the question on the table is: "Are you meeting his needs now?" I've learned that, as a woman of God, you should practice restraint as a way to grow spiritually. This alone will help you to learn how to pay attention. Once you pay close attention it will allow you to hear yourself being negative, critical, demanding, or other things that will not meet your spouse's needs. I believe strongly that, in order to get what you want, you have to give. I'm sure that sometimes you may be tired and feel that you have given enough, but I believe that all marriages, except those that are abusive, deserve a chance to rekindle what was lost since you first met.

When you have met his needs fully and your needs are still NOT being met, at least you can place yourself in a position to make a clear-headed decision regarding your relationship. Although God hates divorce, He does not prevent you from having one. He just provides conditions in Scripture for what has to happen for you to be free from your covenants or not.

Oh, oh, I can read your mind right about now, and I know I am going to get all of the reasons about what men do. I get this! Again, I know it seems unfair, and the things I need to share with you may be difficult to swallow, but they work.

You see, the women who are having the most success in their relationships understand another secret: **It is not about being right or wrong, but about knowing what works and what is useless, about what may be considered effective or ineffective.** Just do what works!

Stop letting things drive you crazy. Focus on what you are able to control: your reactions and mindset. You will have to forgive a man for his ignorance and for not being smart enough to know how to relate to you appropriately. You will teach him and help him out. You will not get turned off, because he doesn't yet have the right skill sets. You will have tolerance. You will be flexible.

An Effective Mindset for You

First Point: A man's dating skills do not translate into what type of husband he will be for you. Great men of God make horrible dating decisions every day. When you let yourself be turned off by his dating skills, you may be missing out on the love of your life. Are you willing to accept this loss? Or will you give it another try?

Second Point: If you take what you are looking for into consideration, **what does the male pool in the church look like for you?** How many men out there will fit your criteria?

Stop fooling yourselves, Ladies! Most of you must change your male-pool criteria in order to increase your chances of finding the love of your life. Make sure you look for qualities and traits that will last for thirty years or more and not for superficial traits that will change with time. Here are some special cases:

The mothers among you who are in your twenties or early thirties must know that most men who do not have kids will prefer not to marry a woman with kids already. This is a fact. It doesn't mean that he won't, but it will not be his preference. This may not be what you want to hear, but it is what you need to know. Start looking for men with children or slightly older men to settle down with. This is what I mean about the male pool.

Those very successful, take-charge types of women among you must realize that many of the professional men you are seeking do not want to come home to a very opinionated woman.

Newsflash: That "got-it-going-on" man you like so much loves passive women. He is looking for a softer landing at home. He seeks the opposite of himself, while these types of women seek a better version of themselves. You will have to adjust to a male who fits your personality best, or be that soft feminine soul that a professional man seeks when landing home.

And, for those of you dating, or tempted to date, a younger man, just know that a thirty-eight-year-old woman with kids already will hardly make it work with a twenty-eight-year-old man who wants a family. I say "hardly" because, if you have money, he may give it a try. Otherwise, you will not be the first or second choice on his list. It doesn't matter how good it is right now.

You see, it is all about priorities and flexibility. This is why I say it may, actually, be easier for you to find a man within your church. In my experience, a man who is really faithful to God and is seeking a woman who is just as faithful may accept many things that other men would not. Because his first priority is to have a woman who shares his beliefs, and perhaps even one who attends the same church. He will change his mind, be flexible, and marry a woman with kids. I have seen this happen.

Last Point: As I said before, very good-looking men have many, many options. If the type of man you seek is not approaching you now, stop fooling yourself into thinking that will change. Just because you approach them, and they sleep with you, doesn't mean anything about a future. Men must show an effort in a relationship, not just show up for a booty call. He left because he had other options, while you were chasing a dead end.

Are you open to following solid advice?

Take a look at the men who do want you. Do you see one of quality in the bunch that you've been overlooking?

Also, just continue reading this book. It will definitely help.

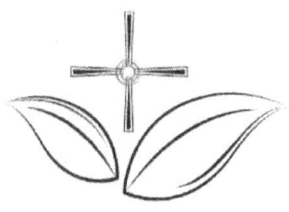

He Just Thinks Like a Man!

In my research, I find that a man doesn't often wake up after a good night's sleep with drama on his mind. He may feel a little troubled over some things, but he is not in a rage. His emotional slate is usually clean when he wakes up—if he got enough sleep. If he did NOT get enough, he may be a little grumpy or quiet, but his actions are rarely uncontrolled.

Let's say it is a Saturday. He may be thinking to himself,

What do I need to do today? Should I have the car serviced? Or chill, maybe work in the yard? I wonder what plans my wife has for us, or what she wants to do today? Maybe she will get her hair done. Then I'll take a good dump and see what's on TV or play basketball with the guys, and then...."

A man RARELY wakes up with drama on his mind.

I've discovered women to be different. Your dreams can be filled with drama and you can wake up this way. I even know a woman who woke up and hit her husband for doing something in her dream—acting as if it had truly happened. I find this is also the way women communicate to themselves and others.

Here is a major point: I always say that when it comes down to the home and relationships, women rule!! It is also why I focus on women because they can get what they want and rule the day with the right approach. A woman can win every time with her skills. All you have to do is view a man properly. Look at him as someone who desires to please you. Think of him as worthy of being praised.

Know this: He does NOT intentionally do things to aggravate you around the house. He is just being a guy, not thinking about too much except making you happy, eating, making money, having sex, paying bills, fixing things, doing his hobby, watching competitive sports, taking a good dump, and chilling. He is thinking, *Just tell me what you want me to do or what you need, dear.*

This is why your best approach towards a man should be direct. Try it. Just say, "Honey, don't do anything today. I want you to spend the day with me," instead of being angry and accusing him, "You don't spend time with me." Or complaining that he didn't remember this or that and doesn't love you. Just tell him what you want and remind him of things that are important to you. Just know that he does think about you and aims to please. Tell him what you want so that he doesn't have to figure it out. It is just that simple. I will address this subject in another way: **"He can't read your mind."**

You may truly believe, *If he aims to please me and loves me, I wouldn't have to remind him of the things that are important to me.* I do find that most women feel this way, but it is not true. His mind is wired differently. Just because he forgot something only means that he simply forgot—NOT that you are NOT important to him. Plus he will feel badly about disappointing you because, to him, that is a sign of failure, and he will beat himself up more than you ever can.

To be clear**, a man who cares about you will do the things he knows you love**. If it is important to you, and you have shared that, he will do it.

Women have also said to me, "My man is so patient, but I yell at him since I believe he should KNOW what to do. I shouldn't have to tell him. I'm working on not yelling, but I still do it."

As you will learn in this book, women in this situation have to be careful. It is really a paradox that could end painfully.

When a man loves his woman, he wants to please her and be present for her emotionally. He is patient, BUT if he can NOT win at all, he will feel like a failure. This is the worst position to put a man in. He will try harder and harder, but at some point he will give up. His feelings of resentment have been building; eventually he will say, "I can't please her, so why try?"

Everything will feel like a test that he can NOT pass. He will come to realize that the issue is NOT with him, because another attractive woman who can see what a good man he is will say something like this, "If my man did half as much as you, I would be so happy," or simply, "She doesn't appreciate you."

Trust me, I know and see it virtually every week, and it has happened to me in the past. I get so many heartbreaking emails daily from these women, even those that have been on the cover of magazines. They say "if he loved me he would _____ , or he wouldn't _____." But again, it was just a test that he couldn't pass, because he DID NOT know what to do. I'll discuss this later in "Love Exam" (Chapter Four). It is a major relationship-destroyer.

You see, there is NO readily available manual for him to study, because the owner of the manual (his woman) will NOT share.

What happens to a woman whose man could never please her? She harbors a continuous cycle of resentment towards all men. She may never marry. Some do change, but there is another side that is NOT pretty. Many become depressed and never recover. I see this, too, and hear their stories.

Help your man win by letting him love you. A smile will help. This is all he can do. He may try, but WILL NOT be able to anticipate everything you want. So, notice his efforts and reward him. Just know that you have only a small window of opportunity, because men will NOT remain in that state of feeling like a failure in love for too long. I get emails saying, "I was just getting there, and NOW he does this to me." Or "Philemon, what can I do now?"

It is hard to do anything after the fact. He may believe that you are changing just to keep him from leaving; this will NOT sit right with him either. Failure is not a good option for a man; he will seek a way to win. Let him win with you. He is worth it and so are you.

A woman who gets this is mature enough and willing to understand the power of relationship dynamics. She is looking for the right approach. Her goal is to understand men. She doesn't expect a man to read her mind. She is aware that her man genuinely wants to please her, but is just being a guy in his thinking! She is direct in her communications and shares what she desires, and he is happy breaking his neck doing those things he knows please her. Be grown and direct and trust me, he will appreciate you so much for this. He just thinks like a man.

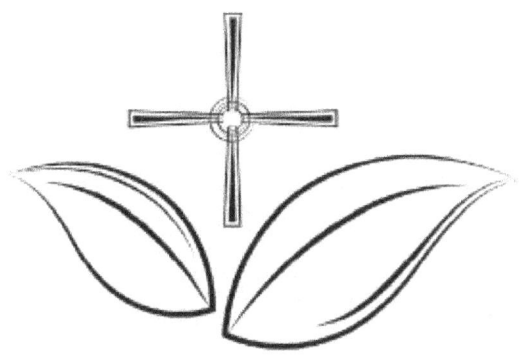

CHAPTER THREE:
Examining Yourself

2 Corinthians 13:5 NIV: *Examine yourselves to see whether you are in the faith; test yourselves. Do you not realize that Christ Jesus is in you—unless, of course, you fail the test?*

A man of God desires a woman who is praised by others for her great character and works.

You may see yourself as an "I-know-what-I-want," accomplished, witty, very conversational type of person with ambitious ways. He may see you as arrogant, bossy, competitive, argumentative, and extremely difficult to deal with. He is seeking a mate to complement him and fit into his life, NOT a competitive partner.

Are You Really Ready?

If Mr. Right walks into your life right now, what will he find? Are you ready for him? Are YOU emotionally available? That is, you do not have negative thoughts about men, and you have the time and energy to put into a relationship. Can you present yourself in a fashion that tells him you are a keeper?

How do you know if you are NOT ready for Mr. Right? Here is a checklist for you:

- ☐ Is your phone still ringing with past relationships—going-nowhere men described as "friends"?
- ☐ Are you still receiving emails from past relationships—going-nowhere men described as "friends"?
- ☐ Are you still receiving text messages from past relationships—going-nowhere men described as "friends"?
- ☐ Are you seen in pictures one-on-one with a variety of men described as "friends"?
- ☐ Are these pictures displayed in your home or on social media sites where your new love interest may see them?

If you checked even one of these, then I ask you, "**Why do you do these things?**"

A MAN OF GOD *is* *Still* A MAN

Is it ego? Does it make you appear valuable? Feel good?

Does it make you feel like he knows that he missed out by not measuring up?

Does it really, really feel good to hear them say great things about you or beg to get you back?

Why do you still allow contact? Do you believe it makes you look valuable to men by being next to other good-looking men on pictures?

If a new love interest looked at your phone's recent call list, what would he find? Calls or texts from a bunch of men? Then you are NOT ready for Mr. Right. The attraction between you will be lost and he will leave, perhaps run away. The research is totally sound on this matter when it comes to men. I've seen so many cases; it makes me sad.

Men of God are walking away because of your past. What do these guy friends mean to you? Nothing, period! They only feed your ego. You allow them to continue to call or communicate just so you can gloat about how they won't leave you alone because of how good you were to them. It's an ego trip. This will not make you look good to a new man of God. This is why he will lose interest and leave.

To prepare for a good man, you have to be, and appear to be, ready and available; you have to be the type of woman he feels can be trusted with his heart. If you are seen on pictures one-on-one with other men on your Facebook, Twitter, or other social network profiles, especially good-looking or muscular men, it could send him the wrong message about you or your type. You also have to implement project "communication silence" from men of your past—those you describe as "friends." In other words, stop the calls now. If you don't, your new man will not say anything, but will realize that you are not ready and not a keeper.

I know you become bored and like to hear men from your past complain about not having you anymore. I know that you get lonely sometimes and take these calls to pass time away. But these men will continue to call when Mr. Right comes along, and it is possible that you will not be able to put a stop to them in time. It could ruin your chances with that new good man and you won't know why. Do not allow this to happen to you. Stop the contact and find another way to amuse yourself and get ready for Mr. Right.

Some good men will allow you time to get rid of all those guy friends who contact you. However, there are so many who will not, and that one time you receive a call in his presence will be the last of your relationship. Also some of these guy friends will not go away quietly and can cause more trouble. Deal with it before Mr. Right comes along. Do not risk it! Get rid of that waste in your life.

A lot of men have told me that they like being cool with their ex-ladies. I totally understand this and have been there before. It is just that those ladies we are cool with could have problems with a new man. When she meets another man, and I'm still calling, it will become a problem for their relationship. Don't take that risk with a new or potential love interest.

Good Person, Bad Mate

This is a subject that baffles so many women of God and it may be hard to understand: YOU CAN BE A GREAT PERSON, BUT A BAD MATE.

Women say to me all the time, "Philemon, I am a good person who loves God, why I can't find a good man of God?" Or, "Why can't I keep the one I'm with?"

I always ask them this question: "You say that you are a very good person, but are you a good mate?" Maybe you do all of the things you believe a man may want or desire, but how are things done? How are words expressed? What about your body language and gestures? Yes, you may go to church, pay your tithes, give to the poor, visit the sick, and volunteer your time. All of this is good and makes you a great person.

But again, are you a great mate to a man?

Do you do the things that he likes or desires?

Duties are what many of us do and especially women who wonder about relationship problems. A man can hire anyone to perform duties; what he needs is a mate, one who operates based on his love language and has the right combination to his love vault.

Good intentions cannot take the place of what you actually do in your relationship. Maybe you did not intend to be controlling, dismissive, fussy, or selfish, but are you committed to changing this behavior once discovered? Actually changing will probably require you to match these counter-productive behaviors to your unmet needs and to figure out how to meet them prior to entering a relationship.

I have a strong belief that a woman can get everything she wants out of her relationship if she gives a man what he needs. Strip the pride, anger, and skepticism and make a heart investment in that man. Give him the treatment he deserves (e.g. love, praise, encouragement). It is like the saying, "Love like you've never been hurt."

Now if the love is not returned, all of the negative energy will rest with him, and he will feel it! Why? Because you did your part and you will have no regrets. It may simply come down to your having conflicting needs.

What I do know? It works!!!! I can't say with one hundred percent certainty that it will work for everyone, but I believe that God has given me this practical process for women. Of those with whom I've shared my approach, the ones who applied the theories have all excelled in their relationships. If the relationship did not work out, they had no personal regrets. This is because they loved like they had never been hurt. When you do not have regrets, you can move on more effectively.

This is the way to heal and to find that special person. You will begin to attract the person you want from the positive aura around you. It's called **the law of spiritual attraction**, recently popularized as "The Secret." Simply put: You attract into your life whatever you think about. Yes, you have heard this before—but again, it works.

The reason you attract negative men is because you are negative in your thinking and you are NOT doing what you are supposed to do to release all of the negative energy around you. This is why I say that you can be a good person, but a bad mate.

Women of faith, I know that you must protect yourselves. It is hard being hurt time after time, again and again. However, you cannot be a prisoner to your past relationships or the hurt/pain they have caused. You must be willing to trust.

I've learned that most women naturally hold back in their relationship to protect themselves from this pain. This need to avoid pain shapes their entire relationship. They will do everything in their power to avoid this pain. Guess what? It is detectable and never works!!! You will get what you think you will get—HURT!!!! Again, you become what you think about.

My goal is to shift your thinking and relationship strategy. I say to you, "Do not be too attached to an outcome. **Make an investment with your heart. Do not hold back!!!**" Holding back, showing so much strength has not worked for you in the past, so try this approach instead. Be independent, but have a sense of sweetness about you. Put the "That-a-boy!" campaign on him. Really believe it and feel it.

Just simply adore that man. It is infectious and he will feel it! Even Mr. Church Player will take notice. He will not want to take advantage of this type of woman. He will respect her. It is hard for men to leave women like this. They are the type men settle down with. They are irreplaceable. I've seen it so many times.

In the dating arena I often see this strong, independent woman who can stand on her own. She may be professional, smart, have a great career, and make her own money. I admire and respect her as a successful, talented woman, but I also get the message that, in essence, she believes she does not really need a man to do anything for her.

Guess what happens when she decides it is time to settle down, to find a mate? She meets a man of God who has it all together. She sees him as a potential mate. Does he agree? What is he feeling? His actions tell me that he does not agree. I can see that she's just too independent for him. He cannot see any way in which she needs him or anything he has to offer her.

Meanwhile, this same man of God meets another independent woman, with the same features as the first, but with a twist. This independent woman has an added sense of sweetness and feminine frailty that attracts him.

I can hear you now, "Philemon! You sound like a chauvinist."

No, I do not mean frailty as in being weak, but a feminine charm that awakens a man's need to protect. I am sharing what men really want and since a man of God is still a man he wants the same. It's up to you if you accept this or not.

What do I mean by feminine frailty? It is more about her energy or spirit, a presence that radiates femininity and creates polarity to masculinity. A woman who allows a man to do things for her that he considers manly and genuinely appreciates what he does. She may be independent in some areas, but enjoys being dependent on a man in other areas. Or, she's willing to share or let go of certain areas of her life in which he excels. She sees what he loves to do and allows him to do it for her. She feels a genuine need to have a man in her life to solve certain problems for her. It may be typical man things—such as flat tires, fixing things, lawn stuff, or whatever areas he excels in or enjoys.

Ladies, we love to solve problems, we just want to fix things for you, make life easier for you. We want you to seek our advice mainly on tangible items. If you are solving all of your own problems, we feel that we do not fit into your life, so how can we pick you as a mate or want to stay in a relationship without it?

I've heard the first type of strong, independent woman call the strong, independent, *feminine* woman "weak in her mind." But she is not!!! I've heard them say, "Oh well, he was just *intimidated* by me."

NO MY SISTER IN CHRIST!!!! It is not intimidation. It is a necessity. HE WANTS TO FEEL NEEDED.

These independent-yet-feminine/frail women are the ones who GET and KEEP that man of God. They make great mates, along with being good people.

 Leave that strong, independent-lady speech behind. Men seek a soft landing, not competition. He likes to solve problems and fix things, so let him! This will make you a good mate for him *and* a good person.

A MAN OF GOD *is Still* A MAN

Your "Just-in-Case" Man

By now you may believe that you are really ready for Mr. Right. You've said "No" to all my questions because you don't have old ex's calling. But, like other women I meet or coach, you may have one very special man. You may call him a "friend." I call him the "**Just-in-Case Man**," and so will your love interest.

Let me be very clear: He does count as a contender for your love. You will NEVER have a SUCCESSFUL, LOVING RELATIONSHIP with another man when you have a "just-in-case-it-doesn't-work-out" man around or on the side.

That hidden cushion person is the one you will pass the time away with when your love interest is unavailable. I know that this can go both ways, but we are talking about why *he* withdraws from the relationship. ☺

Mr. Just-in-Case is a go-to guy when needed. He is usually someone who really cares about you. There is no doubt about this. You feel safe with this man. He will always have your back and be there for you in between relationships or during difficult times in your current relationship. He encourages you and may fix things for you. He is meeting many of your needs, so you don't really notice when Mr. Right is not.

So, why isn't *he* your Mr. Right? Would he like to be? Perhaps he just does not fit your personal profile for the person you feel you deserve, so you've decided he's not the man for you. (Look at the last point I made in "Who's Correcting Men?"—perhaps he's a greater possibility than you give him credit for.)

I get countless emails from hurt women telling me about their love interest in the church who has either left, called things off, or got caught seeing another woman—often in another church. These emails are heart-breaking. I can feel the pain of these women. But guess what?

The first question I usually ask them is about that Just-in-Case Man. I want to know if one exists. To this very day over fifty percent of all the Christian women I've actually had the opportunity to either coach, talk to, or correspond with, always had such a man in their life. WOW!!!

AND YOU ARE WONDERING WHY YOU ARE STILL UNMARRIED, HURT, AND CAN'T FIND THAT SPECIAL MAN? Could it be because you have this man on the side? Women have actually said to me, "I'm not doing this or that to improve our relationship, because I can always jump to him"—Mr. Just-in-Case. This person is always a distraction from their problems.

Just reverse this and tell me, How would you feel if the man you are with had another woman in his life "just in case"?

The reason why these relationships are not working out is often because he found out about the man on the side, or because you act as if you don't care, because you do have Mr. Just-in-Case standing by.

What if you had a "just-in-case" job? How would you act on your current job? You know that you would do just enough and not take any stress from anybody on that job. Please understand that a Just-in-Case Man will definitely keep you from putting in the work on your current relationship. It is the same principle.

 To find the love of your life, you have to be ready and available totally. Stop running to that Just-in-Case Man!

A MAN OF GOD *is Still* A MAN

Furthermore, **all relationships have issues**, so remember:

To have a successful relationship: Give it your all!
Stop running to that Just-in-Case Man!
Stay and work it out.

There cannot be anyone else influencing whether or not you will put up with the little difficulties you may experience in your current relationship. If you are running to your Just-in-Case Man when you are uncertain, instead of working on those issues with your love interest, you will never have success.

If you have a breakup in your relationship, remain ready and available for a new person.

Yes! There will be some lonely days when you desire male companionship, but you will have time to pray, self-reflect, and prepare yourself for the love of your life. It will be well worth it.

Remember, if your love interest finds out about your Just-in-Case Man, he will leave!

Relationship Vita

You may be wondering what in the world does **relationship vita** mean? Well, the word *vita* is Latin meaning "life." Therefore a relationship vita is a fancy way of saying your relationship history. It's like a job resume, but covering your whole life. Instead of listing jobs, it lists those you call your "exes." In talking about what makes you ready for Mr. Right, this subject of relationship history requires a special note.

Men do compare themselves to your ex. However, they will give more weight to ex-husbands and to baby daddies than others. Why? Well, in his mind, it is easier for women to feel safe to cheat with them than just old boyfriends. (If you and your ex-husband do not have kids together, most men will file him in the category of regular boyfriend.) I will go on record and say that everyone reading this book knows someone in the church or has heard about someone cheating with their ex-husband or baby daddy. Therefore, a new man will watch these relationships closely, and if he senses a threat, he will lose that feeling of attraction and will leave.

There is a delicate balance to managing these relationships, especially when children are involved. The new husbands will be around their kids, so the exes will usually have concerns. The key is to blend the adults together as soon as possible. Never project the attitude of "look what God has blessed me with" or "look how much better he is than you." It will not help you adults to treat one

A MAN OF GOD *is* *Still* A MAN

another with respect in front of the children. The best revenge will be your obvious happiness.

Just keep in mind that insecurities and territorial attitudes sometimes raise their ugly heads when two men meet. It will be your job to touch your new man and claim him so that there is NO question that you are with him completely, but respect your children's father. Always, Always, Always, include your new man and never, never, never exclude him from an event. Otherwise, he will feel left out, and the attraction between you will be lost. He will detach himself from your relationship and leave eventually.

Those Other Men (a Major Point to Consider)

I have discovered that most men do not like these one-on-one guy friends you may have. For some reason, your women friends in church feel it is OK to hang with male friends. Yes, you see it on TV, but in reality it is a hidden reason why attraction is lost and men leave relationships. You can call it insecurity or whatever you like, but I've seen high quality men leave because of a woman's guy friend. It doesn't matter if he attends the same church.

Even though you believe these guys are wannabes or friends, a man will always see them as a threat. He will assume that any other man hanging around you is either an ex or a wannabe—even if you reassure him. And, guess what? He may be better able to recognize another man's secret desires than you are. Yes, some men are OK with these types of relationships but make sure that you create the space for him to be honest about his feelings. He may not like the friendship, but is too nice to share this feeling because he doesn't want to come across as an insecure paranoid; especially if he really likes you and the relationship is new.

If the guy friend is truly just a friend and not an ex or your Just-in-Case Man, and if you can't live without this friend, the key is to make sure that your friend becomes *his* friend, too. **Eliminate the territorial threat.**

Honestly Sharing Too Much?

Proverbs 21:23 KJV: *Whoso keepeth his mouth and his tongue keepeth his soul from troubles.*

Are you sharing too much with your mate or man-of-interest in the guise of being honest? This is about how to follow Scripture on guarding your tongue when in a relationship.

Honesty is important, but some kinds of information can be hurtful, confusing, alarming, and can trigger territorial issues.

"I share everything with my mate and leave nothing out" a woman will tell me, quite proudly.

Telling all in this way can work against you. I've noticed that it can be a thin disguise for emotional assault—either consciously or unconsciously.

Are you sometimes not sharing enough? Most certainly. It is a fine line. Discrimination is the key.

Being transparent in a relationship is essential. But it is different from telling all. Bite your tongue. Reflect on the consequences. Then choose your words carefully as you decide what to say on sensitive matters.

Ask yourself, "Why do I have an urge to share _____ [fill in the blank]? Why now?

I notice that when people share some truths, it is really an effort to unburden their soul and transfer the pain to someone else. I see this so much in my practice. For me, it is a form of selfishness.

 You should not irritate your mate with stuff you should simply keep to yourself.

There are examples scattered throughout this book to help you learn when to share information and when to bite your tongue when tempted to share something with your husband or future one. Just know that you are not being dishonest. Most often, truth is best tempered with kindness and given on a "need to know" basis.

This holds true for all sharing of information, with everyone.

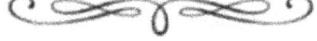

Traditional Mental Boxes

Proverbs 18:22 NLT: *The man who finds a wife finds a treasure, and he receives favor from the* LORD.

I find that this scripture, Proverbs 18:22, stagnates many unmarried women in the Church. It prevents them from taking appropriate actions according to current male psychology. You see, dating is NOT in the Bible because marriages were arranged back then. Since we are NOT arranging marriages anymore, it is best that you punch holes in your mental boxes regarding traditional things you feel men should do. Most women of God feel that attraction is very rational, saying, "You love God and so do I. We go to the same church." However, attraction is not rational, it's emotional.

Most women are waiting for God to do everything for them. Sometimes we want God to change something, but he has given us the ability to do it. This is why wisdom is so important for understanding what is a divine decision and what is a human one. As I stated at the beginning in the "Why This Book" section that God never chooses your mate for you. He gives you complete responsibility.

There are only two options available to you in life. You can wait or you can generate what you desire out of life. You have to be active in your life to generate God's plan.

Think about this. There are two things that usually come to those who only wait without taking direct action.

1. The wrong things (the undesirables)
2. Nothing

You can generate and manifest quality in your life by learning skills and applying them to your situation—in this case, your desire to be married.

> 2 Peter 1:5-8 NIV: ***For this very reason, make every effort to add to your faith goodness; and to goodness, knowledge; and to knowledge, self-control; and to self-control, perseverance; and to perseverance, godliness; and to godliness, mutual affection; and to mutual affection, love. For if you possess these qualities in increasing measure, they will keep you from being ineffective and unproductive in your knowledge of our Lord Jesus Christ.***

Let's gain some knowledge regarding male psychology that's facing women of the church today. You may also want to review "His Life Stages" and "Guy Brands" (Chapter Two) from this perspective.

Point one: Some men are sensitive and require that you call them and be a little more aggressive. If you are sitting back waiting for him to hunt, he will not do it without some calls from you in between. However, I believe that he should be the dominant chaser. If he asks, "Why don't you call me sometimes?" this is your cue that he requires this to feel wanted.

Point two: Some men are not shy, but don't like to bother individuals. A man like this requires a woman to step up to him before he hunts. She has to provide the approval for him to approach her. How do you know if he is interested? Well, he will look at you, but will not make a move. Again, he just doesn't want to come off as being too forward; but he is not really shy.

Point three: Men with lots of options (very good looking and got it going on) may be more relationship-minded than men who are not. They are usually sick of the rat race and do not have anything to prove, because women have always shown them attention. A man like this just wants to meet the woman of his dreams and settle down instead of having to deal with a barrage of women coming after him. Stop projecting your traditional mental boxes on these men, thinking they are heart breakers when they simply want a loving relationship and validation from the woman he loves.

Point four: Just because a man has not been divorced very long does not mean that a relationship with him will not work or that he is on the rebound. Depending on where he is in his life stage, he could be the type who has solid relationship skills and practices them and loves God. However, his former spouse did not. He will be the type who wants to find a woman who will practice these skills and wants to get married as soon as possible. He is not interested in getting over things. He loves being married.

Do NOT overlook this type in point four or make him feel like he is rushing things.

Do NOT turn your back on a man because he is rushing things. The attraction may be lost and he will find someone else to marry.
He is just ripe for marriage.

Yes, it is understood that men who can't be alone may have dependency issues, but do not judge too quickly with your box thinking. The "It's Too-Good-to-Be-True" syndrome could be in play here. You'll be reading more about it in "Negative Thinking." See also "Divorced Man with Children" (Chapter Two).

Uncertainty

1 Peter 5:7 NLT: *Give all your worries and cares to God, for he cares about you.*

Certainty, one of the six basic human needs we talked about earlier, is a primary motivator for many women. Thus uncertainty can drive many to extremes. Does your uncertainty lead you to do any of these?

- Checking a man's cell phone?
- Breaking into his Facebook or email account?
- Checking the house phone to see who has called, just looking for "something"?
- Smelling a man's clothing for abnormal fragrances?
- Recording the phone to see if your husband is talking about you?

Diagnosis: Trust issues. Most would say that you are extremely insecure, but some women believe that this should not be a problem unless a man has something to hide. I've heard of women checking a man's phone on the second date trying to be sure. This is simply unacceptable.

We all need to feel a sense of security that things will be okay. Certainty gives us peace of mind and assurance. We also use different behavioral strategies to meet this need. Some are constructive and others are destructive. For example, when you feel stressed, worried, unsure and uncertain, how do you meet your need for certainty?

Some women meet this need by trying to control their man, constantly making sure they know what he is doing, or by losing their temper. Some overeat just to meet their need for certainty. There are also good ways: praying, reading or reciting scriptures, and faith, as well as physical exercise and positive thinking. For example, saying "I will get through this," or sharing with a friend. All of these are ways to meet the need for certainty.

My question for you: What has to happen for you to feel certain that you can trust a man? He is a man of God and you still don't trust him? Is it possible that this could ever happen in your present state of mind? You see, when you are checking a man's phone and emails, among other things, you are simply testing him to be certain that he is not doing something behind your back.

What if you were given a test that you could never pass? How would you feel? What if you needed to pass this test to get a better job, get a good man, or to vastly improve your life? But the deck is stacked against you? How would this affect you?

Now think about how you are giving your husband or love interest a test that he can never pass because of your constant uncertainty. How do you think he feels?

This is unforgivable to most men. If he finds out what you are doing, even a man of God will never see you the same way and will want out. Any attraction between you will disappear. If you are dating he will leave in a hurry. If married, he may be tempted by someone who makes him feel good in her presence.

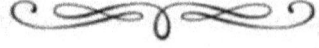

Runaway Mind

1 Peter 5:8 ESV: *Be sober-minded; be watchful. Your adversary the devil prowls around like a roaring lion, seeking someone to devour.*

If there is one constant that most men believe about women, it is their tendency to let their mind run away with them. When racing, the mind can send out strong, crazy, and horrible thoughts. For example, if you text your husband and he does not text right back, you assume the worst.

Yes, men do this, too. As stated in the introduction, I am addressing issues that couples who love God have sought guidance on within their relationship. This is such an issue. Couples have come in hurting from the painful, sometimes tragic, consequences of this process. Sometimes I think of them as having "tragic thoughts," but then have to admit it was not really the thought, but their response to it.

Such thoughts take women places in their minds that appear real to them. They begin by noticing *He's too friendly with Sister Mary* and convince themselves that *My man is thinking of leaving me* or *My husband does not have my back*. It goes on and on.

Based on my experiences while coaching women, I'm beginning to believe that some think that these thoughts are God speaking directly to them. These thoughts are so real to them that some women even act on them or react to them.

I usually suggest that they file them away in their mind under the label of "crazy thoughts" or "opinions," and opinions are not facts. The worst part comes when women act on such thoughts. For example, one may accuse her husband of looking at another woman the wrong way. This then feeds his runaway mind, *Will she leave me?*

One of the biggest complaints I've received from men in a relationship is that they are being accused of inappropriate behavior with another woman in the church, or at work, when it is not true. They feel helpless. You see, how can a man prove that he is not doing anything inappropriate?

And it all started just because of a feeling, thought, or maybe a dream his wife had. This can lead to many problems.

What can you do with your suspicions? The key is to get hard proof or evidence before you act or speak on an issue. Make sure it's not your mind playing tricks on you, playing with your own trust issues.

Many women are so suspicious and paranoid that they drive themselves, and him, crazy. The word "jealous" comes to mind. Yes, that green-eyed monster. And vanity—*How can he do that to me?* Self-righteous anger is still that—red, fiery anger. God's voice can't be heard above the din made by these monstrous feelings, sometimes called "passions of the mind." They may secretly check their husband's emails and pockets, rummage through his car at night, read his credit card statements, and go through his phone calls—even calling the numbers they don't know.

Please understand that you could be hurting your husband's business relationships with others if you are not careful. Stop calling these numbers you don't know, because it will not change anything.

Realize that he may not be doing anything inappropriate at all. Know that, if he sees you doing this, he will never see you the same way again. Your relationship will change.

Now, if he gives you a reason to start snooping—perhaps you notice a major change in his behavior, then I understand why you'd be suspicious. However, be careful how you go about checking it out. Do not start this in the guise of, "I have the right to go through his stuff because he is my husband." Respect his privacy, and expect him to respect yours.

Here is my question, "What will you do if something materializes? Will you leave?" Before you start snooping, have a plan of action. If you find evidence, what will you do?

Don't start looking for evidence until your plan of action is clear and standards are established. You would only make both your lives miserable, especially if you are stuck with each other for financial reasons or because your public image must remain constant in the eyes of the people. Knowing and not having the ability to do anything about it is tragic within itself.

If you find no evidence, what will you do? Perhaps take a look within yourself. Perhaps you have trust issues. Perhaps you can justify them with past experience with other men. My training and experience has shown me that trust issues and jealousy are only symptoms based on what one actually fears. Finding and addressing these underlying fears and honestly getting clear of them is a proven recipe for eliminating such issues.

I also find it helpful to check myself and the women I coach for negative thinking. It is just as destructive as chasing a runaway mind. In the next section I will give you some examples of negative thinking in those who allow it to color their world view.

Negative Thinking

Philippians 4:8 NLT: *And now, dear brothers and sisters, one final thing. Fix your thoughts on what is true, and honorable, and right, and pure, and lovely, and admirable. Think about things that are excellent and worthy of praise.*

Men don't think about what you are not, it is about what you are to them. *My arms are too big, My butt is getting fat, My hair is not right.* This is your negative thinking; not a man's. He does not evaluate you as you do yourself.

Negative thinking begets negativity. Whatever you focus on with a man is how he grows in the relationship. If your focus is on the negative "Jerk," name calling, he will grow in negativity. If you focus on the positive, he will grow in a positive manner.

Here are some examples of negative thinking: *He is too good to be true. Something must be wrong with him. He's forty-five but never married; something must be wrong with him! I wonder if he is crazy, secretly gay or down low? Men who struggle with their sexuality are usually in the church. Could he be a narcissist, a player? Because, you know, you find them in the church too.* Or you may think that something else is wrong with him.

Why do you think this way? Why not believe that God is blessing you, goodwill is coming your way, and take it? Your negative thinking is probably why you are still not married.

Stop buying into the too-good-to-be-true rule. That mindset has kept many of you from getting great deals—missing out on the love of your life.

Here is a quick story. I received an email from a woman who is allowing me to share this story to help others.

This man from another church approached her and was extremely serious about settling down. They met at an office party about a year ago. He was ready to be married and had said to himself that he would settle down with the next good woman of God he met. He simply wanted a wife. Ladies, when a man wants to do something, it doesn't take him long to make a decision and jump right on it!

Well, this woman had the too-good-to-be-true mindset and thought negatively about the whole situation. She said, "Philemon, I believe Satan is trying to trick me or he must be crazy or something. He loves kids too; maybe he is a pedophile. I just don't know about him."

Keep in mind that she wanted to be married, and he was exactly what she was looking for: A man who was willing to commit and was good with kids.

I told her to just trust that maybe God is trying to bless her and to accept the blessing. I also shared with her that men are very simple. When he evolves to the point of wanting to be married, he only has a few simple, personal requirements:

- He wants a woman who loves God.
- He wants a woman who loves and respects him and totally has his back.
- He wants a woman who meets his personal requirements.
- He wants her to be attractive and/or appealing to him.
- He wants to enjoy her company, knowing the attraction is mutual.

Back to the story: She brushed him off and never took him seriously and decided to wait for a man who will walk through her home-church door.

Well, her co-worker who met this man at the same time asked if she will be OK with her going out with him. She gave her consent, thinking that the co-worker can filter out this crazy man and inherit that problem.

Now, one year later, that co-worker and this man's wedding date is set. Not only did her co-worker find a man who would love her two children, but one who is extremely caring. She looked at him as being a blessing instead of a too-good-to-be-true reality. She never thought negatively about him and decided to date him to see what would happen. Well, she found her man of God. It was just that simple.

Many of the answers or solutions to your problems are very simple and may seem too good to be true for you. But if you think they are, you will continue to miss out in life because these wonderful things are simply too good to be real or trusted by you.

As to the first woman in the story, you may say that it wasn't God's will.

I say that negative thinking was destroying her marriage destiny.

To say that it wasn't meant to be is an excuse to make one feel good about not taking charge of their life. You can choose to think differently.

 Our behavior on the outside is determined by the way we feel on the inside.

This is why I strongly recommend personal coaching to clear negative or limiting beliefs. It is extremely difficult to clear them without help.

He Can't Read Your Mind

Guess what? He can't read your mind. This is something that is impossible to do. It is another reason why attraction is lost. Men will leave on this impossibility. And yet, here are examples of what I hear from ladies:

"If I have to ask, then I don't want him."

"If I have to ask, then he doesn't care."

"If I have to ask, then he is not for me."

Do you know what this means when you think like this? You expect this man to read your mind before you can love him. He has to read your mind, or you will make his life havoc. He has to read your mind, or he is not for you. Impossible!

This is a negative and actually crazy belief system that says, "I want him to already know how to love me, or I will leave." Now imagine that for a moment. Let it marinate.

Most women are guilty of expecting a potential to come with an owner's manual for them and to know exactly what it takes for them to feel love. They say, "He has to look around and see what has to be done around my house. If I have to ask, then he doesn't love me. I don't want him. I shouldn't have to ask for this or that. If I have to ask, then he doesn't care, and I don't want him!"

Don't get me wrong, there are some things that are based upon home training and his mama should have taught him. If she didn't, then you can try to train him. Other things may be cultural. His family did things one way, yours another. Money is another sensitive area. As a former financial consultant, I encourage you to settle any differences in this area before marriage. And if his giving you gifts or money makes you feel loved and he doesn't give you anything or not enough, does that mean he doesn't love you? There are always keys to knowing if someone is selfish or self-absorbed. The key to overcoming these apparent obstacles is to share what it takes for you to feel love.

A man often sees things differently, but it has nothing to do with how he feels about you. Most of the time, if you don't ask for what you want, you will not get it. If it makes you feel love when your mate does a certain thing, tell him. Why is this so hard?

If you believe, "I shouldn't have to ask. If I do, he's not for me." If you want him to anticipate your needs or wants, to have an idea what you like, then this belief system will keep you unhappy, unmarried, in constant emotional pain, and—yes—the attraction, the energy in your relationship, will drain away and you will be left without him.

 No one can read your mind. Share with him what it takes to love you. If he won't do those things, then you will have a real answer about how he feels about you.

Show Interest

When he is expressing interest in you, return the interest. You want him to know that you are interested, with dignity of course. You won't have to compete for his time if he is into you; he will call and make an effort to spend time with you. Show interest. One reason he will walk away is that he feels you are not interested. It could be your body language.

So many women say, "I'm a lady and you are not supposed to show interest before he does."

Well if you don't, he will lose his feelings of attraction for you and will leave. **Don't play games.**

Once you get something started, make sure that you keep expressing interest. I understand that you should allow a man to lead. But you can do things, too. Like sending little notes, especially thank you notes or text messages, letting him know that you are thinking about him or appreciate what he is doing.

Here is the problem: Too much space will make him think that you are not that interested, but too much interest will crowd him. Hey, I never said that men are easy—just simple! The only thing that concerns me is what he actually thinks about the relationship. A man could be sticking around because he has a kind spirit.

Now if he is not showing you any interest after you have expressed yours, then it is time to create space because he may not be the one. He may start chasing to get you back. You see, sometimes a man may want to keep you around, for whatever reason, perhaps until he can upgrade to that special woman. He will chase you and make you feel as if he really wants you, but he is only being territorial. All he is doing is trying to keep other men away. You see, he doesn't want to lose what he has with you currently, but he's not interested in stepping up to the next level.

Ladies, it's a game, not always intentional, but you should have standards. Don't play this game. If he wants you, then he should be willing to step it up. If not, just say "NEXT!"

I can hear your question, "How do you tell the difference?" Remember, when the Bible was written, marriages were arranged. That is why the Bible is silent on the steps leading to a marital relationship. You will have to rely on your own God-given skills, honing them by using other resources you trust.

Just know that the man who wants you will be thoughtful and will do, on his own, the small things that show this. The man who is just holding on may be insensitive, negative, not doing small things. There may be a few acts of kindness, but you will have that feeling that his focus is elsewhere. Just listen to that inner voice because it is God speaking and move on.

How to know when God is speaking to you is the subject for another book. Let me just say that allowing the devil to prey on your fears will not manifest what God has for you. God's voice will calm you and won't feed into your negative emotions. If you don't buy into the "It's-Too-Good-to-Be-True!" syndrome, then by God's grace you can use the skills in this book to manifest or attract into your life the love of your life.

Is He Enough?

In my research, certain men were uncomfortable with two questions that are often asked in the beginning of a relationship, especially when done online and over the phone. You may be surprised that these two questions are: **"How tall are you?"** and **"What do you do for a living?"**

Now I am sure you are thinking, "What's wrong? These are legitimate questions." Yes, but they can create a sense of possible inadequacy. Here is why.

He will think for a moment that maybe he is not tall enough for you, or that what he does for a living may not be acceptable. A man with an important job as a maintenance worker, for example, may feel that some women will not find his title fashionable.

Asking these questions can create a negative feeling on your first encounter.

CONSIDER CHANGING YOUR APPROACH!

"How Tall Are You?"

Here is how you ask the tall question. First, if you feel strongly about it, make sure you give the minimum you are willing to accept and don't settle for less. Just know that you could be missing out on the love of your life by rejecting a man based on his height.

You can say, "I am 5'3" and anyone over 5'5" is good for me." He is listening and will feel good if he is over 5'5." He will say,

"Well, I'm taller than 5'5." This approach will not make him uncomfortable (unless he is 5'4). If a man's height is very important to you, and he is too short for your preference, then move on. Make sure, however, that taller men will want you too.

"What do You Do for a Living?"

You want a man who has a job; I get that. Also, I understand that it's an icebreaker. I urge you to consider another approach because, for a lot of men it's a complete turnoff. I've met men returning from a date, saying "Man! That lady is money hungry. She just asked me what I do for a living. It was the first thing out of her mouth. I have a job, period." I have heard this more than you can imagine. However, in all honesty, I've heard this more from minority men than from others.

Men with popular titles are usually the only ones who do not have a problem with this question. They will proudly say, "I'm a doctor,"— or a pilot, or an engineer. However, I've seen some of them indicate displeasure at this question, too.

Instead, simply ask him, "Hey, how was your day? Were you very busy?" or, "Whew! I had a stressful day at work. How was your day?"

If it's on a weekend you can ask, "Do you work weekends, or are you normally off?" Or, "I am so glad this is the weekend and I'm off work. What about you?"

This will start a conversation, and he usually will tell you what he does for a living. If not, then simply wait, because he is not ready to tell you yet.

Socially Incompatible?

Mike and Darlene met online at Christian Singles and seemed to be a perfect match. The chemistry was there, too. Mike felt that he was on top of the world.

Mike is an executive director for a non-profit organization, loves God, and attends many black-tie events for the city and government. He could not wait to show off his new love to all of his friends. They had been dating for three months when one came up.

Well, at the event Mike whispered something in Darlene's ear about one of the individuals there and off she went, talking loudly under her breath saying, "I don't know who they think they are. She 'bet not' come up in my face."

Mike was shocked and trying to shish her, saying that she was too loud. She said, "Don't shish me. I am a grown woman and will speak my mind, I'm saved, but she's about to make me backslide." She wasn't very loud, but loud enough for others to hear.

At the dinner Mike also realized that she chews with her mouth open and smacks out loud while eating.

Where did this woman come from? He wondered. She dressed for success, was smart, had a master's degree in education, but was loud and attitudeish. She was just not fit for this type of event.

Mike's friends were calling her trashy and everything else behind his back. He was embarrassed and upset that this relationship went so wrong.

On the way back in the car Mike asked Darlene "Where did this attitude of yours come from?"

She said, "I hate those types of people and don't' want to be around them anymore."

Mike said, "Well, I see that we cannot make this one work. I have to be around those people. They fund my organization."

Darlene called him a snob and said that she sees that he loves cliques.

Women of God, if you are socially incompatible with a man, it will NOT work. I hear this often from men of God who say that they are meeting women in the church who appear to have everything except social etiquette.

Hey, this is a good time to ask your family and friends if you have good etiquette and table manners.

Are You a Plus-Size Woman?

OK, you have some curves and are carrying extra weight. You are affectionately known as a "Plus-Size Woman." Plus size comes in all different colors, shapes and sizes too.

Let's begin by acknowledging that there are many, many, happily married plus-size women. I am talking here about the ones who are either not married and lonely, or unhappily married and believe it is because of their plus size.

In my research into men in relationships, I've received interesting, controversial responses regarding plus-size women. I say controversial because some will see them as stereotypes, saying plus-size women are easy targets. In fact, I am just passing on what many, many, men have said about their experiences dating plus-size women. I've done the same thing with their responses that I did for men—pooling them into three general "brands." Although the men I interviewed were attracted to these women at first, this is how they described what turned them off:

First brand: "She is always talking about her weight and skinny women. She is either meek about it or extremely vocal with a sassy attitude. It appears that she is self-conscious about her weight and masks it with her attitudes by either not taking my interest seriously or questioning why I want her."

Second brand: "She is nice—sometimes too nice. She gives and gives. She used to bring me food, take care of me when sick, give me money, pay for events most of the time, just do everything for me—

just like my mother."

Did you read the last part? "Just like my mother?" Now, tell me, "What man wants to be romantically involved with his mother?"

Third brand: "She is mean and grouchy. Says she takes no "stuff" from a man, challenges me, argues with me, and fights me (sometimes physically). She has a big mouth and is strong with a sense of confidence in her views on men. I got out of there fast. I was afraid, man!"

That's what I hear from men in a dating relationship with a plus-size woman. Here are my views.

I wonder sometimes how these women got their attitudes about being plus size. It might be the home environment, media-hype, or past experiences with men. I find that women of the third brand have been hurt the most by men in their lives—not just by dates.

One big reason I wonder is that I know plus-size women who do NOT fit into these brands. They have no problems attracting and keeping the love of their life.

On the other hand, women with some of the most amazingly perfect bodies and beauty (according to society) still have men and relationship problems. They think and feel they are the cream of the crop because men drool over them. However, these women are seeking help on why they can't keep a man or attract the man they want. I know because I coach them.

And yet, many women who come to me, not just plus-size women, feel they have to wait until they lose weight to attract a man. "Here is the truth and a secret: **What really gets to a man is your look not your looks!**

Ladies of these three brands, hear me: **You don't have to take things from a man because you are plus size.** You don't have to be so happy to have a man because you are plus size. You don't have to give him all of your money, time, and energy and get nothing in return because you are plus size.

A MAN OF GOD *is* *Still* A MAN

 Total acceptance of yourself is the key. Don't' worry about being a plus-size woman. Just be a plus woman of faith. So many guys will love you just as you are now. Know that you are worthy.

Yes, you should be the best you can be to feel good and healthy. But never let your size keep you from taking the right actions to place yourself in the view of a quality man of God.

All you have to do is be with the person you are trying to attract and use the ideas and tips in this book to develop some relationship skills. This alone will give you the confidence to change your love life.

Strong and Independent?

"I'm Ms. Independent!" Some women have been taking that statement too far. Why do you have to tell a man that you are strong and independent? I've found in my research that so many men hate what that expression has come to represent.

Here is a question from a man: "Hey Philemon, I went to a speed-dating function recently. Every woman I ran into kept telling me that she is 'a strong and independent woman.' Excuse me, but what does that mean?"

He continued, "Take it from me, all the women I have dated in the past who have said this were nothing but trouble. Why is that statement important to say when you first meet a man?"

So, Ladies, there you have it. Saying that you are a strong, independent woman should be avoided, especially early in a relationship. It could be misunderstood and most men do not care to hear it. It destroys any attraction between you and is another reason why a man may leave a relationship or never get involved.

A MAN OF GOD *is* *Still* A MAN

Disrespecting-Ex Dilemma

I often receive calls or emails from women seeking my advice because they feel disrespected in their marriage or relationship. However, when they describe what their husband or potential is doing, only a small number of them meet my criteria of what is actually being disrespectful of her.

The majority of complaints are based on outside influences: his mom, his ex, his baby mama, his child, his family member or his friend. Someone did something that upset her, and SHE believes her husband should have stood up for her, but he didn't. Most of the time the disrespect in her mind involves his ex, the mother of his children, affectionately known as the "baby mama."

The only interesting part to me is that he is treating her right personally, but gets the blunt of the outbursts and chastisement by his wife based on what the baby mama is doing. Many even split or divorce because of this scenario.

Ladies, your husband has a dilemma: Either respond as you wish (although he doesn't see what you're upset about) or take the risk of doing nothing and making you unhappy. It is a lose-lose proposition for him.

Know this:

- People see things differently all the time.
- Understand that when your husband says he doesn't care about anything his baby mama does, just believe

him because 9.9 times out of 10 it is true.

- Most men could care less about what someone else is doing around them, as long it does not affect what goes on between you and him.

Just know that men are constantly calculating if they are winning or losing within a relationship. If you are unhappy, he will feel like a failure, thus not winning. If you are NOT able to show him how he can win, he is losing, which places a strain on your relationship and makes it impossible to maintain the attraction he once felt. He will leave or become totally detached. There is no in-between in this situation.

Men can only respond to issues they CAN actually see. They must understand that it is occurring as you see it before responding appropriately as you wish. If you want to have a happy marriage, don't expect your husband to take actions or accuse him of inaction because you feel disrespected or have an issue with someone in his life. If he cannot see it, he just doesn't. It is that simple! All you are left with is a disagreement. Treat it as such because he is NOT personally disrespecting you. Disagreements will happen in a relationship and must be managed.

On the flip side, if he shares that he sees the disrespect and still allows it to happen, THEN your inaction claim has some merit. However, this may present another dilemma, depending upon his relationship with the other party. Just make sure you do not fight simply because you believe his response should have been harsher. This will be just another disagreement that no one can win.

Expecting a man of God to act on issues he cannot see does NOT work! It's how he treats you personally that counts. However, he should recognize and acknowledge your feelings and have empathy for them.

He may pick up on it at some point, especially after you bring it to his attention. What he does then depends upon his relationship with the other party. So long as he is treating you well, don't force an action. Each must give their best in a marriage. Otherwise, one is attempting to control another to act on something they just can't see. This is a losing scenario in any relationship.

Your World View

Matthew 7:1-2 NLT: *Do not judge others, and you will not be judged. For you will be treated as you treat others. The standard you use in judging is the standard by which you will be judged.*

One of the biggest mistakes you can make is to attempt to make your husband or a potential conform to your world view. That view could be "A man should…" do something totally subjective and based on how you see the situation. You may be thinking, "I expect my man to do this or that because this is the way it should be done." This is laying expectations on him.

Newsflash: Men do not like to be around women with overwhelming expectations. Men know that if these expectations are not met, these women will lose their mind and go off. That pressure is one of the main things that will cause him to leave.

Women of God ask, "What can I do? He is so frustrating!"

Listen to yourself. Remember the Bible verse above, ***Do not judge others***…. Can you see how you are judging him, discounting his views?

Consider this: He is a man of God. Perhaps he is listening within and setting his priorities accordingly. Also, growing up, his mama may have trained him—to do things differently from how your mama trained you. When noticing these differences between you, have you simply asked his point of view?

What ticks you off about your husband? When he is

performing a task, and it is not being done the way you want, how do you respond? These are indicators that it is all about your world view. Simply acknowledging the idea of "world view" helped me a lot in responding to such situations. And when I discover that my view differs from someone with whom I need to live or work, I remember the question that the Lord asks of the children of Israel, ***Can two people walk together without agreeing on the direction?*** (Amos 3:3 NLT)

 Your husband or potential has his own approach to situations. When you stop making your opinions law, there can be a reconnection, an opportunity for you to form a stronger bond with your man of God.

This Man Is So Immature!

Claims that a man is "So Immature!" go hand and hand with "Your World View." I often hear something like this from frustrated women:

"I do everything by myself with NO HELP! I work all day, cook, clean, look after the kids, pay bills and make all of the decisions in the home. He just sits around watching football, playing video games, or wanting to hang with his friends. He is so immature and won't help me with the kids or do anything around the house. When I say something to him about this, he sits there being quiet. He won't say anything! The kids love him, but he is sorry and so immature! This is driving me crazy. What did I do to deserve this karma? Help!"

Does this sound familiar to you? I'm sure if you have kids, you may have this story personally or know someone who does. What if I told you that once the kids and dad are interviewed, you will often get a totally different story?

"Mom comes home yelling because things around the house are not done right. We clean up, but it is not a good job according to her. She yells at dad, but when he yells back, she starts crying, screaming, "No one helps me around here," and calls him names and goes to the bedroom.

When he cooks, she says "The kids shouldn't eat that stuff," or "That was not cooked right." The rooms are cleaned and bed made, but it is not done right. Dad did not help us kids with our homework right. He did pay the bills, but it was not done right, because he forgot to do this or that.

Dad took us to get ice cream and, when we got back, mom was mad because our rooms were not cleaned right. Mom is always upset."

Do you see a pattern here? There is one word that should stand out to you now, and that word is "RIGHT!" If it is NOT up to your standards, it is NOT done right, and, by your definition, it is not "done." Like the t-shirts out there:

> **If Mama ain't happy, ain't NOBODY happy!**

If things aren't exactly the way you envision them, then you are NOT happy!

Ladies, it is NOT that he is immature. A man just knows how to cope with the stress of life by creating outlets. He can relax and let things go undone. You can't, because you feel that your work is never done, and that it must be done to a certain standard. It's the standard that is stressing you out and affecting your relationship, not his non-actions.

Men will shut down if they feel NOTHING they do is "right." It means he is NOT winning. An unhappy woman is the worst thing EVER to a man. Once he feels he can't make you happy, usually he will plan his escape or do dumb things.

While you may be creating karma with all your yelling, running a household has little to do with karma. When you have a home, especially with kids, the work is NEVER really done. There is always something more to do. You finish one project only to be faced with another one immediately. What's more, the laundry will never be done, dinner must be cooked, and there will always be some dirty dishes to wash.

May I share some advice?

 Learn to let some things go for another day. Enjoy yourself, your husband, your children, regardless of the circumstances or what you have to complete or accomplish. Laugh more!

When you reflect back on your life later, you will realize that most of what you fussed about was NOT that serious! Shift your thinking as to the importance of your role as a mom and wife. Enjoy this time when the children are young enough to enjoy being with you.

Appreciating and recognizing effort is the key to correcting and improving the standards of those you feel need improvement. You may actually burn off some karma by changing your attitude. Instead of: "I do everything by myself with NO HELP!" Say, **"I play an important role in the lives of my kids and husband and will enjoy this precious time I have with them."** It is more empowering, and it works!!!

 A man of God, who is praised and appreciated by others, but NOT by his wife, will be feeling unfulfilled in his marriage. This places him in a weak and dangerous position, subject to great temptation to misbehave.

This has been a common denominator of men of God who have fallen from grace because of sexual encounters with other women. In every case the man turned to a woman who praised and appreciated him, one who also catered to his sexual desires as a man, not just as a man of God.

 Praise and appreciate your man of God as much as other women, or he will turn to one of them to fulfill his unmet needs.

Exposing a Man of God?

> Ephesians 5:11 NLT: *Take no part in the worthless deeds of evil and darkness; instead, expose them.*
>
> 1 Timothy 5:19-20 NLT *Do not listen to an accusation against an elder unless it is confirmed by two or three witnesses. Those who sin should be reprimanded in front of the whole church; this will serve as a strong warning to others.*
>
> Galatians 6:1 NLT: *Dear brothers and sisters, if another believer is overcome by some sin, you who are godly should gently and humbly help that person back onto the right path.*

Some think that they are too smart to get caught in their sins, but fate has several ways of exposing them. We can see in Ezekiel 8 one manner in which God exposes the secret sins of people who may act righteously in public, but are walking in darkness.

The point is that there are clear scriptures stating that we are to expose sin. However, I've learned that one must have wisdom in doing this, because, in some cases nowadays, it can have extremely harmful effects. We simply need the wisdom of God when exposing men of God, especially those with status.

In this section my concern is more about why you want to expose and plan a course of action before you proceed. I've placed this in Chapter Three ("Examining Yourself") because it really gets to the core of the differences between logic or reasoning and emotional behaviors. This relates directly to how a woman should examine herself in order to make appropriate decisions when faced with betrayal or wrongdoings by a man of God.

Some men of God who are leaders often have a personal identity that can be quite different from their public one. They may watch TV shows that may surprise others; they may laugh when comedians on TV are using vulgar language, among other entertainment enjoyments. In essence, they are men and human and cautious.

Yes, they are extremely careful about those they allow into their private space. They will go out of town to do things they enjoy in order to avoid judgment from others. This is more about their concerns of offending those in the ministry than actually being hypocritical. You will find that many with status or fame operate this way; however, the behavior of men of God—especially ministers—is judged with even more scrutiny.

Occasionally, some men of God with status will take their behavior to another level and do sinful things that, if exposed, could possibly ruin their marriage, relationship if dating, career in the ministry, and reputation. This usually has more to do with sexual immorality than anything else. In most cases in a marriage, it has to do with infidelity.

When his wife, or in some instances a woman he is dating, discovers the sexual immorality or cheating on his part, all Hell usually breaks out. Let me share this: In all cases in which women of God have called me after discovering that their man—who was supposed to be "of God," as they say—has been cheating it was presented as a five-alarm fire. When this happens, I spend most of my time with them attempting to put out the flames and preventing them from taking destructive actions, knowing from experience that they would regret such action later and wish it could be taken back.

Their inclination is a desire to hurt him in any way, and exposure is their weapon. They also feel that they have scriptures to back them up. They want to share it on social media, with church members, family, and just about anyone, in order to get back at them. Just talking about what they want to do seems to ease their pain. They don't yet see the full range of consequences of following through on their plans. This is why, from a relationship perspective, I believe this is the wrong approach.

On the one hand, there are scriptures describing what action you can take if a sexual immorality happens in your marriage. But they also encourage you to consider what is best. (Ephesians 5:10 ***Carefully determine what pleases the Lord*** and 5:15 ***So be careful how you live. Don't live like fools, but like those who are wise.***)

Therefore, I pray you have more restraint before making hasty decisions. There is another scripture one can look to for guidance in this situation:

Galatians 6:1 NLT, ***Dear brothers and sisters, if another believer is overcome by some sin, you who are godly should gently and humbly help that person back onto the right path.***

This can be used, and I encourage a woman of God to have emotional maturity and the strength of God in these cases. This will prevent her from taking harmful actions that could be like committing suicide to her way of life and possibly her children's.

One should take a calm approach to such matters. This is what I usually recommend:

1. First, although you are hurting, consider Galatians 6:1 and NOT exposing him unless not doing so would cause harm to others.

2. It is not a good idea to force him to share his infidelity with others by going before the church to say "I have sinned." Allow this to be his desire. You uncovered his sin; it is exposed. If he is forced, it could create extreme dissonance or stress that can have a detrimental effect on his health and life. Some men of God have committed suicide, died of a heart attack, or become gravely ill when their sins were exposed and they were forced to share their wrongs in public.

3. Encourage counseling; but do not force him. Let it be his decision.
4. The affair is a private matter, unless it has a direct global effect on others. Don't just react emotionally because he cheated on you and scriptures are there to back you up if you expose him.
5. Realize that you are NOT a victim, but a witness, to his bad action.

Take a pause, go into prayer, and get help for yourself. Coaching is a great solution. It will help you think matters through a lot more carefully. In most cases I've noticed that exposing him could be action seeking revenge. This is a violation of Scripture, too. Romans 12:19 NLT states, ***never take revenge***.

Yes, infidelity is painful, but outing him could possibly add more to your pain when done in haste and when you are unprepared for the results. Again, in some cases women have destroyed their way of life because of the need to hurt him by exposure. Having sound judgment, emotional fitness, and the wisdom of God on how to proceed are the keys.

CHAPTER FOUR:
Relationship Destroyers

A man may not marry a woman for reasons that some may believe are insane, but they can be real to him.

When a man of God asks you not to do or wear something, pay attention. It could be triggering a global belief he has from the past. If something you do or wear matches that belief, he may walk away because you broke one of his personal, non-negotiable rules.

Compromising and Dysfunctional Needs

I've shared in Chapter Two about how important it is to meet his needs and explained the concept of the six basic human needs. When applying this knowledge, there is something about compromising that must be understood or it can destroy a relationship.

You see, we often hear that one must compromise within a relationship. I've said it myself on many occasions. However, the more I study and grow as a student of what drives human behavior, the more I've re-adjusted my thinking around this concept. Why?

1. I've learned that **if a compromise does not meet the needs** of an individual, even if one believes it is a fair agreement, that relationship is still doomed long term.
2. I've also learned that compromising works well when dealing with strategic issues such as house work, among other things within a relationship, but not really anywhere else.

What works? It is all about meeting needs, learning to build and maintain friendship while strengthening the positive vs negative effects in that relationship. These concepts I provide in depth to my coaching clients.

Sadly, in coaching couples, I find that this approach does not work when the negative issues in their relationship overwhelm the positive. I teach that in a healthy relationship there must be at least five positives for every negative. This is based on solid research from the Gottman Institute. I've coached women of God (men too) with such **dysfunctional individual needs** that their loving mate has not been able to meet them and both are very unhappy.

For example, because of trust issues, being insecure, or the need to feel important, a person may need their mate to do a particular thing. But while they are doing it, the mate is responding to them in a negative manner because they have this negative emotion. It can be a no-win situation and a mess!

Please don't run out and just believe that your husband or future one has dysfunctional needs because you don't want to do something he requires of you. You may believe, "This is why I can't win in our relationship." This could be true. But it is only when what they are asking of you is based on emotional instability that it can be categorized as dysfunctional.

By dysfunctional needs I mean those that are so extreme that it is impossible to meet them; they can destroy a relationship. To expand on "Meeting His Needs" (Chapter Two) regarding the six basic human needs, there are **two dominant needs** that are most likely to become dysfunctional. It happens when one is driven to feel complete certainty and the need to be or feel significant in their relationships.

Yes, having an extremely strong need for both **certainty** and **significance** can be a huge problem. When these two extreme needs clash, when they are that dominant in one's life, they are impossible for anyone to meet. Don't get me wrong, they are important needs, but if this is what is driving a person, it usually ends in doom and gloom, with no hope of finding happiness anywhere.

These are the needs that fuel trust issues, insecurities, and usually everything that creates havoc in relationships. When a person is driven by both of these needs, a loving mate may do everything to meet them at first, but usually burns out in the long term.

A dysfunctional vehicle for meeting the needs of an emotionally dysfunctional person is what is destroying relationships nowadays, even in the church. It doesn't matter who you are or what you have accomplished because this is a matter of the heart. This is the area where most have fewer skills in dealing with their greatest fears of being hurt or not feeling like they are worthy enough to be loved. Meeting needs with this type of person is extremely difficult or virtually impossible.

If you are NOT putting in the work on yourself and developing life skills to cope with matters of the heart and maintaining a relationship, you will NEVER be happy in a relationship, nor will anyone be happy with you.

Even for a person of faith, God can NOT put this work in for you, nor can He bless you over your non-work. It is your responsibility, so it is best that you refrain from saying, "He is working on me." This is often an excuse for you to do nothing and feel good about it.

God wants you to trust Him *and* for YOU to help yourself. 2 Thessalonians 3:10 speaks about work and eating. I believe this is the same principle for benefiting in anything else, including relationships. Also in James 2:18 you will see how having faith without working on yourself is dysfunctional within itself.

If you truly want a lasting, happy, relationship, you must put in the WORK on yourself so that your needs are NOT so difficult to meet!!!!

The Love Exam

Many people in a marriage or love relationship have an exam—a love exam—used to see if they are loved. We go over this exam in our heads and may even ask our mates directly. For some the exam is always in play. For others it only surfaces when their mate has disappointed them. These are actually their personal rules for love. Many relationships fail because one mate cannot pass the other's love exam. Therefore these tests are relationship destroyers.

In some cases the test was borrowed from a parent, family member, a TV show, a book, or even a movie—perhaps even unconsciously. It was not something the person actually chose.

Here are some examples from my coaching sessions:

- If he loves me, he will stop and text or call me during the day all the time, no matter what he is doing.
- If he loves me, he will focus on me when we talk and never place me on hold—even if there is a work-related call.
- If you love me, you will agree with me no matter what.
- If he loves me, he will really take care of me if I'm upset and crying.
- I only know that he loves me if he still loves me when

I'm falling apart.

- If she loves me, she has to support me in my career and understand that I'm doing this for her and the family.
- If she loves me, she would never share our personal information with others.
- If you love me you have to anticipate my needs before I ask.
- If she loves me she will express it when around friends and family and show me appreciation in front of them.
- If you love me, then when you go to a store you will bring me back my favorite ____ as a sign that you were thinking about me. If you forget, I know you don't really love me.

These are just a few tests often found in marriages or relationships. Our spouses or future ones often fail at them. Very few are using a test that their mate can satisfy.

How to create your own valid test that the love of your life can actually pass? The key is to get a piece of paper right now and write down your test(s). You have to be really honest with yourself.

First let's think about the format of these exams:

He must love me in spite of _____.
If he loves me, he will _____.
If he loves me, he will do this for me: _____.
I only know that I'm loved if he _____.
If he does this: _____, then he doesn't love me.

Now that you know the format, write down your test. We all have one. Again, be honest with yourself because you may have more than one test. Inquire within yourself.

A MAN OF GOD *is Still* A MAN

Here is one way to pull out what is inside of you, a way to brainstorm your love exam. Just fill in the blanks in the above list. Another way is to ask yourself this question many times until you run out of answers: ***If he loves me, what will he do?*** Do this quickly and write the first thing that comes to mind, instead of thinking hard. Just start writing. Or, ask a friend to write as you talk. This process will help you understand what kinds of tests you are giving, or will give, the love of your life.

Here's another way: Imagine you are speaking directly to him, saying:

If you love me, you will_____.

Complete this sentence. Now do it again and again until nothing more comes to mind.

Now if you are still having trouble coming up with anything, here is another question to ask yourself to bring it out:

When you do _____, I know you don't love me.

Again, repeat this over and over until you get it all out.

This is your current love exam.

Read it through. Consider how these test questions influence your behavior. Do you do certain things on purpose to see if you are loved?

Now, if you are a woman and you feel loved when a man consoles you, consider this: Are you, perhaps unconsciously, finding things to get upset about? Are you often upset and crying when he's around?

He could love you tremendously from the bottom of his heart, but when you are sad or unhappy, a man naturally feels like a failure.

If this happens too often, he will feel that you are always upset at your core and will become frustrated with himself. But his feelings will be easy to misinterpret as frustration with you and your unhappy emotions. This man will think that he has failed you and will stop taking care of you when you are upset because nothing he does helps. Then you will think that he doesn't love you, because he is not taking care of you.

Can you see how these tests can hurt a relationship? How can he pass? Such a test will most likely ruin what could have been a relationship leading to marriage. The resentments and frustrations will build up and destroy that possibility along with the relationship.

These tests are how so many Christian marriages end in divorce. You see, as I stated before, men of God are asked to make sacrifices for their marriages and to maintain restraint and discipline, regardless of what is going on in their homes, even if they are unhappy. However this is a test, too. Many are failing and divorcing and leaving their life-long church home because of shame or guilt. They could no longer tolerate the resentment that had built up and, in some cases, was causing health issues.

This is why relationship skills are so important. The sacrifices will be learning to implement strategies instead of waiting for something to happen that usually never comes because of a lack of skills. This is especially true in areas where the Bible is silent on how to handle the situation.

The key is to know what your tests are and make sure the love of your life can pass them. Throw out the others, no matter the source. Tell yourself that they are NOT true.

Shifting Communications

> Amos 3:3 NLT: *Can two people walk together without agreeing on the direction?*

Both men and women destroy relationships with their shifting communications. Let me explain how this happens and give you a technique to use that will improve your relationship drastically.

Most do not know how the conversation dynamics at work between two people can shift an entire relationship. One of the best ways to destroy a current or future relationship is to shift communications by blocking emotional or general proposals within a conversation. In most cases when a problem is presented by a husband, wife, or a potential spouse, it is related to their inability to communicate effectively. You may hear, "We have a communication problem."

Most never understand that within conversations we are often making proposals, and the response to these usually reflects the overall health of a relationship.

This section is to help you become a better communicator by learning how to accept proposals. If you are having reoccurring arguments, as many couples do, I'm sure it has a lot to do with blocking proposals within the conversation sequence. The goal is to learn how to elevate your communications to successfully navigate in your relationship. Couples or unmarried individuals may want to seek coaching on this issue for detailed strategies, but I will provide you with some insights that you can apply right now. This is based on the work of Dr. John Gottman of the Gottman Institute on emotional bids.

Do you often wonder, *Why am I not able to communicate what I'm really feeling? Why is there so much miscommunication?*

It is because either you misunderstood your current or future husband's proposals, or you failed to make a proposal to him that shows how much he is loved by you.

What is a proposal? A proposal is a statement that always invites further communication.

What is a block? A block counters the information presented in the proposal.

Proposal: "I have a taste for spaghetti and meatballs today"

Block: "That's so fattening."

This response is a block because it counters the proposal with a contrary opinion. Even if there is no response, just silence, it still blocks the proposal. The same is true if you turn away or roll your eyes. Blocks happen all the time in romantic relationships and cause all types of problems.

Now, instead of blocking the proposal, what if the response is the following:

Proposal: "I have a taste for spaghetti and meatballs today"

Response: "I know this great Italian restaurant" or "That sounds great. Maybe we can go to this Italian restaurant I know. I can see myself eating chicken and pasta."

This response returns the proposal with a proposal. Remember, you want to invite further communication instead of making the person feel attacked or bad about bringing up the subject. Here is another one.

Proposal: "These people on this job are driving me crazy. They are lazy and putting all the work on me. I'm so frustrated."

Block: "Why don't you just tell the supervisor instead of complaining about it? That is how I would handle a situation like that.

How will this response make him feel? He should have never shared his day with you or vented about his frustrations. He will not want to share his thoughts or frustrations with you in future. Even if you feel you are stating a fact, it will still come across as criticism and will cause hurt feelings. It can also lead to an argument. This man will NOT feel good in your presence.

If he loves you, he may keep on making proposals for a while, hoping you will return one. However, he will continue only to the point when resentment kicks in and smothers his hopes. Then he will end the relationship.

What if the response goes like this?

Proposal: "These people on this job are driving me crazy. They are lazy and putting all the work on me. I'm so frustrated."

Response: "I'm sorry. Why don't I give you a backrub to relieve some of your frustrations?"

What you are communicating in this response is that you are sorry for his experience, understand his feelings, and that you'd like to do something to make him feel better. You must also understand how your mate receives love and replace my example of a back rub with that method.

Do you get the picture? This is a way to elevate your communications to a level that invites more connection instead of one that provokes fights. Blocking proposals is a sure way to destroy a relationship. There are in-depth ways to formulate proposals and to avoid blocking them. One of my couple's communications workshops is the key to learning how to become an expert at this.

The "Not Me Too!" Syndrome?

No! Not me too! I am NOT swelling his head. I only lift up the name of Jesus, not his. Why should I praise him? Other women tell him how wonderful he is all the time, but he will NOT hear this from me. Yes, he is a great man of God. He speaks well, and people love him, but I'm not a church groupie and not slobbering all over him like these other women. I'm bringing him down a notch. He hears that other stuff all the time."

OK, in my Fred Sanford voice: "Are you crazy?" Women of faith! NEVER, EVER allow other women to say quality things about your man that you have NOT said to him OFTEN. And be sure to say it to him in front of THEM.

I don't understand the mentality of women who are so concerned about how their man will respond to such admiring women. Are you competing with him? Or trying to keep him in a certain mindset around you?

I see a pattern in this that destroys marriages and relationships. And it is so easy to STOP if you let go of this "NOT me too!" mentality, whether it's based on pride or something else. Why is it so important to NOT praise your man the way other women do?

A Real Case

Husband (a minister): "I feel good when I'm around her or talking to her [his lover]."

A MAN OF GOD *is* *Still* A MAN

He cheated with this woman and is now considering filing for a divorce and leaving his church home just to be with her.

His wife is extremely upset and wants him back, although she is also depressed that he cheated and is considering a divorce.

Situation: This quality man with his talent, smarts, and great looks, is an amazing speaker and very effective at bringing the word of God to his home church's congregation. He is only a minister with the potential to become a pastor.

Discovery: His wife felt and saw all of these qualities in him, but because other women were praising him, she had developed this "NOT me TOO!" attitude towards him. She would NOT say those things that make a man feel good in her presence.

My Interview:

Me: Do you also see in him the qualities that other women praise him for?"

Wife: "Yes, but I don't like being just like other women. I don't need to tell him what he hears all the time."

Me: Even though he is wrong for cheating, do you feel you played a role in this situation?

Wife: I'm just shocked and blown away that he would do this to me. Not him of all people. I'm not the one who sinned. I knew these women blew up his head. I'm shocked.

Me: Because he is a minister and loves God?

Wife: Yes, he must be faking. I mean, he is the last person I would think would do something like this.

Me: My dear, even though he is a man of God, he is still a man. Are you open to seeing the big picture of the role each of you played in this relationship so that ownership can be taken for the results?

As I was sitting there with empathy one day, I had time to ponder my experiences in this matter. I was thinking, *Wow, this is a crazy attitude to have, but it exists and, even worse, I see this pattern all the time even in the church.*

 Women of faith, if your current or future husband gets attention from other women, be a "ME MORE" type of woman. Give it up for him even MORE than they do. He really only cares when he hears it from you.

I strongly advise you to do this as a way to avoid his cheating as the man in the example above.

 If a man of God cheats, keep in mind: This was his decision. It was NOT your fault! He has to be responsible for his own actions. Any excuse he provides is just that, an excuse.

Your Husband vs Your Pastor?

Numbers 30:16 NLT: *These are the regulations the Lord gave Moses concerning relationships between a man and his wife....*

Never take your pastor's advice over your husband's. You can destroy your marriage by going against your husband; and, according to Scripture, you will be out of God's order too. The book of Numbers 30:1-15 shares a list of rules that the Lord gave Moses regarding accountability for pledges, vows made under oath to the Lord. Not only is a man responsible for his own vows, but also for those made by his wife and unmarried daughters living at home. If the man objects to the woman's vow, it is nullified; she does not have to fulfill it. If the man agrees, then it stands. But, if she does not fulfill it, then God will hold HIM accountable and **He will be punished for her guilt.** (Numbers 30:15 NLT)

The story of Timothy and his mother Eunice provides insights on God's view *(Acts 16:1-5)*. Eunice was a Jew and knew that God commanded every Jewish baby boy to be circumcised. If he were not, the covenant would be broken and that Soul cut off from his people.

However, Timothy was not circumcised, because his father, a Greek, did not permit it. Yet God honored the faith of Eunice, and greatly used her son Timothy. The law of being subject to her husband supersedes the law of circumcision. God held the father, NOT the mother accountable and accepted his decision. A woman submitting to her husband, even when she believes his decisions are wrong, shows great strength; and God rewards such strength of character.

It should be noted that Scripture does not provide any conditions indicating that a woman doesn't have to submit to her husband. It should be noted that Scripture does not provide any conditions indicating that a woman doesn't have to submit to her husband. However, the following scriptures:

Ephesians 5:21 (NLT): ***submit to one another***.... and

Philippians 2:3 (ESV): ***Do nothing from rivalry or conceit, but in humility count others more significant than yourselves***, and Colossians 3:19 (NLT): ***Husbands, love your wives and never treat them harshly***, provide guidance and a clear picture on God's model for marriages and our loving relationships. It is not a license for a man of God to gloat in some false identity of manhood to emotionally humiliate or abuse his wife.

This is why it is extremely important that a woman of God must **choose her husband carefully**, because she is charged to submit to this man regardless. It doesn't mean that a wife must violate any laws or remain in an abusive relationship, but overall she has to submit to him in order to be aligned with Scripture.

When Things Go Bad

Romans 8:28 NLT: *And we know that God causes everything to work together for the good of those who love God and are called according to his purpose for them.*

Divorce usually happens when things go bad in a marriage. Everyone knows that God hates divorce but it still happens. I don't sugar-coat issues. Every issue I'm addressing comes directly from at least several cases in my coaching practice that involved men and women of God. Therefore, I know these things happen, although they are not always discussed within Christian communities.

What I've noticed in the cases that end in divorce is that the relationship was destroyed long before that. So let's look at this topic, what to do when things go wrong, from the perspective of letting go in terms of how you treat your husband. This also applies to those dating because women get hurt in these relationships, too.

Just know that I'm not encouraging divorce; however, I do believe that sometimes it is a good thing to create space to clear heads. With this in mind I say to you: **"Let it go, or Leave!"**

Yes, remove yourself from the relationship to clear your head. You may be thinking:

> *He doesn't deserve forgiveness now.*
> *I can't pretend that it didn't happen.*

I don't want him to think I'm a pushover or weak.
He must be punished.

And if you said these things to me, I would ask you:

>How do you relate to your husband with these feelings?
>
>What's the purpose for staying when you can't treat him well?
>
>Are you staying so you can implement your "Holding-on-to-What-You-Did-to-Me" campaign?

I've learned that it is extremely safe to hold on to past actions. Why is it safe?

1. It provides an excuse for your ever-changing emotional moods.
2. It gives you a reason to be mad, which meets your need for certainty and to feel significant.
3. It keeps you safe so you can have an excuse why NOT to trust, or why you shouldn't trust or love in the first place.
4. Maybe it gives you a reason to keep feeling sorry for yourself—the "Why Me?" syndrome.
5. It prevents you from loving deeply, because there is a fear of being hurt anyway. So why do it?

My precious women of faith, these are excuses! Why do you need these excuses? What is driving you? Here's what experience has taught me:

- So many women do NOT experience love in their life, because of FEAR!
- Too many are afraid of being hurt; therefore they live their life skeptical and filled with emotional drama about men in general. "The Bad-Attitude-towards-Men" syndrome.

- Because of this fear, they make accusations all the time when in a relationship and run him away to start the cycle all over again.

- They keep selling themselves on the idea of why they SHOULD NOT love a man, because all men_____ (You fill in the blank.)

- They want everything to be completely right in their relationship. They need to feel absolutely certain that they are loved and will NOT be hurt before they will give love fully. (With this attitude attraction does not develop and most men will not pursue a relationship with such women.)

Here is a NEWSFLASH!!!!

- You will NEVER have love or be comfortable in a marriage or relationship with these thoughts or actions.

- You have to be willing to take the risk of being hurt again and love him anyway if you ever expect to gain his love. There is NO OTHER way. This is why it is very important to choose carefully the man you will love.

- Only those who love regardless of what they receive experience love in their life.

- Those who trade for love, saying "You do this for me, and I'll give you that," NEVER experience true love in their lives. Why? Because they were trading, and it was NOT given freely.

When hurt, you have choices:

1. If your husband hurts you, you can leave! God did not command you to stay, but Scripture does set prohibitions to remarrying. You may have just made a bad choice. If you are not able to leave right now, it should be clear that you are leaving.

2. If you decided to stay, you apparently made a good choice, but he was not always at his best. You MUST let it all go and start loving again right now. You can share your pain, but love him through it. A worthy man will feel it deeply and will NOT want to hurt you. I recommend that you get help.
3. If you are unsure, there has to be a plan of action so that your mate will know what to expect. Never keep him hanging.
4. BUT, never use your uncertainty of whether you will leave or stay to punish. That's revenge and violates Romans 12:19: ...*never take revenge.* Revenge never serves anyone in a relationship long term. Your best revenge is your happiness.

Please understand that it is OK to let it go. You are making a sound love investment in a person you feel is worthy even when he was NOT at his best. You are NOT a laughing stock when taking a risk on love, you are the exception. Don't listen to anyone else, because it is your love life at risk, not theirs. Fight for love and happiness.

Forgiveness is the key when things go bad. Let it go, work it out, and keep your husband.
The other option is to leave.
It should be just that simple.

Why complicate it? I understand that we are bound by religious principles and prohibitions. Just don't use them as an excuse to stay and punish.

No Calls Yet?

You just met this great Christian man, had a date, but he has not called back. Wow! What happened? How you respond can make or break the possibility of this turning into a long-term relationship.

First, consider this: Just because he seemed nice, appeared Christ-like and gentlemanly, does not mean he is really that way. Some of the biggest frauds start off this way. You need more data to know for sure. So don't get all excited and lose your focus. You have more work to do before you can exhale.

Then, Ladies, please stop jumping to conclusions if you have not received a call in a couple of days, especially after a first date. It could be because he has cold feet temporarily and does not want to seem desperate (Yes, men who love God can play hard to get, too.) Also he could be processing whether he feels you are what God wants for him. Some men feel that women act differently if you make them wait; that a woman will become more interested in a man who doesn't pursue her. (Yes, this is a form of mind game; Christians play them too.)

Maybe he is not in a position to call or text. He may be very busy or sick or just trying to get over an ex. And, yes, he could have discovered that he is not attracted to you. There could be a number of factors—things you can change and things you do not have any control over. So why bother to fret over no phone call? Just relax. Do not call him! If he is interested, he will call. It is just that simple.

Hey, you have a life too.

Allow a few days. If he does not call, then it's on him. Don't beat yourself up. You could have avoided a major crash in your love life. If he is playing games in the beginning, it is a sign of more games to come.

Some men think that women love them more, or that they look more attractive, if they tease you with their attention. When they finally do call, these types of men don't give you any reasons for not calling sooner. Just don't buy into it because you want to train your future husband, in a nice way, to understand that you are not interested in playing games.

Say, "So how have you been? Is everything OK with ya?"

If he does not explain or say anything about what is going on with him, it is a sign that he can be evasive or too private to share. How can you learn about a man who will not share or who is too private? If you put up with this, he will always keep you on the edge, making you think that he might walk out of your life for some petty thing.

Before you get all technical, just make sure that you are prepared and ready for your Mr. Right. It could be because of your behavior on the date. Whatever the case may be, learn from it, improve, and move on.

Teasing a Man

Philippians 2:4 ESV: *Let each of you look not only to your own interests, but also to the interests of others.*

Never make fun of your husband or man of interest in public—about anything! Not his hair, clothes, shoes, or any mistake he makes. It is a deal-breaker to embarrass your husband (or any man you care about, for that matter) in public.

Many men are more sensitive than you think, so let me point out an area that can create anger in your husband, and he may never tell you. What is it? Well, making fun of him (teasing) in front of others, especially your family.

Here is an example.

A group of you are playing volleyball at a family function. Your husband jumps up to hit the ball and misses badly. Now there could be teasing going on by other family members or friends.

Do not join in—never!

Defend your husband! Say, "Y'all leave my man alone." Then say something nice about him

"My man is _____." Then stop and give him a kiss, if possible.

I don't care if it is your sister, your mom, or your best friend—**never let anyone make fun of him** while he is in your presence.

Now, I know that family members may make fun of each other, and you can get by when he is not around—but never in front of others outside of your immediate family. Some men don't like to be teased in front of their kids either.

 **Teasing? Be careful.** Your relationship may be in jeopardy. He may never discuss this matter with you, but will start acting up, even being cruel, because you bruised his ego. The attraction between you is gone and he will leave

How Do You Respond?

Proverbs 15:1 NIV: *A gentle answer turns away wrath, but a harsh word stirs up anger.*

How do you respond to your husband or love interest when you disagree with what he is doing or saying? Do you remember Proverbs 15:1 or do you respond with criticism? If you want to change your relationship with him overnight, the first thing you can do is **STOP** criticizing! Criticism destroys relationships by creating distance between you and making a man feel that he is not achieving.

Remember a man of God is still a man. That means he is competitive. Minute by minute he is gauging whether or not he is achieving. Achieving what? His goal. And what is that? Pleasing you!! But your criticism turns it into a battle that he is NOT winning!

In other words, stop being combative in your conversations. I understand that this can go both ways and is more easily said than done, but changing how you respond to him will help you connect deeply with him in a special way. It can make him not ever want to leave you. Learn other ways to respond to situations. This book is full of ideas. For example, see "Meeting His Needs" (Chapter Two).

When about to burst with a critical, angry comment, what can you do instead? Personally, I find it helps to ask myself,

What is it that she needs in this moment? Is she seeking certainty? Connection? Love? What can I do or say that will help to meet this need?

Then, when life is calmer, begin building that strong connection. First, understand that your most effective approach to dealing with issues in your relationship is to talk about things you both want. Next, discuss what is interfering with your having what you want, instead of talking about what's wrong. This will keep you both out of combat mode.

In addition, know this: Just because you have never heard of something before does not make it the end game. I hear this often on my blog from women who say, "That's crazy! I've never heard of this before." Does this mean that the world revolves around you, your experiences and thought process? Just because you have never heard of a particular issue before doesn't mean that it never happened or doesn't exist.

This is how you can create problems in your relationship. Just know that what is going on could be true in the current situation, and it is best that you try to understand.

How Would You Respond?

Here is an example. Imagine you are getting dressed to go out for dinner. Your husband tells you that he doesn't like something you are wearing. He says, "It makes my skin crawl."

If you dismiss his comment (thinking *How bizarre!*) and decide to wear it anyway, then all evening your husband, the one you are with, will feel his skin crawling, and he will not want to be with you. It is just that simple. He could have a mild phobia.

What sorts of things might this be? Anything! Because it is based on his unique life experiences. However, listening to men talking with me and other men at church about women who turn them off, I can tell you that it is often something regarding how a woman looks and her attire. It may relate to their image of a Jezebel or, more often, to a traumatic experience with women at a young age, as described in "His Global Beliefs" (Chapter Two.)

You may understand, or you may discount his belief. You may use this to criticize or tease him. This only serves to chip away at your relationship. How do women make this mistake? I'll tell you how: by looking for ways to make him wrong. Remember his emotional calculations, the mental mapping he does to see how you fit into his life? (See "A Secret about Men" in Chapter Two.)

Yes, you read, study, have great ideas, and are a great debater—I get this. But stop using those skills on your husband or potential. First, no one wants to be wrong anyway. So explain how he can feel good with you or about you if he is made out to be wrong and you right. Yes, you will win the argument, but eventually you will lose him. This doesn't mean you cannot exchange ideas or disagree, but the way you do so makes a difference.

Think about this. Before you say something to him, ask yourself this question,

Am I criticizing, encouraging, asking a question, or sharing or exchanging information?"

Don't just criticize. Try to understand his point of view. All of the other approaches are OK, and you can get the information you need from them. Just stop criticizing. Again, I am not saying that you can't disagree.

Next, When Your Needs Clash, How Do You Respond?

Imagine that your date is Lewis, a construction worker, and you have been planning a private evening with him all day long. You actually took off work to make this evening very special. He is scheduled to arrive around 7:00 p.m. Around 5:00 p.m. he calls to tell you that he isn't feeling very well, is tired, and wants to call it a night. He asks if you would be OK with this.

How would you respond?

Emotionally? Or will you understand his situation and have a different approach?

Responding emotionally will make you focus on all the work

you have done, taking off work, and will make it all about you.

Now say that you put yourself in his shoes and know that he has a very stressful, intricate, and physically demanding job. Let's say that you respond by saying, "Honey, I am so sorry that your day has been difficult. Why don't you get some rest and call me later? I am missing and thinking of you."

How do you believe he will respond? You will have just created a deeper connection with this potential mate simply because you understood his situation.

Yes, you will hurt and be upset that you worked hard making preparations. You may be feeling very emotional about this matter. Just add intelligence to that emotion and score big with him. It is simple. You have so much power just by using the proper strategy in your relationship.

Challenging His Manhood

Proverbs 21:19 NLT: *It's better to live alone in the desert than with a quarrelsome, complaining wife.*

When a woman is trying to make a man conform to her worldview, I often hear the man say, 'She makes me feel less than a man." Challenging his manhood in this way is another reason he will become detached and leave.

Here are some questions for you:

- Do you think that you are smarter than your husband or potential?
- Do you feel that you can perform a task better?
- Are you undermining your husband's ideas and approach to issues?
- Do you listen to your husband?

Here is an example: John was on the phone calling a hotel about their reservation. Jodie was listening to his conversation and started interrupting, saying, "Give them the confirmation number. Tell them that we are not paying an additional fee. Tell them that we work too hard for this." Say this…; say that…, all in John's ear about how he should handle the issue.

John said, "OK, honey, I got this. I can handle this!"
When he got off the phone, Jodie asked, "Well, what did they say?"

Grilling him: Didn't you tell them this…? Didn't you tell them that…?

What happened here? Well, Jodie just undermined her husband's approach to business by second-guessing what he was doing. She felt that her skills were more suitable to handle the task better. Also, Jodie did not listen to her husband. He said, "I got this!"

Women, let him do the task! Do not interfere! If there was something that he forgot to say, you can point it out in the right tone. Then he can pick up the phone to clarify or fix the problem. He does not feel that he knows everything; he will listen. Just allow him to do the job. Be a team player, not a take-over mate. You do not need to take over the task.

MEN HATE THIS!

These are ways you challenge his manhood. Men hate your commanding tone. Your husband is not one of your employees or children.

Here are examples of comments and tones that challenge his manhood:

> "Didn't I tell you to take out the garbage?"

> "Go pick up my clothes from the dry cleaner."

> "You need to fix the doorbell; it's acting up."

> "Why didn't you just call the bank?
> It would have been the easier approach."

> "Why don't you just call a mechanic and let him fix it?
> They know more about this than you."

One more point. If an issue occurs, such as a home or car-repair problem (or another area in which he takes an interest), make sure you show him that you totally accept his input by letting him handle it. Do not second-guess him by working on the problem by yourself.

And NEVER bring to the table another man's ideas. That's like telling him, "You are not capable of handling your manly duties."

Here is an example of how you may challenge your man's ideas with another man's: "Philemon told me the reason why we are having this problem is because of this or that."

He may think to himself, "Who is this Philemon? He's just a man like me!" Then he may rebel against that good idea only because his ego has been bruised.

I know that this may seem childish, but I am telling you ladies what my studies of the average man show. It is also based on all of the calls I've received from women complaining about how stubborn their man is about an idea. Most of them bruised their man's ego, and this is why they were having problems.

Now there is a way to implement another point of view, but you have to walk carefully when dealing with men. Always acknowledge his ideas, follow with a compliment, and then make suggestions.

PHILEMON

He Won't Lead

1 Timothy 2:11-13 NLT: *Women should learn quietly and submissively. I do not let women teach men or have authority over them. Let them listen quietly. For God made Adam, and afterward he made Eve.*

Who is taking charge of your relationship? I mentioned earlier that God has given men authority over women. The Bible verse above is often quoted. Some women are fighting against this order in their relationship. I believe they are doing this because, nowadays, women are encouraged to take charge. At the same time women complain to me about how their husband or potential won't lead, take action, or show more initiative. These are the questions I ask them:

"Do you seek outside counsel?"

"Do you make most of the decisions in your marriage?"

"Do you always take charge?"

"Are you assertive?"

If you answered "Yes" to any of these questions, then you are an Alpha Woman, considered dominant. Yet, if you want your husband to lead and take more initiative, here is the million-dollar question: "How can he?" What you call assertive, he calls bossy!

If you are not yet married, seeking that special someone, then be alert to this, too. Bossiness may be one of the things that comes through as you let down your guards. It may be why you are sitting in church desiring a mate to no avail.

Men often complain about the feeling of being controlled, the inability to get their point across, and of being the victim of constant insults. Yes! This happens in the church. Men complain that their **wives, women of God, are seeking advice or counsel from outside sources without their permission.** They also feel that they just cannot do things right. A man of God will shut down because of this.

Why? Well, for one thing, we are talking about a "man of God." Your wanting to control everything sets up a conflict between what both of you know the Bible says and what is actually happening between you. Because God holds him responsible and gives him authority over you as his wife, but he wants to please you, and you are obviously displeased. This sets up conflicting priorities or values for him. He loves God, and he also loves you. (This also looks like a case of your wanting your cake and eating it too.)

Let's walk through how a man of God maps this out. He knows he's been slipping on the biblical side by allowing you to control everything. Now, however, you are still unhappy. You want him to take charge and plan trips, dates, and events. But when he does, you interject your opinions, attempt to take over the project, or complain about how he is doing it. He is in a no-win situation. What else can he do but leave?

Many women of God in this situation share with me how their husband does not know how to do certain things; he requires her help. This is the reason given for interfering with him when he does try to lead, and why she is overseeing what he does. Does this sound familiar?

 **Leadership is not about doing it ALL.** Nor has it anything to do with competency. The leader does not have to be smarter, more talented, or more spiritual than the followers. Leadership only requires having the ability to make a statement.

How does he become the leader of your family? When he says, "We are going to do this tomorrow at 7 pm and that's it," you accept his decision. This makes him the leader and leaders delegate. Effective leaders delegate more. They get to know who can do what well and then back off. They don't hover.

If you know how to do something better, and he is aware of that, he may ask you to do it. You may want to ask, "How can I help?" to indicate your cooperation and submission.

If you are a take-charge woman of God, and if you want to have a relationship with a take-charge man of God, you must stop taking charge and be the flexible one, the submissive one. You know what the Bible says. Also, in this book you are learning about a man's natural desire to please the woman he loves, fulfilling his responsibilities to God to lead, love, and care for her.

When you second-guess his opinions, his approach to matters, and his decisions, he is losing in this relationship and will not want to be with you. Please understand that your way is not always better, but if you subconsciously believe this, the relationship is doomed. This undermines the attraction between you. He will leave.

Not only is the concept of one leader, one follower, in a partnership a key part of the Bible, it is a basic concept in every leadership class I've ever taken—in Christian and secular settings. Research supports the Bible in this, showing that relationships work best with polarity—a balance between opposites. One must be dominant, the other flexible, i.e. submissive.

That men are natural-born leaders and women natural followers was once conventional wisdom. Both men and women were respected for playing their very demanding roles well. Nowadays this conventional wisdom is no longer accepted. Young men and women today rarely have the skills to play these traditional roles.

Let's face it. Men in this country are just not dominant anymore; they are not being encouraged to lead. Women no longer trust enough to follow and are becoming more and more dominant in many settings, even within the family. Both men and women are enrolling in classes on how to lead (communicate) and how to follow (surrender, trust). Employers often send employees—male and female—to training in these areas.

We must address this issue because it exists throughout the church. Despite the clear authority God gives to men in the Bible, many men and women of God are still struggling with how to live in today's world while following Scripture. This is one of the relationship challenges in today's church, an area in which to consider what adjustments can be made to bring harmony to the home. I have observed couples doing this and still keeping to God's law.

As described above, some couples are re-defining how the husband, a man of God, leads. She acknowledges that he is ultimately responsible, as the Bible says, while each takes on tasks in their areas of strength, working for a common goal.

A variation on this occurs when the woman is a take-charge person and the husband is OK with it. If that is you, just be happy! If the home is operating smoothly, then let that be the goal. Try not to force him to take more initiative than he wants to. Not only is this kind of assertiveness clearly against Scripture, but you will be disappointed. I say this because how it is working now may never change in your household. This is his style of leadership. If he is not asserting himself, it is probably because he is content with what you have planned and relieved that you are taking care of it. Of course, as a woman of God, you will be ready to follow him anytime he indicates he wants to handle something.

The Bible story of Deborah comes to mind. The fourth chapter of Judges tells of how Deborah became a judge when Israel lived in a time of great moral decline due to a lack of strong national leadership. God appointed Deborah to the highest public office in the land. Even Barak, a mighty Hebrew warrior, knew that the Lord had chosen to speak through Deborah and said that she should accompany him to battle.

This strong woman was allowed to use her leadership skills to benefit her people. If he is also allowing you to do that, congratulations! That is his way of leading—using the skills of others.

If you are still determined to make him lead, then this is extremely important:

Do not take this man to the pastor or counselor without his permission!

If you have an issue on which you want to seek outside counsel, ask him if it is OK for both of you to seek help together.

If he says, "No!"

DO NOT go by yourself behind his back.

Instead, ask him if it is OK for you to go for yourself.

This approach is in keeping with the Bible's mandate, *the wife must respect her husband* (Ephesians 5:33 NLT, NIV).

Rather than being adversarial, showing respect for his point of view and for his reluctance to seek outside counsel may allow you to engage him in the process. Ask his help in setting a goal, selecting the person to see, and evaluating the results. This should be acceptable to him. If you go, be sure to report back to him on the help you receive.

I have seen this work for couples who want to follow Scripture and meet the demands of today's church. It can work for you, too.

Giving Unsolicited Advice

Luke 6:31 NLT: *Do to others what you would want them to do to you.*

You just read about taking charge. Now let me share one of the biggest mistakes a woman, or any person for that matter, can make: giving unsolicited advice. People just don't like it and especially men. It is disliked so much because of how it relates to **Drama Cycles**, the dramatic cycles into which people in a relationship often get swept up. I'm going to go a little deep with you on this because it is needed and will make sense in the end.

In order to better understand these cycles, Stephen Karpman, a well-respected psychiatrist, designed a model in the shape of an inverted triangle. Karpman identified three roles that people play in these drama cycles, placing one at each corner of the triangle: Persecutor and Rescuer on top and Victim on the bottom.

> **Persecutor**: a role taken on when someone blames others for not doing things right or for not taking more responsibility for their actions. (Sometimes called "Perpetrator" or "Aggressor.")
>
> **Victim**: a role taken on by someone after something happens to them or is done to them.
>
> **Rescuer**: a role taken on by someone attempting to fix something for someone else, something they see as being "broken."

Playing these roles is one of the most common ongoing drama cycles that people in a relationship can find themselves in. This is what makes people co-dependent. These are what we call "games" and are another reason why a man will leave, because these games will destroy the attraction between you.

The only way out of such a cycle in a relationship is to take on two additional positions or roles:

Observer: a role you play when you take a step back and simply notice your own behavior, looking at what is really going on in order to find a solution to the problem

Creator: a role that suggests that you create your own system in getting your needs met. You decide to STOP being part of a co-dependent drama cycle and simply create the life you want.

Now you may be wondering, *What does this have to do with giving unsolicited advice?* Well, I'm glad you are thinking this way. Here is an example of how this can lead to a drama cycle.

Whenever you give advice or offer your opinion on solving a problem for someone else without permission, without being asked, you are placing that person in the role of **Victim** in a drama triangle and you are assuming the role of **Rescuer**. This is because you are sending a message or suggestion that he cannot solve his problem himself; that you are the **Rescuer** and have the solutions or resources needed for his problem.

Now this may be the case; and your goal may be only to help. However, it will not be received that way because you did not gain his permission for your advice. This problem is huge in male and female dynamics. I often hear women I coach say, "Philemon, he won't listen to me or my advice." They do not understand why he is reacting this way. You may be wondering, too.

Well, using the drama cycle model, if he rejects your advice, you have placed him in the role of **Persecutor**. This places you in the role of **Victim** because of his rejection. On the other hand, if he accepts your advice, he may feel less than a man or beneath you, as well as feeling dependent because he needs you to solve his problems. Is this making sense to you now?

I hope this explanation gives you some perspective on how your unsolicited advice can place a man in a victim's role and how, in that position, he cannot feel good in your presence.

I'm sure you are thinking a million dollar question, "**Philemon, how do I help or offer my advice?**" Glad you may be thinking this. Simply ask for his permission to give advice. This places him in an empowering position. Something like "I'm sure you have considered everything in this situation. I was wondering. Is it OK for me to make a suggestion?" That gives him the power to say yes or no and places him in control. Be sure to wait for his answer, accept it, and bite your tongue if he says, "No!"

Another approach is to say "Hey you can reject it or not, and I'm OK with it, but wondering if I can offer a suggestion." I'm sure you have the picture now.

Here is the key. Don't be so pressed to give advice. If he says, "I've got this" or "I can handle it," just let it go because he is not giving you his permission. He is stepping up, being a man, and handling things himself.

And, do not take it personally. He's a man, and men like to solve their own problems.

You want him to take the lead? Let him!

Fussy

Luke 12:26 NIV: *Since you cannot do this very little thing, why do you worry about the rest?*

Are you constantly shouting or raising your voice, complaining or being argumentative? If so, you are considered a fussy woman. You are ruled by your emotions and react by yelling at others. A man will take notice of fussy women, even if the fussing is not directed at him. It will destroy the attraction and he will leave in a heart-beat, leaving you to wonder what happened.

Just know that being fussy is very annoying and can really piss off a man, or worse, embarrass him if you fuss in public. This is a deal breaker and will create unhappiness, poor treatment from him (if you are stuck due to finances), or he will simply leave.

Please note that there is more than one approach to solving problems, and your way is just another option. Also, no one wants to be wrong, and your tactic to make sure that you are right will have an adverse effect on your relationship. We can all be fussy at times and a work in progress, but some women take this to a whole new level in their relationship.

Do Not Describe Your Ex

Recently, I watched a man of God lose total interest in a woman he had been extremely excited about one hour earlier. Why? She made a huge mistake. She described her ex and other men who expressed interest in her to this man. I am sure she felt that it would increase her stock by attempting to make this man think that other caliber men wanted her, but it had the reverse affect.

Alice met Brian online at a Christian dating site and they started communicating just to discover that they worked in the same office building. They both loved God and were extremely interested in each other. Alice was 5'3" tall with average build and looks; Brian was a 5'10" customer service rep of the same build.

While at lunch one day, Alice told Brian that her last boyfriend was a 6'3" bodybuilder and worked for the mayor's office. She also said that another man she went out with played baseball for a minor league team, and she described him as very good looking. This was a huge mistake!

I noticed that Brian looked strange when approaching me after the date, so I asked him what happened. He went from being totally interested to telling me that he felt it wouldn't work.

Alice, on the other hand, was excited and told me that he was everything she wanted, from spiritual values and looks to personality. She was still very interested in him. She felt that this could be a long-term relationship developing. She is in for a big surprise.

Brian said that he lost interest because of not being remotely like the men she dated in the past. He wondered how he could compete with something that he is not. However, Alice couldn't care less about those types of men or their status. She was just making conversation.

 Do not describe other men to your husband or your intended. If you must, then talk about his character, not his looks, or body, or his status. It could be the difference between your getting and keeping this man of God, or losing him in a hurry.

You can turn this around on the man and say that he needs to be more confident or less insecure. Just don't make Alice's mistake. It is up to you.

Your Projections

Are you projecting your thoughts onto a man? Are you attempting to guess what is going on with him instead of asking? Most experts think this only happens after being in a long-term relationship with a person. But, projecting your thoughts or ideas based on your experiences in previous relationships can also occur in a new one. This will make a man of God not want to marry you and has led to divorce.

Remember, you are responsible for your own feelings and thoughts.

Projection is a defense mechanism that we all use. It is the behavior of taking something of ourselves and placing it away from us, onto others. Yes, we can sometimes project positive and sometimes negative aspects of ourselves.

Sometimes our projection is the act of not wanting to acknowledge something about ourselves. Instead, we turn it around and place it onto another. For example, "It is not about the mistake I made, which may be stupid; it's that you are critical of everything I do!"

Sometimes we project our experiences onto another. A woman may say, "My mother was crazy at times, but I could handle her when we disagreed. Therefore, I can use this same tactic with my co-worker when she acts crazy."

The issue with projecting negative parts of ourselves is that we still suffer from them. In the first example above, instead of feeling inadequate (our true feeling), we hurt with the feeling that everyone is critical of us. While we escape feelings of inadequacy and defenselessness, we nonetheless still suffer and feel uneasy.

The more energy you put into avoiding the realization that you have weaknesses, the more difficult it is to face them eventually. Projections can ruin your relationship, destroying the attraction, and he will leave.

Your Characterizations

Do not characterize your husband. He will not be able to pop out of character in your mind. *He is always late. He gets this wrong all the time. He is forgetful. He is constantly this or that.* Yes, this goes both ways, but we are talking about why a man of God will no longer feel the attraction and will leave the relationship. LOL

Instead, try this: Make sure you see him with fresh eyes each day. Remember that a man just wants to be your hero. He wants you to respect, appreciate, and acknowledge him. When you do, he will want to please you even more. Instead of expecting negative behavior from him, expect improvement, love, and helpfulness.

Saying negative things about what he is always doing, because you have characterized him that way, hurts. It also locks him into a box if he believes your assessment.

Refrain from doing this, and apply the law of spiritual attraction we talked about in "Good Person, Bad Mate." What you see, what you expect, is what you get. So look at him as if he is a new man, always. Notice his improvements. Focus on his strengths.

 Keep in mind that people change, especially after awareness. Look at him with fresh eyes all the time. Notice and acknowledge his changes.

Expectations and Disappointments

Romans 12:9-10 NLT: *Don't just pretend to love others. Really love them. Hate what is wrong. Hold tightly to what is good. Love each other with genuine affection and take delight in honoring each other.*

Can you handle disappointments? They happen when you have expectations, and most expectations are unrealistic. Why unrealistic? Well good men have flaws. The key is to be willing to accept his flaws because you want him to accept yours. I hope you do know that you have flaws. If not, let me remind you of a few I've heard from so many men over the years that I know many of you do these things:

- Changing your mind fluidly.
- Because details matter to you, sometimes you over share
- Carrying on those catty conversations while he's there, listening (perhaps because he's waiting for your attention)
- Expecting him to come home from his job and listen to details about yours—what you did, who said what, and how they don't like you
- Holding long, detailed, conversations about a wedding and its colors, or who's having a baby or divorcing and why

A MAN OF GOD *is Still* A MAN

- Some of you are messy, too, and can destroy a bathroom.

- You can be fussy at times with tragic thoughts and may wake up accusing him of doing something because you had a dream.

- Sneaking and going through a man's stuff when he is not looking or is sleeping

- Acting like you are his mother and giving orders

Yes, there are exceptions, but need I say more? **You cannot expect a man to be better than you are.** Some women make this mistake often. Most of the time a woman has a vision of how she wants a man to act. If he comes up short, she expresses her disappointments.

Remember when I said earlier that men make emotional calculations? Just know that things happen in a relationship and that he sees your flaws, too. So you must learn how to manage disappointments which can build into resentments. A man just wants to feel safe, too, and to know how long he will be in the dog house if he makes a mistake.

I'm not referring to unacceptable behavior, but to issues like forgetting to do something, not listening to your conversation, or getting distracted when you talk, all of which make you feel he is disinterested. He may want to watch a huge play-off football game, but you planned an evening with your out-of-town family member months prior to meeting him. Some events come up without notice. How could he know that his favorite team will make it this far in the NFL playoffs? It is best that you know how to manage disappointments—or his feelings for you will change.

Here is something you must consider. When he disappoints you, assess it this way: **Is this worth breaking off the relationship for?** If not, accept it as a mistake or flaw you can live with and don't pounce on him about it.

Relationship Habits

Luke 12:26 NIV: Since you cannot do this very little thing, why do you worry about the rest?

A man will not want to be with you if he feels that you are too nitpicky, especially about his habits. For the most part, a new relationship does not have habits. However, both you and he do have them. While dating, he will notice all of your habits from how you eat and how you behave at a movie to if you are neat. He will also notice your patterns—e.g. if you are late all the time, if you blow your nose in public, if you talk so much that he can't get a word in, among other things.

We talked about your expectations and disappointments in the last section, and how you are also noticing what he does.

However, here is the key that he will consider in making his emotional calculation: "**Can I tolerate this habit?**" If not, he will leave. You, of course, will do the same regarding him.

Men feel that women often turn small habits into what they view as "bad behavior" or a red flag, when it was just something misunderstood or extremely trivial.

For example, you may be horrified by his behavior in a restaurant, and share this with a friend, "Girlfriend, he dropped that fork on the floor and picked it up and started eating again. I about died!"

What does this have to do with how he will treat you?

A MAN OF GOD *is* *Still* A MAN

Making statements like this can become a habit of finding bad in everything he does. This is finger pointing, a form of contempt that quickly saps the life, the attraction, out of a relationship. It's a bad habit that will make him leave.

Over-the-Top Behavior

Are you guilty of "over–the-top" behavior? What is extremely unappealing and drives men crazy is a whining and complaining woman. It could be nasty put-downs or criticism of others. She simply complains about anything that is going on in the world—about waiters, parking spaces, co-workers, or anything not going the way she sees things.

Just as you label some of his behavior "bad," he considers this misbehaving—and the "over-the-top woman" does this in public and in private.

These women are extremely particular and require special treatment, e.g. she may need a special umbrella, a special spoon, can't do anything without makeup, whines simply because a person spills plain water. She has to have something before anything can be done; otherwise, the fun stops for everyone.

Afraid to break a nail? Can't do fun things wearing pumps? A man of God will tag you as simply "over-the-top." Yes, he will want to leave!

A MAN OF GOD *is Still* A MAN

He Is NOT Your Girlfriend

I receive a host of complaints from men of God in my research regarding their wife or love interest talking to them as if they are girlfriends. I know that you are comfortable with your husband or man of interest and feel that you can share anything with him, but No! You cannot!

Even if he asks questions about your past, especially things you have done of a sexual nature in a previous marriage or before giving your life to Christ, be very careful of what you say.

As your husband, all he really wants to know is whether or not he is the best in the pleasing area. So say something that makes him think that he is your best or change the subject. Do not answer his questions directly unless you can make him the best in the bedroom. Learn how to be a little evasive. You can say "I'm not comfortable talking about that; however, you are the best thing that ever happened to me."

If he is a man of interest, telling him too much about your past could simply turn him off to considering you as his wife. Don't do it! You can say, "God has brought me a long way." Period. That's enough.

Also, please do not show your husband or man of interest pictures of what women call "Eye Candy" that your work colleagues or girlfriends may send you via email or text. What is eye candy? They are pictures of good-looking men with these cut bodies or muscular physiques. Yes, many women of God get those eye candy texts and emails from their friends, too; however, mainly younger Christians. Sometimes they receive texts of men who are actually nude, showing the goodies. Just know that NO man likes this—even if he is cut himself.

You cannot say to your husband or future husband something about another man. For example,

- He is that cute guy with the bald head.
- He is that guy with the pretty eyes.
- He is that tall, good-looking man who works for UPS.
- He is a cute doctor.
- [Even worse!] He has a big one in that picture.

Ladies, you cannot say such things!

You are probably thinking, "Philemon, he is just insecure!" At least that is what I often hear from ladies regarding their man or while debating this issue. Well, this is one reason he will not say anything, because he does not want you to think that he is jealous or insecure.

However, you may be right that he is insecure because some are, but many are not. He is **not** your girlfriend, and you should never do this—even if he says that it's OK. You could risk planting a seed in his heart that will never go away. That man of interest could walk out of your life, and you won't have a clue why. I've seen men of God walk away because of issues like this.

If you do make this mistake, quickly remove any concern from his mind by complimenting him. Example: Let's say that you said to a friend, "Oh, he's cute!" and then you realize that your husband is listening. What should you do? Well, quickly close his mind by saying, "But no one is as handsome to me as my hubbie." You get the picture. You must close his mind from wandering all over the place, especially if that man you commented on has it going on in the looks or style department.

Let me tell you how this could affect a man. Recently a professional Christian counselor I know got married. Right before sex one night, his brand-new wife showed him eye-candy that her girlfriend had just sent via email as a joke. Guess what happened? He simply smiled, but was really hurt inside. The worst part was that he went limp. She asked him what was wrong. Being a counselor, he decided to share his pain. She was apologetic, and the problem was resolved. But this could have been avoided.

Now, what if he was not the type to communicate his pain right off? What type of problem are you inviting into your relationship?

Ladies, men are not wired to talk about what they are feeling right off. Most are just not good at talking about personal issues or comfortable talking about feelings, period. Men are just not good at it!

I understand that talking about feelings usually comes easily for women. Also I know that you want answers to your questions fast, but please know that we are not wired this way. Sure, you get frustrated because he is not communicating, but you cannot rewire a man's natural behavior. It is best that you simply understand and do not force the issue.

By forcing the issue, you risk planting seeds in his heart and mind where negative vines will grow around it. If this happens, he will never see you the same way again. Maybe he will just walk away, thinking that you are not the woman for him.

Remember, he is NOT your girlfriend. It is best not to share such information with your husband or love interest. Also, again, do not describe another man using terms like cute, good looking, big muscles, nice teeth, pretty eyes, or good-smelling. Find other adjectives. Are you guilty of this? Just don't do it! Problems often start this way.

Mind Games

Mind games are very subtle but dangerous. They create insecurities. I often notice something in women's behavior that fits this category and relates to relationships. I wonder if many of you reading this book do something similar. When people call me about their personal relationship, I pay close attention to these behaviors. I have also noticed them while around others. It seems that many women are doing the same thing.

When I ask the women why they do this, most don't have an answer except to say, "I don't keep things from my husband or future husband." What I'm about to share is not really bad, but I'm wondering why it is being done so often.

OK, I am sure that you are saying, "Enough, Philemon, what are you noticing?" Again, it is not really big, but what I have discovered is that these kinds of comments can plant seeds of suspicion in your husband, and they will blossom later when problems arise.

Here it is: Why do women tell their man about compliments they receive from other men on the job, at church, the mall, or other places?

Let me see if you recognize any of these comments:

- "You know what happened today? This UPS man whistled at me. I guess I was looking cute. But, you know, I only have eyes for you, honey."

- "Everybody said that I was looking cute today. You know how men are on the job, they look at me, but I don't pay them any attention."

- "People said that I looked different today, and then this man asked me if I was married or involved. I told him yes. He ain't getting any play here."

Sound familiar? Please know that men do this too, but we are talking about understanding the natural side of a spiritual man. (LOL).

When you say things like this, you are actually telling your mate:

> "You can be replaced quickly
> if you don't appreciate me or act right."

> "Other men want me right now."

> "You need to realize what you have in me."

Make sense yet? I hope so, because it may be difficult for me to put into words exactly what I see. What I do know and recognize is that men will always bring it back up during an argument or problem in the relationship.

For example, let's see if any of these are familiar:

- "I don't know WHAT you do. What about that dude at work who is always in your face complimenting you? What about him?"

- "Why are you dressing all up today? I bet it is because you want that dude who asked if you were married, or involved, to say something again."

When there are problems, all of the compliments you received from other men and shared with your mate are thrown right back in your face. So, again, why are you giving him these words to use later?

I have a question, "Do you tell him these things because you are subconsciously trying to get a reaction, or are you just insecure yourself?" You can piss him off with this stuff, just as it pisses you off. You are creating an environment for him to feel more insecure or uncomfortable.

Personally, I believe that we all want our mate to know and

think that they already have the best, and the reason to think this is because others want what they have. Is this so wrong? Well, I do know that it is thrown right back in our face when we have problems in our relationship.

What we are doing is playing mind games. It is just that simple.

Vague Explanations

You just read about how you can be creating insecurities in your relationship. Now I want to share more ways that men feel that you are driving them crazy.

"You keep me on the edge." This is what so many men feel or say when their woman uses vague explanations regarding her daily life. You may not even be aware that you express yourself in this fashion. Please consider the ramifications of having your man's mind wander with your vague explanations.

As noted in the previous topic, being insecure is a major problem in relationships, but you could be creating more insecurity by the way you explain unknown facts to your husband.

I know he usually complains about your giving him too much information about your life. There is a general belief that women do go more into detail than men. But in this case, more information is needed to avoid an issue, and most women clam up!

Ladies, first know that a man is always looking for outside threats to himself and his relationship, especially in regards to another man. So, whenever you are explaining things that happened on your job or at church or anywhere—and he was not there—make sure that you provide details and names to allow him to place a person with a known event. It is human nature to want to keep situations in perspective.

Jerica's Vague Explanations

Spencer and Jerica have been dating for almost two years, and he feels that Jerica is the one who God has for him and wants to marry her. She has a child already, and he helps her out fixing things around her place and maintaining her car.

His one concern is that Jerica keeps him on the edge all the time by how she explains, or leaves out, details of what is going on in her life, especially at work and other places. Jerica doesn't like to drop names and considers herself a private person. She doesn't understand what she is doing wrong.

For example, one day she called Spencer and said the following, "I need to get some new belts for my car. Gary told me that my belts look worn out and should be replaced, or my belt pulley is going bad."

Do you see any problems in how Jerica provided information on this event?

Well, you should know by now that men are territorial and Spencer's mind started wandering, and he began to think to himself, "Who is Gary? Why is he spending time with the woman I want to marry? Why is he looking at her car?" Maybe Gary thinks Jerica is interested in him, too. He begins to feel uneasy, assessing threats and thinking the worst.

Now, here is what actually happened: Jerica drove to work and started noticing a sound that had not happened before. Spencer had recently had her car serviced and was told that he could probably go another six months before having the belts replaced. When Jerica drove in, Gary, a co-worker who is 30 years her senior and about to retire in two months, heard the noise and asked if he could look under the hood. He noticed that the sound was coming from her belts and told her to get them checked out.

If she had given Spencer this explanation, telling him who Gary is, it would not have been a problem at all. Instead, it started an argument because, when he asked her about this man, she was not in the mood for the "third degree." She felt it was crazy to think she was interested in two men because she loves God. But Spencer is still a man, and no man wants another man taking care of the woman he wants to marry.

A MAN OF GOD *is* *Still* A MAN

Well, they spent the next two weeks barely speaking. Spencer was simply on edge about this event because he was about to ask Jerica to marry him. But now? Neither of them was feeling very loving towards the other. This could have been avoided if she had provided more details on the event up front. Since it was not the first time this had happened, and because she did not respect his point of view, I'd say that between her **vague explanations** and his **runaway mind** they did not make a promising match.

Simply Insecure?

OK, Ladies, I know that you think that this is too much and that a man like Spencer is simply insecure. You also may think that he should have trusted her and not acted this way, because he should have known her better.

I get this and understand that, in a perfect relationship world, this type of misunderstanding shouldn't happen. But we know that no one is perfect. Just know that **you have the power to ease his mind at all times** and should do so without hesitation. It will not hurt you to provide more details in your explanations.

You can be private with someone else, but when it comes to your current or future husband, drop names, special circumstances, just to ease his wandering mind and to keep it from running away with him. He will love you for this, and it will prevent a tense relationship.

I know many other men who left a woman because she was too vague. The women were left wondering what exactly went wrong. Many times a man will not say a word. Why? Well, he doesn't want you to think that he is insecure; so he will just leave or stop calling. Men of God are still men and should be treated as such.

It is not about anything you may think that keeps your husband or future husband with you and happy. **It is about the way you make him feel, period.**

Moochers

"I want someone in my life. Men just see me as a friend. Men just leave me without saying anything. I'm a good Christian person and help others out, so why can't I find someone special who will stick around?"

Have you asked yourself these questions? If not, then this message is NOT for you.

But I discovered an interesting pattern with good caring women of faith who just can't seem to keep a man interested. They have no problems meeting new men. It is just that, when they do meet someone, he usually quickly places her in the friend category, or he just loses interest and leaves. "Why?" these women ask me.

Are you ready for this? Well, it is often because of "moochers." Those people to whom you lend money, allow to live with you on and off, or maybe that doing-nothing brother or son—all able-bodied grown-ups who are just taking. Yes, it is your Christian duty to help others, but there is a limit.

When a man assesses a woman for consideration as a wife, he looks at her other relationships for possible conflicts. He will appreciate the fact that you are a caring and good person, but will NOT like the way you always put yourself out and do things for these able-bodied, mooching family members. He will NEVER say anything about this to you, but will say to himself, *This is not the woman for me* and will move on.

You may ask, "What do you mean 'doing things for'?" Well,

- Paying their bills
- Preparing their meals
- Giving them keys to your place and allowing them to come over, hang out, and go into YOUR fridge
- Helping them find a new place and cleaning it up
- Going with them for business transactions
- Just doing things that grown folks, especially men, should do for themselves

If you have people in your life like this, and especially if they are men, most quality men will keep on stepping or will put you in the friend category! You will not be the woman he will want to spend his life with. A man cannot have this going on in his household, even if it is your own money! He will not have the heart to come between you and that family member. Therefore he will leave.

Clean this up! Prepare your life for a quality man of God. Stop doing these things for able-bodied grown folk. Don't get me wrong. It is okay to help, but not to be totally engaged in doing things for these functioning, grown, moochers.

Freeloading Friends

I have always been curious as to why so many women have to show proof to their friends that their man is good. It seems like a salesperson type of approach to selling their mate to others. I guess wanting others to like your mate or to be happy for you is normal human behavior.

They will tell their friends, e.g., "He took me here or there. He did this for me; he did that for me. My man is this or that. He bought me this and that."

This kind of talk always leads to one worse thing: freeloading friends. This is when your girlfriends ask you and your man out so that they can get FREE drinks or dinner. Also these girlfriends will ask you and your man to take them on a trip so that he can pick up the tab. Freeloading girlfriends! Sometimes family members do this, too.

The Story of Mike and Tara

Mike and Tara have been dating for several months now; it is going quite well. However, Tara's friends are really suspicious of Mike simply because he seems too good to be true and attends another church. He is very attentive, thoughtful, and quite caring.

Tara's best friends, Kim and Diana, simply do not like Mike, and it is driving her crazy. These are her girls, her prayer partners, and the ones she's been hanging with all of her life. She wants her friends to be happy for her, but they are not there yet.

A MAN OF GOD *is* *Still* A MAN

Mike decided to purchase tickets for all of them to see Tyler Perry's *Madea Goes to Jail*. When they found out, they jumped for joy. So, off to the play they went. It was a hot July night and unforgettable. They laughed all night long.

The next day, Kim calls Tara and says, "You know, Mike is not bad after all. I think he really cares about you, and I like him now."

Tara jumped up and shouted with excitement! She was relieved, WHEW! Problem solved.

Guess what happened next? Kim and Diana started calling Tara all the time about going out together again. "Hey, girl, why don't you and Mike join us here or there?" Do you know why? They expected Mike to pick up the tab for every evening!

Tara felt so much pressure that she would slip him money so that it could appear that he was funding the night. Mike did not like this, and it created distance in the relationship. Tara was happy because she felt that everything was coming together and that the relationship was getting stronger.

Well, suddenly Mike pulled away from her and did not explain why. He told her that the relationship was moving in a direction that he was not expecting. He also said that she was wonderful, but it was not working for him. Tara was devastated!

She felt that things were going great and could not figure out what was the problem. But as you read this story, you know the problem: those free-loading friends were destroying the relationship.

How could Mike ask Tara to choose between her childhood friends and him? It wasn't going to happen. He never even mentioned it; just pulled away. Kim and Diana comforted her and said, "We knew that he was just like the others. God was protecting you from him, girrrlll." To this very day, this cycle of nonsense is still going on in that circle.

Mike is now engaged to be married to a wonderful woman of God who does not allow her friends to come between them.

Do not let your freeloading friends or family members run a good man away.

Meddling

We have been discussing some of the ways in which you personally can contribute to destroying your relationship and ways to prevent this. We have examined everything from how you can challenge his manhood by trying to make him conform to your world view to responding to him critically and indulging your trust issues. But it can go a little further.

Let's consider complications added to your relationship challenges by others in your life: family, friends, or exes.

If you really want a man to leave, then allow others to meddle and butt into your relationship. It will kill the attraction between you. Ladies, some of you have family members messing in your relationship. You know who they are. It may be your sister, brother, cousin, uncle, or aunt. Or, perhaps friends in whom you usually confide.

Are any of them calling, wanting details about what is going on in your relationship? And do you call any of them, telling them your business, especially when there are problems? This encourages their meddling. Stop it!

Be aware of anyone in your life who is always butting in, calling, and saying that someone said this or that when it is not true. They are just simply plain ole messy. You need to put them in their place or risk losing your husband or man of interest.

As I said, in "Challenging His Manhood," one of the worst

things you can do to your husband or potential is to second-guess his opinions or advice by seeking help from another man. This really bruises a man's ego; and yet, women do it all the time. I don't care if it is your father. If you feel that his opinion or advice is not on solid ground, just don't let on that you sought opinions elsewhere. Protect his sense of manhood all the time.

A big complaint I've received from men is that their woman never takes their advice. They tell me, "I told her the same thing, but she won't listen to me." Ladies, try to avoid this behavior because it hurts him and it may be destroying your relationship.

The Story of Brandy and Ray

Brandy (age 30) and Ray (age 33) were engaged to be married, but one day Ray suddenly left very angrily and called off the relationship. According to Brandy, she did not have a clue as to what the problem was, even though Ray had shared his concern. He was a quiet man, not very talkative. He didn't say things over and over again, but he loved Brandy. Here is the story.

Brandy's car broke down and Ray took action to get the vehicle fixed, arranging transportation for her. When her father found out, he called Ray and wanted details on what action he was taking to resolve the problem. He replied, "Mr. Gwinn, I have everything taken care of. I took her vehicle to MetroPlex Automotive."

Brandy's dad said, "I've never heard of this company and do not want my daughter stranded because you are using a shade-tree mechanic."

Ray explained that his family has used this company for many years, and that they have an impeccable reputation for quality and price. He said, "They are considered a gem in the automotive repair industry."

Brandy's dad said, "Well, what's their location and phone number? I want to call the Better Business Bureau to see if they have any complaints." Then he asked Ray, "What problem did they find with the vehicle?"

These types of comments had been going back and forth constantly throughout his relationship with Brandy. On several occasions Ray had told her that he did not like her father interfering. Brandy felt that her dad was just concerned because he loves her.

He said, "Yeah, I know, but you are thirty years old and I've got this. I will be your provider. I will pay the bills, not your dad."

She responded by saying, "Oh Ray, you should get over it and stop being so insecure."

Well, Ray called off the engagement because he had taken all he could. Brandy was extremely hurt, but to this very day she believes that he was insecure and wrong.

Ladies, can you see what is wrong with this picture? Instead of letting her dad butt in, Brandy should have told her dad, "I am about to be married. I love and appreciate you, but Ray is the man looking after me now." But she could not do this, and so Ray left.

Why He Stopped Calling

We have talked a lot about why a man will stop calling. Often it is to give himself time to process something that happened. He is making his emotional calculations, creating a mental map of where your relationship is going. I will now add to this subject, speaking directly about why he stopped calling.

As soon as a woman realizes that she really likes the man she is dating, that he may be "the one," she panics, wondering:

Should I do this?

Is he interested in someone else?

Does he like this or that?

Her mind is racing so fast that she over-analyzes everything. Her need for certainty in a relationship has taken over. The only way to calm her growing anxiety is to find out the answers to her questions.

Suddenly, this need for answers monopolizes her attention every time she is with him. She begins asking him those "Am-I-wasting-my-time?" questions I mentioned earlier. Her behavior changes completely. Instead of increasing the connection and growing it naturally, she tries to force it into a stable status. What are the results? He is left wondering:

Whatever happened to this special woman I was interested in?

She is not the woman I thought she was.

She is wrong for me.

Then he loses interest and stops calling. It is too hard to make her happy, too much work.

I'm going to continue to repeat this: **A man likes being around a woman who makes him feel good.** A man will watch a game with you if you make him feel good about it. You need to be fun to hang out with.

A friend was introduced to this nice lady who was smart, educated, funny, outgoing, and made him feel pretty good at first. Their conversations were great. He would call her often during the day, and she called him—hey, he was interested.

This was the initial stage of the relationship. Then, suddenly, he stopped calling. When she called him, he just clicked "ignore." He was conflicted, but still somewhat interested.

She texted him. He did not respond because he was trying to collect his thoughts. Then he texted her and said that he would call her tomorrow. He simply needed a break. Before you get mad keep reading.

The next day he called her. She was noticeably irritable and began to ask him a series of questions. He cut her off because of a meeting and said that he would call her back.

He believed in keeping his word, so he called her later. She started in again. He said right then, "I am sorry but this is not working for me. I think that you are a nice person, but not the one for me."

I am sure that she was baffled and bewildered, but it was how he felt. He wasn't going to lead her on. She said, "I felt that you would be different," and hung up the phone.

He was going to explain his reasons in detail, but she did not allow him to. Well, she never listened attentively anyway, unless he was answering her questions.

Why did he stop calling?

1. She went into panic mode, started nagging all the time, and was moving very fast, being very demanding: "When are we…? How long will it be…? I would love to have this. I can't wait until we take our first weekend trip; separate rooms, of course. A man has to get me at least three carats if he wants to marry me."
2. He was thinking that he could not afford her.
3. She was too much work. When he was with her, she had the overly talking bug, nagging and asking all these questions without giving him any room to breathe. She was not a good listener.
4. Her lifestyle was not conducive to having a relationship. She worked too much and did not have time for one.
5. She did not know how to simply hang out in a relaxed setting without getting to the business of the relationship. "I need to know this. Tell me about that."
6. It was a job interview, not a relationship.

I know that you have read books that say that you must gather information from men. Ladies, there is a way to do this without interrogating him and making yourself less attractive.

He wasn't forcing her to do anything or to jump into bed. He wanted someone who can relax, have fun, have great conversations, and learn about him in this setting. And that is how she was in the beginning. Then she turned into an attorney and started cross-examining him.

Two weeks passed. He decided to call her to explain his reasons for not calling. He felt that maybe she would be calmer by then. This could have been a great exit interview. Well, the girlfriend, peer-pressure, talking points had kicked in. You know, this "strong-independent-woman stuff." She was angry and non-responsive.

He stated clearly that this was not an attempt to get back into her life. He felt that they could help each other by explaining their actions, if she was interested.

She said she was, and he described how she had changed from being this fun, attractive, woman whom he was enjoying getting to know into a pushy, rude, inquisitor. The seeds this planted in his head would not go away, so he doesn't see their getting back to what they had in the beginning.

Her comments: "I am sorry! I am going to be me. I need to understand the man I am with. I have been hurt too many times not to get all of the information that I need, when I need it."

This confirmed his worst fears. Although he had seen her as smart, educated, funny at times, and outgoing, he could no longer feel good in her presence. He did not want to hang-out with her any more. He felt that she would never listen to his concerns or desires. She wasn't willing to balance her need for information with what he wanted: building a relationship in a relaxed setting. This is why he stopped calling. It has now been three years. She is still going through this cycle with other men.

Relationship books have given this woman more ammunition. Many of them include questions every woman should ask before getting too deep into a relationship. These books are her Bible now. She feels vindicated.

As I see it, individuals like her will use whatever they can to support a failed argument. In defense of relationship books, I haven't read any that advise a woman to be an aggressive interrogator, instead of having fun connecting and growing the relationship.

Getting back to this story, let's look at what he did to prevent this and what pushed him over the edge. When she first got off into this questioning mode, he would change the subject to a TV show or some other current event, anything other than answering her questions.

He asked politely, "Can we talk about something else? I've been having serious talks all day and want to relax now."

What was her response? "Okay." Then ten (10) minutes later she would go back to the questioning again. It was no fun for him. She did not make him feel good; he did not want to hang out with her any more.

Stop panicking about a potential relationship, seeking certainty in a relationship too fast by asking tons of questions. Attempt to grow the connection naturally. Asking questions is great and necessary, but when excessive it feels like a job interview instead of a connection. Men like someone who they can hang-out with, too, and if you are interrogating all the time, then it's a no go.

Conversation and interrogation are two different things. What she wanted was her questions answered all at once in order to make a decision about him. What decision? There was nothing on the table yet but intrigue and this started less than a week before. Now she wanted to force a relationship by demand, without knowing if they could actually enjoy each other's company first. She actually wanted the same thing he did—a loving relationship—but she did not know how to get there.

 Understand this: Just because you want to know doesn't mean that you will get an answer from a man that day. If you force it, the door could get shut permanently.

Cheating

I've saved this relationship destroyer for last because it's a big one. In my experience growing up in the church and as a coach, this one act has been the number one cause for divorce in the church and why some fall from grace. Yes, "turning their backs on God" or "backsliding" as we say in my church. This is sadly and often the result of cheating. Marriage is a covenant between a man, a woman, and God. In addition, Scripture clearly expresses God's preference in this regard: ***I hate divorce!*** (Malachi 2:16 NLT).

Yes, Christian women cheat too. You already know that this could destroy a relationship, that's a no-brainer. This section is designed for you to understand the position in which you have placed this man of God and what has to be done to ease the pain. You will not get everything that you need to recover in this section, but it is a great start and will help.

Please understand that there is hardly any advice for men of God when their wives cheat on them, but lots of information for women of God when a man does. However, in our society, women are almost as likely to cheat on their spouses as men. This has become a proven fact.

You can NOT say that "Satan is targeting our marriage," because his target is not the marriage anymore; he already won this battle when the wife cheated. Now he is coming after this man of God and will attempt to weaken his faith in God.

A man of God who has been cheated on will have to manage

his emotions, especially anger and shame. Yes, he will be angry but in Ephesians 4:26 the Bible states: ***Be ye angry, and sin not...** (KJV)*. Therefore it is OK for him to be angry. But shame is a constant threat to him because others will blame him by saying what he didn't do in his marriage. Since you cheated on him, you may be blaming him, too. It is NOT his fault that you cheated, but yours. No one can make you unfaithful; it is a matter of choice.

Being unhappy is not an excuse, nor is what he is not doing. It may actually be true, but is not an excuse for cheating. You cheated because you chose to. Do not make him the cause for your sin.

Do not attempt to force him into therapy. He will not be in the right state of mind to have you take the lead in this matter. Let him make this decision on his own. In addition, counseling can dredge up some pretty painful things. People don't love admitting to their spouses their deep feelings: that perhaps they were not their first choice, they are inadequate in the bedroom, or they are dissatisfied with any number of things that could be the underlying causes for what happened. But it is extremely important for the two of you to get into a coaching or counseling program in order for you to survive infidelity.

The only way your marriage can recover from this act is for you to admit that your own lack of restraint caused you to cheat, not that he was a bad husband. This will benefit you spiritually, too, because repentance is the essence of healing this relationship.

If you are remorseful, it may prevent him from seeking revenge, which would be a mistake on his part.

So where are you? Adultery is the state of your marriage right now, and there's precedence as to what is available to him via Scripture.

There is a discussion with Christ and the Pharisees in Matthew 19 in which Jesus refers to God's original purposes for marriage. He is asked, **Why then did Moses command to GIVE HER A CERTIFICATE OF DIVORCE AND SEND her AWAY?**

Jesus then answers, **Because of your hardness of heart Moses permitted you to divorce your wives; but from the beginning it has not been this way. And I say to you, whoever divorces his wife, except for immorality, and marries another woman commits adultery** (Matthew 19:7-9 NASB).

When interpreting such passages in the Bible, it is clear that God never ordained or created the institution of divorce. Man did.

The issue for you is what is believed in your ministry about when one can divorce and remarry. Most believe that if there is sexual immorality on anyone's part, the other is free to divorce and marry again. This is the dilemma you are in right now.

You are in damage-control mode. Let me make a few suggestions for what you can do.

First, what you should know is that nothing in your experience has prepared you for the mission of controlling the damage you caused when you cheated.

Cheating is not the biggest issue right now, because it has already happened. Rather, how you should handle yourself right now is paramount. It has been my experience that more damage is done after an affair than by the affair itself. The goal is to take this act of disgrace and change it into a story of repentance and redemption.

Because your cheating has been exposed, you will be facing judgment, contempt, and guilt. This is not a time for a waddle in self-pity, but a time for a plan of action to save your marriage. You want to limit the impact of this huge ordeal and place yourself in a position to ask for a second chance.

What Should You Do First?

Stay in constant prayer. Ask for forgiveness and manage your expectations of reconciliation. There is a process to recovering from cheating, especially as a woman, because men have the most difficult time dealing with infidelity. Be prepared to undergo a few of these difficulties:

A MAN OF GOD *is Still* A MAN

The Hot-seat: You will be experiencing embarrassment and extreme discomfort, but the good news? This is temporary. There will be harsh judgment from friends and family and other church members. They may even become hostile towards you. Just know that judgments are only someone's views and should NEVER be treated as what is true.

Anger at a huge level, but he should not sin. In most cases, you may have never seen your husband as capable of getting this angry. Nothing ignites anger more than infidelity. It can be fierce, especially coming from a man. Anger is a symptom of hurt, and this is good because one has to care in order for it to hurt. If there is NO anger, I would be concerned that the relationship will be over.

Negative Outcomes: Sleeping on the couch, hotel rooms, and possible separation from the family. This will be more about how much of it, from small to huge, but it will be temporary too.

Evidence of Pain: You will see the pain you caused. He may cry and crawl up in a fetal position with pain. One never sees the true cost of having an affair until it is exposed.

Tons of Investigative-style Questions. Nothing you say will be believed. Buckle up because this hot-seat will last a while. Regardless of how many times you are questioned, even in the middle of the night, just stay humble and calm when you are directly under fire. Never get defensive or aggressive. Staying calm pays off, and be as honest as you can. If you are consistent in your responses, the questions will stop. At this point, you have asked God for forgiveness, so do not regress. Do NOT lie to him anymore.

Up and Down Emotions: One minute he may feel hopeful and next his rage will ignite again. This could continue for a while. There will be highs and lows. Never fight this. Just go through the storm.

Bashing: Even though he is not to sin when angry, you may still get lots of criticism from him. Every mistake you made will come to the forefront, and all of your flaws and faults will come out of his mouth. You will feel you can't win, but remember that you will feel discomfort. Just know that he over-looked those flaws and stood by you. Be hopeful that he will do it again. Mostly you will be bashing yourself. There will be a battle with your own guilt and regrets, especially when it is exposed in the church.

 The key to making the recovery process faster and possibly helping you get the marriage back on track, is this secret sauce: **Being Genuine**.

Yes, sincerity! If your husband can feel your sincerity—that you are sincerely sorry for what you did, he will be more inclined to give you a second chance. Remember, he has to feel it, not you.

CHAPTER FIVE:

The Bed Undefiled

1 Corinthians 7:3-5 NLT: *The husband should fulfill his wife's sexual needs, and the wife should fulfill her husband's needs. The wife gives authority over her body to her husband, and the husband gives authority over his body to his wife.*

Do not deprive each other of sexual relations, unless you both agree to refrain from sexual intimacy for a limited time so you can give yourselves more completely to prayer. Afterward, you should come together again so that Satan won't be able to tempt you because of your lack of self-control.

Lack of sexual spontaneity is frustrating to men. You have to be able to sneak a quickie to take the edge off your husband from time to time or he can become frustrated creating the conditions for weakness in this area.

Let's Be Clear about Sex

Honesty is the key to having clarity about men. Therefore, I must tell the truth. Religion teaches men to feel guilty about their sexual nature, whether a man of God will admit it or not. Some men of God display and have the necessary restraint as Scripture requires. For most, this guilt is designed to regulate and suppress his sexual appetite, as we will discuss in "Sexual Appetite."

Here is the problem: **Testosterone is immune to guilt.** What does this mean for a man of God? His goal is not to allow the animal instinct within to take over, but to allow what feeds the soul and spirit to take precedence. Many reference the Holy Spirit to keep them grounded.

As a woman, there is something you must know about men. It may anger you, and women of faith sometimes try to ignore this, but it has been researched and researched by many. In *The Truth about Men Will Set You Free: The New Science of Love and Dating* by researcher Dr. Pat Allen she reveals her results, what she calls the Rule of Mating:

> "Love is what females give sex for."

> "Sex is what guys give love for."

If this angers you, please understand that sex is God's gift. It is not wrong that women give sex to get and keep love, and men give love to get and keep sex. It is best to accept this exchange of love and sex because it brings us to what love really means within a marriage. Love is saying "I will do it" and keeping your word. How couples keep these agreements is how one can measure their love. Men and women of God are no different.

Research also shows that men who produce less testosterone are more likely to be married, and men who produce more testosterone are more likely to divorce. Why? Because a man who produces more testosterone is more likely to engage in extramarital sex, even if he is a man of God. This is why so many have gotten into sexual trouble. I will talk about this more in this section.

So listen up women of faith: Don't play with sex in your marriage. If your man wants more sex, it's because of higher testosterone, but research shows that when he connects with his woman, his testosterone actually lowers. This is what keeps him from wandering. Just try not to EVER turn him down. If you must, make sure you express your desire to please him in that moment. Share how you will love him at another time, and express your desire for him. This is another way to protect your marriage.

The reason Satan capitalizes on one of God's greatest gifts (sex) is because of the attitudes people of faith have surrounding it. Those who love God and are married should be the biggest supporters of great sex within marriage. This will allow the next generations to desire and be eager to experience such ecstasy in marriage. Nevertheless, they hear messages that paint sex as gross or nasty to say the least.

Some married women of faith are even getting together and sharing how they shun sex with their husbands. They say, "Make him do dishes and other household work for sex, but only treat him once a week." This has to stop because it allows Satan to expand these cracks within marriages and creates havoc within them. Don't play with sex in your marriage!

Also, as I said before, I won't hold back in this book. Therefore, let me say that I know some of you reading this go to Church faithfully and say you love God. You may even hold a high position in the Church, perhaps you are a pastor. Yet, you are privately and sinfully having sex before marriage. I know because women sleeping with you are asking for my advice in my coaching practice.

In this chapter, "The Bed Undefiled," I will be explaining sexual issues. We all know that sexual intercourse is properly expressed in marriage only between a husband and wife (1 Corinthians 7:2-3). Even though these issues affect unmarried people sinfully having sex, I will be covering this topic as it was designed by God: within a marriage. This is much needed information.

Sexless Marriages

Sexless marriage is a lot more common than one may believe. Although it is not as common as some believe. I've heard some ridiculous numbers on sexless marriage, e.g. forty percent when it is defined broadly. More reliable estimates are that between fifteen and twenty percent of marriages are sexless. That's having sex less than ten times per year. Some couples may be sexless, but do not consider themselves as such. This is because one spouse travels, is in the military, or has been relocated to another city. But when they are together, sex is frequent.

Let's look at the truly sexless marriages. What makes them so? And, if you are in one, what do you want to do about it?

First, I find it curious that those giving advice on this are women sex experts, and they seem to believe in minimizing sex in marriage. **You will hear things like:**

"The wife is tired, resentful, has too much housework."

"You should time sex when she is about to have her period."

"She wants freedom to say when she wants sex."

"They tell men to find out how much sex your wife desires. If it is once a week, and you want four times per week, take the one time and masturbate in between."

If you are in a truly sexless marriage, is it mutual? Or is one of you suffering from unmet sexual needs?

No, I don't need to analyze your responses or other possible scenarios. Here is what I'm going to say about this subject: **There must be honest communication when discussing this issue of your needs.** Meanwhile, remember what you just read about hormones. It is too dangerous to NOT meet each other's sexual needs, because sex is the NUMBER ONE reason given for meeting these needs elsewhere. There are cultures within which this is an acceptable option, but ours is not one of them.

In our culture, advocating Christian family values, we want to share our lives with a godly person who has the same values and agrees to follow Scripture in how we live our lives together. We see marriage as a gift God gives men and women of faith for fulfilling their natural needs.

If this is what you want, then remember what we have said about cheating on both sides and make sure needs are met to prevent this temptation. You need to communicate honestly with one another and just find a way to make it happen in your marriage, as described in 1 Corinthians 7:3-5.

A MAN OF GOD *is* *Still* A MAN

Sex Always on His Mind

Proverbs 5:18-20 NLT: *Let your wife be a fountain of blessing for you. Rejoice in the wife of your youth. She is a loving deer, a graceful doe. Let her breasts satisfy you always. May you always be captivated by her love.*

"Sex is always on your mind!" Do you say this to your husband? Or are you the one who can NOT get enough sex? There are women who seem to stress their husband with THEIR never-dwindling sex drive, meaning that they can NEVER be satisfied. This can be a huge problem, but not always.

If your husband is always ready when you are, then there is no issue, because there is NO pressure. He is just ready when you are. But if your husband constantly nags you, even after having sex a few hours ago, then there may be some psychological issues surrounding sex with him that should be addressed.

For the record, people usually focus on what needs are lacking in their life and relationship, e.g. not enough sex, not feeling important in a relationship, not being enough. Once those needs are satisfied, usually they will change their focus.

That said, the **NUMBER ONE COMPLAINT** I receive from married men

"I DO NOT GET ENOUGH SEX!"

In dealing with this issue, it has been my experience that some married women are dropping the ball when it comes to sex with their husband. **I constantly hear on their side:**

- He focuses on sex too much.
- I need more love and commitment from him.
- Where is the romance? He used to be romantic.
- If he helps me around the house or with the children, I'll give him more sex.
- Every time I want to cuddle he wants sex. [A sign that he is not getting enough.]
- Men want sex too much and will do it (cheat) anyway, regardless of what I do.

Most of these excuses are limiting beliefs and invisible sabotagers that are destroying relationships.

I have to be honest. I've found that SOME women use sex as a way to CONTROL their relationship. This is dangerous, a disaster waiting to happen. However I'm not against bargaining or compromising to get more sex, but make sure you have read "Compromising and Dysfunctional Needs," one of the relationship destroyers described in Chapter Four. For example, if you need more help, give your man a task; he will do it willingly, knowing that more sex is coming. I don't believe most men have a problem with that, as long as they can see how this could help you and him in the process. However, this is trading for sex and could cause more problems especially when it is not given freely.

But know this: Every person has a recipe that triggers a loving response from them based on human needs and their own rules. Many call them "love languages." The primary love language for most men is physical touch. YES, SEX! Therefore if you are trying to control him with what triggers his love towards you, it is simply a recipe for losing that man—if not literally, then emotionally. Just make sure that you do NOT play with the way he feels love, e.g. physical touch.

Also, please understand that once or twice a week is NOT enough sex for most men; three times per week is average. If he needs it more than three times, it's OK to try to reach an agreement. (Again, make sure you read the section on compromising.) Maybe he can help around the house to increase that number. Let me repeat this. You should NEVER play around with your husband's desire to feel loved by you.

I understand that being in the mood is not always easy when so much is going on around you, e.g. the kids, work, etc. Your husband should be your ally—your personal go-to guy, especially in times of stress. However, a sexually frustrated man can NOT be an effective listener and will not be able to provide you with the emotional support you need. Love him, sex him up, and watch how much more he will give right back to you all the love and attention you need.

Now let's address sexual appetite in the next section.

Sexual Appetite

"Not enough sex."

"A woman who is ashamed of her body."

"A woman complaining about body parts."

"A woman who is not liberated in the bedroom."

"A woman who cannot receive."

These are the main complaints of men. Based on my experience, one of the main reasons why a man of God strays or leaves has to do with his sexual appetite or her lack of sexual desire. However, this is the most under-discussed topic with couples.

For example, there are so many women who just want to give and give in the bedroom, but cannot receive. A man has a strong need to accomplish a major goal while in the bedroom.

Your husband needs and wants you to reach an orgasm. He understands that there will be times that you will not, but this has to be the exception. His ego is tied to his performance in the bedroom. Men keep score. Winning means you're having an orgasm. Losing means you did not have an orgasm. You rejected his gift. Therefore, you must learn how to receive, so that he can give or perform. The end is that he can give you what he believes is a massive orgasm.

Whether we like to acknowledge it or not, our sexual appetite underlies much of what we do. It underlies why men are concerned about status and height, and why women are more concerned about their appearance—being beautiful. It is human nature, how we evolved as a species. Our behavior is shaped by our past. In order for us to survive, we have to reproduce. Believe it or not, Nature does not care how we populate the earth and reproduce, just as long as it is done. This process shapes our sexual behavior.

Nowadays individuals, especially men, are forced to live by rules that go against their natural tendencies. As mentioned before, the number one complaint of men is that they are not getting enough sex, that they are forced to use willpower and self-restraint to tame their desires. Here is the problem: it is not natural. This is why so many get caught cheating among other things. If you are not willing to address your husband's sexual appetite and his willingness to suppress it, your relationship MAY lead to infidelity, or he will leave, and that is a fact.

Please Note: Compromising only works to a point as long as it suppresses his desire enough that his willpower and self-restraint can manage it. However, if the compromise is not suppressing that sexual appetite enough, he will be tempted to go elsewhere.

In my coaching practice, I address the sexual appetite issue directly and up close. I do not allow one mate to create excuses as to why they are more sexually reserved. I explain to them that, whether or not their mate understands the situation does not deter the appetite; the desire is still there. I ask them, **what do you expect your mate to do?**

Allow your man to be open and upfront about his sexual appetite. Do not be ashamed of your body and complain about body parts. This is unattractive to men.

Lack of sexual spontaneity is frustrating to men. You have to be able to sneak a quickie to take the edge off your husband from time to time or he can become frustrated creating the conditions for weakness in this area.

"**I like it, but it is too much trouble trying to get it**." This is a complaint men have about their wives who cannot be spontaneous.

For these women, everything has to be in order before having sex. It takes so long that he will not want to go through the trouble. Men have complained about wanting (i.e. physically needing) their woman for a quickie to take the edge off, but she would not because the time was not right for her. Men love women who can sneak in the bathroom or closet for a quickie—even if people are around. Just being able to sneak is a major turn-on for men; without this sexual spontaneity most men are frustrated, and this is where trouble starts.

I privately surveyed hundreds of men of God among thousands responding to a multiple-choice questionnaire. When asked "What makes a woman incredible?" You may be surprised what answer was checked one hundred percent of the time: "A Proverbs-31 woman with porn-star-like skills in the bedroom." Yes, this came from even pastors. Now you have it.

A MAN OF GOD *is* *Still* A MAN

His Sexual Performance

A man can become frustrated simply because he feels that he is under-performing in the bedroom. This can be all in his mind, but for some reason, if that belief exists, it's dangerous because he may want to test his performance with someone else. It is really a form of protection of his ego to cheat before he thinks his wife will leave. Again, it can be all in his mind.

Men have a certain way they perform in the bedroom, as well as having a certain type of erection that they believe provides the best performance. Additionally, they seek a certain type of reaction when having sex. If a man is not able to reach that type of erection, hear a certain sound or reaction from you, perform a certain technique, or handle his sexual business as he believes he can, he may question his performance or think that you may feel that he is not doing it right.

This can bruise his ego tremendously and create all types of mind chatter—explanations or questions about his performances. Signs that this is happening include the "Did you cum?" question. Or, he may say something like, "Are we good?" He is seeking a reaction out of you regarding his performance.

If you are slow to understand where he is coming from, or not able to discuss exactly how the sex was for you, his mind will continue wondering about his performance. If you are not the expressive type in the bedroom, it could create weakness and may explain why he is tempted to seek sexual validation elsewhere.

It's Just Biology!

Your husband is so into you and really enjoying the moment. It is building up until he has a massive release. Yes, he ejaculates. Next he is sleepy and acts as if he does not want you to touch him or seems to not want to be in the same room. He may actually want to be alone and go to sleep. You become upset thinking he is inconsiderate, that he just came to bed to get what he wanted and now is no longer paying any attention to you.

What just happened was a biological event that can be measured. How? By measuring oxytocin and testosterone hormone levels.

A man needs a high dose of oxytocin in order to ejaculate. After the ejaculation, however, his level rapidly decreases. The letdown makes him feel drained and sluggish. Next, his testosterone levels increase and create the feeling of wanting to be alone. He just wants to sleep!

Most women, on the other hand, still have high levels of oxytocin and will be relaxed and some will sleep. If she is not tired, however, she will also have the feeling of wanting to be close or affectionate. This is because the oxytocin is enhanced by her estrogen.

However, I have noticed that some women who have been extremely hurt or had negative relationship-influences growing up will have the exact symptoms as men in this case. However, when checked out medically, they also have low oxytocin levels and other hormonal issues.

A MAN OF GOD *is* *Still* A MAN

When you understand the why behind something, it should make it easier to accept. So understand that your husband is not being inconsiderate, it is something that happens on a chemical level. Don't blame him for something that happens naturally.

Godly Men Cheating?

Women ask me this question practically every day, "Why do godly men sin and cheat?"

First, let me say this: Any reason a man will give for cheating is an excuse to make himself feel good about his actions. Instead of shifting responsibility towards the right person, himself, he will attempt to shift the blame to the spouse, explaining how it occurred because of her actions. Everything he may say could be absolutely true, but his cheating was still wrong and his action was improper. He should take total responsibility.

In a nutshell, everything you will read about the excuses he provides are all about meeting his needs. Even if you are compromising or have an agreement in place about sex, if the agreement is NOT meeting his sexual needs, it is an ingredient for cheating either physically or emotionally.

Know this: You are NOT at fault for his inability to embrace enough honesty to share his needs with you. You should see yourself as a witness instead of a victim of his actions. He did not give YOU the chance to satisfy these needs prior to his attempting to solve his problems outside of his marriage.

But why do godly men sin and cheat? I wondered that myself and wanted to get some perspective, so included it in my research. Let's look at what I learned from listening to hundreds of religious men who cheated on their wives because of unmet needs. There are two parts for you to read: this section and the next, "Power in the

Blood."

You may disagree with the findings, but I'm only reporting what I like to refer to as "heartfelt responses to cheating." Keep in mind that there are men who go to church regularly, but will still cheat no matter what you do, and none of those men were in this research. This research was conducted with men who expressed love for God and were genuinely disturbed by what they had done. They seemed to really love their wives, but cheated anyway.

Why did they risk it all? I will say that it should be understood that scientists have proven that when we are aroused, the part of the brain that regulates judgment turns off. Yes, when in our heat-of-the-moment emotions, we don't always make the best decisions.

Therefore as Matthew 26:41 (NLT) states, **Keep watch and pray, so that you will not give in to temptation. For the spirit is willing, but the body is weak!** This should be a main factor to flee from temptation in the first place.

Other common denominators among family men who cheat include these:

First, consider the primal animal side of the man at play. His values level or system of thinking is at a point of feeling powerful to where he wants what he wants. In that moment of heat he does not care about the consequences. Additionally, the major ways by which most men validate themselves are via sex, their sexual performances, and a woman's response. The psychology around this phenomenon, even when they love their wives, is paramount to understanding why a family man who says he loves God may cheat.

Second, I've also discovered that the majority of men who do not seem to validate themselves via sex are the ones most often cheated on by wives who really love them. Yes, lack of attention can make a woman cheat, too. Also, some men have a low libido, which can be frustrating to women desiring more sex than they do. In most of these cases, I've found that their disinterest in sex was health-related, e.g. meds or low testosterone levels. See the suggestions below to resolve the problem.

Reasons Men of God Give for Cheating

Here are the reasons the men in my study gave for cheating on the wives they loved. These reasons reveal ways in which you can validate your man and his sexual performance.

"Sex seems like a chore to my wife."

"Sex is scheduled because of our kids."

"Sex is lacking."

"Sexual stimulation is lacking or insufficient."
(a key to poor erections, especially to older men)

"She does not initiate sex."

"She does not respond to me sexually, or not enough for me to believe she really enjoys it."

"She seems to not feel my penis or it is not big enough or perfect for her."

"I am unable to make my wife have an orgasm via penetration."

"She doesn't believe my penis is the king of pleasuring."

"She doesn't meet my needs for sex."

"She doesn't want to have sex again and I do."
(See the next section on this after-sex urge.)

Will your husband say some of these same things about you? Then you are not validating him and are at risk of his cheating on you.

The tone of the men participating in my study was not about bashing their wives. They were describing their actual feelings. They said they had been trying to suppress these feelings because they knew she was a good woman. You see, Ladies, for these men, it did not matter that his wife works, is often busy dealing with the kids, and doing many other things as a super mom. He sees that and loves her for it. However, understanding and loving her for these reasons is not in the same compartment of the brain as sex. He recognizes all that she is doing and feels guilty when he still needs sexual validation from her. Therefore, when she is too busy and the opportunity arises, he weakens and tries to fulfill this need elsewhere.

In this study and with other family men of God, I find that most understand and know how to arouse their wives, and they are doing those things. But they said she is not responding. He wants his mate to stimulate him by really wanting it without having to romance her every time. He feels that, because he is protecting and providing for his family, she should be willing to allow him a quickie to take the edge off sometimes before work. He wants her to desire him badly. He wants her to think it's big. In his mind, on a subconscious level, he deserves to be validated by her. And if he's not getting that, and the opportunity arises, he may yield to temptation. These men said they were either sorely tempted or actually going elsewhere for sexual validation.

Every man in my research who cheated on his wife had the same common denominators: The other woman validated and stimulated him by reallllllllllly wanting him sexually because she was ready with usually NO romance work. She would practically beg to see him so she could have him sexually. She wasn't prettier, smarter, didn't have a better body, nor did she in any way measure up to the quality of his wife in his mind. She just totally validated him sexually, and because this was missing in his marriage, his lower head took the wheel from his upper head and jeopardized his relationship with God, his wife, and family.

For the record, men are visual; some of those men did report cheating because his woman let herself go in the appearance area. But NEVER simply because she picked up weight having his kids as most women believe. The letting herself go was the key.

This is what I discovered in my research. These are their answers. You can accept them or not. However, if you are NOT validating your husband, and don't act like you want him sexually, you are at risk of getting cheated on because he greatly needs his penis to be desired.

Never think that your husband loves God too much to not cheat. He is still a man and can be subject to sexual temptations. Too many wives I've coach who have been cheated on said, "I couldn't imagine this man doing it; he's always into the Word." Again, he's still a man and it can happen to your marriage, so try to insulate it with implementing strategies.

Note: Most men of God won't cheat sexually, but some will cheat emotionally by hardly ever coming home and by staying married to their work, church, or ministry, rather than cheating with a woman. Either way, he stays where he is validated. However, it may not stay that way over a longer period. This is usually how he is able to connect with another woman and divorce you for her. But there is one more thing you must consider: "Power in the Blood."

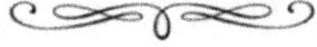

A MAN OF GOD *is Still* A MAN

Power in the Blood

OK, I'm going to say it! One of the most important things to a man other than being connected to God ,work, or family is how hard can he become before and during sex. It doesn't matter who he is!!!!! I said that I will NOT hold back in this book and I'm not!!! You see, this is his ultimate validation. Show me a man who is having difficulties in that area, and I will show you a man who is doing everything in his power to fix it. Also, he will usually avoid contact with his wife until it is fixed. He will not want to have sex, or not as frequently.

Therefore you have men of God—even in their twenties—taking ED meds (erectile dysfunction), e.g. Viagra, Levitra and Cialis, testosterone boosters, just because it gives them a more powerful erection. If not by prescription, then they borrow them from friends or buy them online. Otherwise, they are using herbals or vitamins that they think will do the same thing. Every man reading this knows that I'm telling the truth!!!

Men will try almost anything to get as hard as possible for his wife during sex. Some use aspirin to thin the blood. Others have a special ritual they go through thinking it makes them harder. Why? Well, it validates him by making him feel powerful and important. He will think to himself, *Man it was harder than a brick. I could punch a hole in the wall with it.* Men reading this know I'm telling the truth!!!!

Why is this message important? It is about the effects of what these additions to making him harder could have on your marriage.

Yes, it is tied to sex, and it doesn't matter how old the man is. I have cases where the man is sixty-nine and this is happening.

If he is taking these pills, or whatever ritual he uses to have sex with you at night, ninety-five percent of the time he will want more sex within a few hours, or early that morning, and maybe even the next day. Sometimes the power of this erection is not tied to sexual urges or satisfaction, but just tied to a powerful, chemically induced, erection that he simply DOES NOT want to waste. He badly wants to use it again. Men, you know I'm telling the truth!!

Women of God, it is my goal to provide you with solid information. I'm here to help you understand some of the factors of marital problems. This one issue has led to unexplained extramarital affairs and cheating simply because a man wanted to use that extremely hard erection again.

I know what you are going to say because I hear it all the time: these mini sermons about the inappropriateness of this, and how "He should...," and "Why don't...."

Instead of saying those things, think about what this additional information can do for your marriage. It is about validating him in the area where he wants it most: in his sexual performance.

When your husband's penis is extremely hard during sex, yes it could involve many factors, not only ED meds. Yes, he desires you. Yes, you turn him on. Yes, you are enough for him. BUT, never, ever, think that just because you put it on him so much last night that it is impossible for him to NOT want any the next day or in some cases within a few hours. Usually it is the next day, but sometimes he needs it two days in a row.

So what should you do? Even though you may be tired, if possible, check in with your husband because most men will not want to share with you that he is taking these meds, or whatever he does. He doesn't want you to know!!! Do NOT ASK!!!! Just perform this test:

> Wake-up a few minutes early or later that night and touch his penis or stimulate him in some way. If it gets

extremely hard again, if you can, hop right on it and bring it down because the effects of those meds at work around other women can cause temptations.

Yes, most men of God have restraint and can wait until later but if he is not getting enough sex, it may be difficult. Tease him that day to let him know how much you want him. He'll wait with anticipation.

Warning: Do NOT lead him to think you are going to give him some and then NOT do it because you had a bad day or your mood changed. If he is expecting sex, you'd better give it to him, or his attitude will change on you. If you teased and made him believe sex was going to happen that day or night, give it to him regardless of your mood. If you are not able, the way you say "No" is the key, because you have to say it with total understanding that you want him. Do NOT play with sex with you husband, period.

Please note: He will NOT come off his ritual, so you will have to conform and make the adjustment. Again, men get their validation via sex, and you want him to be validated by you in this area, not by anyone else. This is extremely important to a man and, regardless of what you think, he will want his penis as hard as it can become. Therefore he will do just about anything to make it that way. I just want you to be aware of how to take precautions to prevent temptation from occurring because of his desire of wanting to use it again.

It Hardened But Falls

"He goes limp during sex and I feel blamed!"

"He goes limp during sex and blames me!"

"He can't get it up and I was so crushed—and frustrated!"

These are some of the comments I often get from women on this subject, and it is heartfelt.

First, we all know that there are medical reasons why a man can go limp or not get it up. The simple answer is to go to the doctor to resolve this. Again, it should be just that simple. But why won't a man go to the doctor about this? Let me share a few reasons.

If your husband goes limp when with you, but he is getting hard when you are not around (not cheating, but getting aroused), something else is going on. This is the main reason why MOST men will NOT go to the doctor; he is getting hard and aroused and YOU are not around. So he believes that NOTHING is wrong with him. I've heard this so many times that it is crazy. But he will NOT say anything about it, because he doesn't know what to say. First, he is feeling bad because of his thought life, but also, it is embarrassing for some men of God to talk about their sexual desires or appetite.

Ladies, a man going limp during sex is major to him, and your response SHOULD be more about communication than blame. However, when it comes to sex, everyone seems too sensitive to discuss it—one of the major reasons why validation-cheating starts and marriages break up. I always say that the essence of a man's feeling like a man is tied to how hard of an erection he can get. So yes, his ability or inability to get it up and stay up must be handled delicately.

Is it possible for you to discuss this matter with candor and without hurt feelings? Yes, you will be able to discuss this and other sensitive matters candidly, just as I do throughout this book. But let's consider a few things first.

1. **Erection Time-Frame**. Some men, even in their 30s, but especially older ones, could have a rock-hard erection that may last a few minutes, maybe up to 30 minutes, when aroused. But, if you require lots of foreplay to get YOU ready, it means that he has to put in work. For some men it means that you were not ready when he was. You did not desire him when he was aroused and desiring you. Many will go limp during the foreplay process. He will often get angry because in his mind, his hard-on earlier could have pleased you. But he had to put in work to get you ready and it went away. Something could change for him mentally and he could go limp, e.g. "She's never ready. Why do I have to put in all of this work?"

Please understand this: There has to be both communication and compromises that meet needs in order to discuss this issue with candor.

2. **Sexual Position**: Your desired position for maximum pleasure can cause him to go limp. Example: Do you like to be on top? Men can go limp in that position at times. In that position, it takes a rock-hard erection. Men hate losing their erection, so that's why he will want to turn you over to get it back hard again. Changing position is the key here.

Men reading this know that if an erection is not rock-hard, his wife won't be able to be on top without it going limp. However, it doesn't mean that he can NOT make it work from a different position. This again is where communication has to take place. Because we have two issues here: You get your maximum pleasure being on top and he knows this, but he wants to stay hard, and also knows that it can't stay hard in that position all the time. You may have to change it up a bit, to get him really aroused so that you can get back in the position you desire for maximum pleasure.

3. "**Take off my panties**": Do you ask your husband to take off your panties when in bed all the time? This one may seem weird, but your husband could go limp. You see, several men have shared with me that this is an issue. They say: "I hate when I have to take off her panties all the time. I just want her to get in the bed already naked sometimes." When they think about this, and see those panties on, they may go limp or lose desire. So every once in a while, take off your own panties, as a way to say, "I want you!"

4. **Never Sexy**: "My wife never wears anything sexy to bed, and she won't let me see her fully naked. It was OK for a while, but now it's a turnoff."

5. **Movement**: If you are NOT a virgin, you will have had different sexual experiences with a different mate or two. Those other mates may have wanted you to move during sex, but perhaps this makes your current husband go limp. He may require his wife to be totally still and to allow him to do all the work. Again, this is where communication comes in.

6. **Odor**: "Her stuff stinks. It is a major turnoff."

7. **She Is Not Wet**: "She is no longer getting wet, so it's hard to get aroused. When I touch her, it's dry. I need her to be able to get wet."

8. **Bringing Up Other Men.** I know you may feel comfortable talking about things with your husband, but you can't bring conversations about another man into the bedroom before sex—not even casual talk about what the pastor said at church. A man does NOT want to be thinking about another man while in his bedroom. He can become turned off and go limp. Even if you have a complaint about another man, talk about it after sex, not before.

It's Fatigue

Here is a dynamic that can anger a man. We just talked about why it went limp. I want to build on what I said about the erection time-frame. There is another reason why a man may not be able to get as hard as he likes during sex. It is the concept of "fatigue." His pleasure tool may be fatigued from being hard, waiting for you all day. It is a muscle after all, so by the time he actually gets to have sex, it is too sore to get as hard as he believes you want or need it to be.

As I've said, men get validation from sex, so it is best to give it to him when he desires it, especially if you can see the arousal. I know that sometimes this cannot happen, but do not allow this to be the norm. In other words, **Stop saying "NO!"**

If a man is extremely burning with desire, his pleasure tool can be so fully erect that he feels it will burst. He is extremely aroused and wants you right now!!! Often he may hear, "Not now," or "Tomorrow" or another excuse.

However, after desiring sex so much from his wife, by the time he gets some, it does not get as hard as he likes, or worse: he cannot please you! How frustrating for both of you, but especially for him, knowing that, if he could have gotten sex in time, his performance would have been far better.

Ladies, allowing this to happen presents a very risky dynamic in your marriage: he won't feel validated. If you constantly leave him this way or are constantly saying "NO!" it will cause a weakness in your relationship. Most likely, at least eventually, he will find another vehicle to meet his need for sexual validation.

At this point you are probably wanting to tell me your point of view—that he must understand the things you go through. Believe me, he does.

I simply want you to acknowledge this FACT: **a man, your husband, requires sexual validation.** If you listen to his request from this point of view, you will KNOW why HIS NEED is a key to achieving YOUR GOAL of keeping the man of God you love happy.

Even a faithful husband, and especially a man of God who is highly motivated to observe God's laws, does NOT have the strength to hold out indefinitely. Testosterone and his physical, masculine, nature will win out and, given an opportunity, he WILL fall. Don't let this happen in your marriage.

Premature Ejaculation

We are adults here, so let us face another fact about the bed undefiled: premature ejaculation can be a problem in marriages. Most people of God are too shy to talk about this subject, not realizing that it can destroy a marriage if there is no communication.

Many women have questions regarding why their husband just cannot hold it long enough for them to be pleasured by sex. In other words, he ejaculates too fast, before she can get to have an orgasm. He is left feeling ashamed. (Yes, that is what he feels, because he was not able to please you. For pleasing you is his ultimate goal.)

Well, this happens, especially to men of God having sex for the first time or after a long time.

Just know that vaginas come in all shapes and sizes and some inner walls can create an environment that makes the head of the man's sexual organ more sensitive than others. Here are **seven reasons for premature ejaculation**:

1. When a woman gets very wet, some men can't take that and will ejaculate too fast.
2. If a woman's vagina is very tight and very wet, some men can't handle this and will ejaculate too fast.
3. If the vagina is very tight and then all of a sudden becomes very open, wet, and loose, some men cannot take this shock and will ejaculate too fast.

4. If you have a wide-open vagina without gripping power, he will fall off into it and simply ejaculate too fast. It will be over when it started.

5. Some men can't handle women making too much noise; they lose their concentration and ejaculate too fast.

6. Some women make movements during sex. If a man is not used to this, he will ejaculate extremely fast. You will be surprised how many women have told me that their man does not want them to move. As stated before, he can also go limp, perhaps because of premature ejaculation.

7. Some men cannot handle the in-and-out fast-pumping sex. They are not usually used to this and will ejaculate too fast if you are into it.

These things happen all the time. In other words, it depends on how sensitive a man's sexual organ is, and how much control he has. Trust me, men work very hard on this control and need your help sometimes.

Here is how to tell: When a man stops moving, he is trying not to ejaculate or is tired. If you are not ready for him to ejaculate, maybe have him change positions or do something to take his mind off the act for a minute.

If he ejaculated already, just keep in mind that the penis will remain hard for a few seconds afterwards, and especially if he is using ED meds. However, it will be difficult for him to continue after ejaculation if you stop. If you continue, some men can bounce back, but most will have to wait a while.

Another thing to know, Ladies, is this: Men are taught to think about something else instead of being with you (NOT ANOTHER WOMAN) and this is why he may not want to be all kissy, kissy, or focusing on you. Why? This may make him ejaculate too fast. Men are taught to build a computer, play baseball, practice shooting free throws, or prepare an opening statement for a trial. He does whatever he can to keep his focus off the act so that he can keep himself from ejaculating too fast.

Most men work to master the art of concentration and self-control. They want to be the best sexual partner for their wife.

Here is how you can help. If you are NOT a virgin, it is best to communicate to your husband what you like before sex. If you like it slow and he is fast-pumping, then you will have problems. If you like him to move and he can't last long like that, then that can be a problem.

As in other aspects of sharing your lives, one of you is probably more willing or able to adapt. Being open to change, creative, willing to try new things are keys to a successful marriage and to sharing a bed undefiled with your husband, the man of God you love. It will allow you to do your part in making sure that both your needs and his are met.

Oral Sex?

I can hear some of you right now saying: "That's just nasty."

This subject may be more a matter of perspective than anything else, but you be the judge. Many pastors and ministers use the word lasciviousness to explain its inappropriateness. They mean that this is a gross form of wickedness that has **sexual** overtones in many cases. They suggest that the act of oral sex starts in a sinful heart (Mark 7:21-22) and manifests itself in fleshly (carnal) actions (Galatians 5:19), and can lead to a state of being "past feeling" which means to be spiritually numb (Ephesians 4:19). As I said earlier, this book is not for or about the men or women referred to in these verses.

In my study and research into this subject, I have conversed with extremely well-educated pastors, other educated spiritual leaders, and biblical scholars. They shared with me that there is nowhere in the Bible that forbids oral sex or even discusses it. According to them, there is no biblical evidence that it is a sin against God for a husband and wife to express love for each other in this way.

I don't believe in adding my own theology when the Bible is silent on a subject, because my opinions may be different than others. Therefore, **according to these scholars,** what you decide to do is **up to you and your husband.**

The book of Leviticus, which mentions many sex-related

prohibitions and rules for the Israelites, never mentions it either. I've learned that scholars see no reason to believe that expressing affection for one's mate in this way is forbidden or would necessarily harm one's walk with God.

Again, I know that some have tried to make a biblical issue out of what parts of the body a married couple can and cannot kiss. In their minds, there is only one biblical form of sexual expression in marriage: sexual intercourse. They attempt to defend their viewpoint on biblical grounds—trying to make it into a holiness issue. However, none of them have been able to show where in Scripture such limits are put on the sexual relationship of a godly husband and wife, or even on priests (who were forbidden to do many things).

This issue is also a **generational** one; **older ministers** have great disdain for the act itself. Feeling incredulous, they ask, "How could anyone put their mouth on that…..?"

Most knowledgeable and spiritually mature Christians realize that God is the author of sex, love, and every part and sensation of the human body, and that He intended the relationship between husband and wife to be loving, sensuous, joyful, creative, and full of pleasure.

Some claim that oral sex in marriage is wrong because they associate it with Sodom and Gomorrah. According to Bible scholars, this comparison is misguided and offensive. It is quite clear that Sodom's problems had nothing to do with how godly, loving marriage partners were expressing their affection for each other.

To the contrary, there was a total lack of godly, loving, heterosexual, marriage partners in Sodom (save Lot and his wife). Serious students of the Bible know that the kind of things that were going on in Sodom were done by extremely ungodly people, expressing enormous selfishness, total lack of love, extreme spiritual depravity, and major rebellion against God. In other words, the sex lives of godly husbands and wives were not an issue in these cities, nor did it have anything to do with its destruction.

The basic principles concerning the enjoyment of sex in marriage are found in 1 Corinthians 7:3-5.

It Doesn't Fit

OK, women of faith, this is a subject that we must talk about. I've already said a lot about sex, but there is one more thing. Without proper knowledge of this matter, this topic can make or break your marriage.

Here it goes: Learn how to keep or make it tighter with proper gripping (Kegel exercises). You know what I mean by "it"—that private part. Now I'm sure that you have heard this before, but let me tell you this from a male perspective and research: MEN DO NOT LIKE IT IF THEY CANNOT FEEL YOU, TOO. They want it to be a good fit.

I've also heard women complain in sessions about their husband, saying: "It's not big enough. I can't feel him anymore" (or never could). "We waited until marriage, but I have a problem: I can't feel him. He's too small." I always say the following, "The problem could be you. Have you made proper preparation to keep it tighter and your muscle strong?"

Many women in my relationship groups love to pinpoint the problem as men not being big enough. This is possible and maybe why we have all of these "make it bigger" enhancement commercials out there. But I guarantee you this, Ladies, the woman with the most gripping power keeps her husband happy. I've learned that after having kids, or as a woman grows older, her gripping muscle can become loose without proper strengthening. Also, if you use toys or had multiple partners prior to salvation, you can become accustomed to the size of whatever type of stimulation you have been receiving.

If you used these toys in the past, you may have lost some sensation. When it becomes time for you and your husband to have sex, it may be harder for him to stimulate you or to feel you. However, if there has been much time in between doing this, it should not be a problem.

This issue has led some husbands to start thinking that his wife is having an affair with a man much larger than him. He will say, "Man, she has become so wide open." It has caused all types of discord in marriages when it is not true.

A man told me recently that he believed that his wife of seven years was cheating with her ex-husband. I asked, "Why?" He said, "I can't feel her any more. Her vagina was tighter before. And one-time she slipped and said that her ex-husband was extremely large." He said it took some time for him to get over hearing that from her. She was forty-three and he was forty-five. Well, she was not cheating, but her gripping muscle was weak. I told him that he needed to have a conversation with her about this matter and explained what was going on. I also said that, as women age, their gripping muscle becomes weak if not properly exercised. To make a long story short, the matter was resolved. There are plenty of techniques online for you to study about how to make it tighter. Google "Kegel exercises."

I only want to add that, if you are doing your part, it could be true that he is smaller. Then, there has to be some discussion about how to work around this issue.

One of the most interesting things in male psychology is that if you accuse a man of doing acts frequently, something primal inside of him can actually create the desire to do it or think about it strongly. Therefore, your jealousy can actually make him do or think about doing something he has never thought about before.

PHILEMON

CHAPTER SIX:

Love Hints

 If he says he is okay, believe him. Just because you are not okay, are feeling uneasy, is not relevant. He can be silent and happy. So stop asking.

The Truth about Love

1 Corinthians 13:4-7 NLT: *Love is patient and kind. Love is not jealous or boastful or proud or rude. It does not demand its own way. It is not irritable, and it keeps no record of being wronged. It does not rejoice about injustice but rejoices whenever the truth wins out. Love never gives up, never loses faith, is always hopeful, and endures through every circumstance.*

Corinthians 13:4-7, "the love chapter" explains and defines love for us. The key point to consider is that love encompasses all of the traits given, not some. Yes, those of us who know the Word and this scripture may at times falter, but this is the standard we are to strive for.

There are **four types of love** based on Scripture and often referred to by the Biblical Greek words:

> **Philia**: Friendship or brotherly love
>
> **Eros**: Fleshly love, the physical or sensual
>
> **Storge**: Family love or the bond among mothers, fathers, sisters and brothers
>
> **Agape**: Divine love, selfless, sacrificial, unconditional love

To make any permanent relationship possible, one must have Agape love.

It's the only love that makes marriage to the death possible.

This is because love is only "Agape" when you give love unconditionally—without a reason, without any expectations.

I know this may seem difficult to understand, but consider the truth about the real meaning of love: it's when you choose to commit to meeting a person's needs and to anticipating their future needs for life without ANY expectations. It's a decision! This is why one needs Agape love. It is the only type of love that will allow you to keep your marriage vows.

Love is NOT an emotion, it is a law. A law has no feelings about what happens. It's a system of enforceable rules and guidelines. We are commanded by Scripture to love in this way.

Love is simply a choice, an act of will, something you give value to. Therefore, if a man says that he loves you, put it to the test.

Ask him: "Does this means that you are willing to meet my current needs and to anticipate my future needs for life without ANY expectations?"

His response will say it all. Just know that if you are to accept his love and his hand in marriage, you will follow the scripture in Ephesians 5:22-33 and submit to him as you do the Lord, right? Yes, you are not off the hook, but I think you see my point.

One should never create conditions for love, because the very condition you set will be what destroys that relationship. You will never find anywhere in Scripture where God shared why he loves us. He just does. If you create conditions for your love, there will be expectations and having expectations leads to disappointments. Disappointments create division and detachment that almost always leads to divorce.

This lack of love, not being committed to love and the family is exactly what is destroying the fabric of our society. It is so important for one to understand love prior to getting married and starting a family. Collectively poor decisions can affect the state of an entire community and cause its destruction. This is how powerful love is to society.

The Commitment: Is He Ready?

There is no magic wand for predicting the future of a relationship, but we can ask questions that may reveal where a person is right now. This is the power of questions.

When first getting to know a man, the most effective way to know how he is thinking is to get him talking about his overall ambitions in life. This will usually involve what he does to make money or what he wants to do. For example, "I want to be a music producer or disaster worker."

The trick is to discover if his overall blueprint is aligned to having a relationship. This is extremely important. By using this strategy, you will learn so much more than you can through those "Am-I-wasting-my-time?" types of questions mentioned earlier.

Revealing questions to ask: If he has a business or is in school or whatever his situation, casually ask something like:

"What are you plans for your career?"

"Where do you want to take your business?"

"How far are you seeking to go with this?"

Then sit back, relax, and LISTEN with interest. Be sure to show great interest—he may be the man you will spend the rest of your life with.

A MAN OF GOD *is Still* A MAN

His response will give you an immediate feel for his blueprint in life. Even on your first date, you will be able to calculate if there is stability there and room for a relationship.

Just sit back and let him reveal all you need to know about how a serious relationship WITH YOU might fit into his life. From this you will know how a serious relationship WITH HIM will fit into yours.

Testing the Commitment

The best way to find out how committed a man is to your relationship is by giving him a test. The simple tests below will help you determine exactly where a man may be with you. Are you feeling impatient? Wondering where this relationship is going? Then this is a good time to give him these tests.

Envision Test: Is he envisioning you as part of his future? Ask him a question about doing something later in the year, such as Christmas or some other holiday. This will tell you whether or not he is predicting that your relationship is going anywhere. This is an excellent way to know which stage he sees the relationship in.

Integrating Test: Have you met his friends yet? His family? A man who is not serious will keep you separate from anything that is constant in his life. This is why so many such men do not date women in their own church. They don't want their friends and family to witness the mess when they end the relationship.

Therefore, if you do date a man from another church, be sure to let him know that you are very interested in attending his church. See how he reacts.

And even if he's in your church, if he is not integrating you into his other long-term relationships, take it as a red flag.

Consideration Test: Do his actions match his words? Whatever he says about the relationship, do not believe him unless his actions match. Ask yourself, *Does he involve or consider me in the*

A MAN OF GOD *is* *Still* A MAN

decisions of his life? Does he include me in things he is doing?

If he really likes you and is serious about you, you will become part of the blueprint he is creating for his life. He will take you into consideration whenever he makes decisions or plans.

If not, then he is not serious about you. He won't need to say a word.

PHILEMON

Find, Attract, a Man of God

Proverbs 18:22 NLT: *The man who finds a wife finds a treasure, and he receives favor from the LORD.*

Proverbs 18:22 is probably the most misunderstood text in the Bible. As I pointed out in "Traditional Mental Boxes" (Chapter Three), this scripture stagnates many unattached women in the Church. It only states that finding a wife is good. Scripture, in general, is silent on how to do this and never discusses what women should NOT do.

Why? Again, in Bible times marriages were arranged and socio-economic factors were considered far more important than feelings. A woman was often not even consulted. Nowadays, however, women are making marital decisions almost entirely alone. This is why they need strategies. I will provide some in this section.

"How can I find and attract a Christian man?" This is one of the major questions I get from women of faith. Before I answer this question let me say something I feel is extremely important.

Pastors and religious leaders often tell people to bury themselves so deeply in God that He has to interrupt them in order to send them that special person he has prepared for them. Their reasoning is that if you seek a man on your own, it could get you off your path. In other words, they say that, if you walk the path of righteousness, you will eventually cross paths with the man God has for you; that both of you will be on the same path.

I do believe this —but with a twist. I believe one should seek God's kingdom first and be in alignment with his will. I do believe that you can cross paths with a man of God on that journey.

Where I differ is in my awareness that times have changed. Most of the pastors and religious leaders giving this advice have been married so long that they would not have a clue how to navigate the dating scene today. Because they are leaders, and usually men, it is easier for them to just walk up to a woman in the church and say, "God told me that you are my wife."

It is just that simple for them. But it is NOT that way for a woman. NOT YOU!!!! Because so much has changed, because rules have changed, men are more cautious nowadays because they are afraid of being accused of harassment if they say anything to you. Yes, it does require some work on your part.

I feel that Scripture backs this up. For example, in 1 Corinthians 7 (KJV):

> [1] ... *It is good for a man not to touch* [live in marriage with] *a woman.*
>
> [2] *Nevertheless, to avoid fornication, let every man have his own wife, and let every woman have her own husband.*
>
> . . . . .
>
> [9] *But if they cannot contain, let them marry: for it is better to marry than to burn.*

What is this saying actually? I believe it is clear that God has given you a choice. He does NOT choose your mate for you, YOU do! But he helps in many ways via His word. You can use the principles found in Proverbs 4:7 (NIV): **Get wisdom. Though it cost all you have, get understanding.** You can pay for help.

You see, that perfect mate for you will align with your purpose in life. However, in order to choose correctly, you must acquire and apply the right knowledge. Scripture tells us to gain wisdom and understanding and that true knowledge allows problems to be solved and avoided.

Relationship knowledge can help you in choosing a mate in the same way that mechanical knowledge is quite useful if a vehicle breaks down. It is the same with all of life's problems and issues. All knowledge belongs to God and he gives it to us to solve, mend, repair, or fix things that are broken and to protect ourselves from the difficulties of life.

Therefore, don't sit there stagnating, waiting for God to act, or wondering what actions you should take to find your Mr. Right. In reading this book you are acquiring the proper knowledge to choose your mate wisely, because God has given that choice to you.

So what approach should you take? I have a few possibilities:

Christian dating sites are often one of the things many are already trying. These sites can be a positive resource to meet someone. I know many women who have found their husbands this way. WARNING: Of course, you must be discerning because certain men are only pretending to be looking for that special woman. They are actually looking for only vulnerable, gullible women to take advantage of. It happens on all internet sites. Therefore you should always meet him in a public place and let your family or friends know your plans.

The technique that I would love to share with you will place you in a proactive position for meeting men who attract you. The screening process in this technique is different, because this system will attract ALL quality men—NOT necessarily men of God. You see, what you want is a pool of quality men, including, most certainly, men of God.

You may resist this technique, as do many women of faith. They will never approach a man directly. They believe it is going against Proverbs 18:22. Let me assure you, that is far from the truth and taken out of the biblical context. The women of today need another way for finding and attracting men. The technique I want you to try first is from a workshop I offer called "Find, Catch and Keep Him." In this workshop I offer far too many details to include here, but I will share a few essential tips and encourage you to begin using them immediately.

This technique has six (6) steps!

1. Take the initiative.

2. Change your location habits.
3. Understand male psychology.
4. Get close.
5. Encourage initiative.
6. Say something.

Yes! You may have noticed. This simple technique includes many of the secrets I have already taught you. Here is your opportunity to apply your new-found understanding, to practice your skills, and to find ways to make them your own. Now, let's look at them together, one at a time.

1. Take Initiative, Take *the* Initiative

Men of God are everywhere. You need only to connect with them. Just as when you are looking for a job, put yourself in a position to be seen by a man and then approach him. Yes, take the initiative! Be the one to approach (I will tell you more about how to do this in the next steps.)

Stop banking on those who share stories about a sister in the church who just prayed and prayed and her husband walked in the door and found her. It can happen, but unlikely.

Whenever I hear this story, I always ask, "Who is she? What is her name? When did this happen?" You see, I want to meet her and find out exactly what she did. Unfortunately, many of those repeating this story could not name her, although they said she was in their own church. After twenty (20) years of looking into this, I've met very few of these women.

Let's just say that this happens to one woman in every church. How many women will be left out? You see, if you wait to be approached, it is possible that only those men you don't want will be approaching you. You will NOT be the chooser.

What if you could pick the man who captures your interest? This will only happen if you take the initiative and approach him. It's like the dropping of the handkerchief as our grandmothers once did years ago to capture a man's attention. This is the reason why I say that, as a woman of God, you must implement the strategy of taking initiative so God can bless your efforts.

2. Change Your Location Habits

Do you go to the same places each week? The same church meetings? Change it up a bit. Visit other churches.

In order to meet a quality man you must make it your business to establish a ritual of taking a small action each day. Yes, I'm saying that you must carve out time to place yourself in a position to be seen and available in search of love. God will bless your efforts.

For example: "Every Tuesday for 2 hours I will go to different places in search of love." YOU WON'T BE FOUND SITTING ON THE COUCH.

3. Understand Male Psychology

Do you know that the more a man is interested in you, the less likely it is that he will approach? He could believe that you are amazing, but will never approach. Why? He does not want you to think that he is a jerk and wants something. He just doesn't want to be too aggressive.

You have to provide him with the permission needed to approach. A man can base his identity on what women think of him. Now you know why I said in step one for you to take initiative.

4. Get Close

It is extremely risky for a man to come over to where you are. It is your job to mitigate that risk, to make it easier for him. Proximity is the key.

5. Encourage His Initiative

Just smiling will not work. You have to look and smile with an approving expression. It is OK to flirt with him in this way—using this type of smile.

6. Say Something

A MAN OF GOD *is* Still A MAN

To some guys, you will have to say the first words. It really doesn't matter what you say. However, it should be delivered properly.

As soon as a man hears you speak **in this way**, he will know that he has your approval to speak to you. What way? You can pay him a compliment. For example,

"I love that watch. You have great taste."

"You seem like you have great taste, what's a nice restaurant around here?"

The key to succeeding with this technique is to recognize how much things have changed and to adopt a proactive approach to your love life. Remember that God has given you the choice, and He will direct your path if this is your desire. You do not have to complicate this with excuses, e.g. "God has not sent my mate. "

Desiring complete certainty or guarantees is why so many are unmarried today. They are NOT willing to risk heartbreak or disappointments. Therefore, a subconscious wall is built too high for anyone to climb, even those who are willing. I call this wall a **"self-made love sabotager."** It is based on fear. If you want to attract a man of God ask yourself,

How high is my wall?

What defenses have I built to keep it in place and to protect it?

What stories must I tell myself to keep this wall in tact?

Do I use God as an excuse for my inaction?

It is time for you to do something different and learn what truly drives your decisions, what you are truly afraid of, what's keeping you mateless.

I truly believe that God will give you the desires of your heart. But, WHAT IS IT YOU DESIRE?

Think about this: I believe that if your heart has a wall built around it, it means you DESIRE and seek protection from pain MORE THAN ANYTHING ELSE! That has become your "heart's desire." That is your true goal.

THIS is what prevents you from finding and attracting a man of God. THIS is what prevents you from recognizing the man of God for you. In fact, God is giving you this protection because it is your desire to avoid pain. Trust God, take action, and He will direct your path. *Seek his will in all you do and he will show you which path to take.* (Proverbs 3:6 NLT)

Shifting into a Full Relationship

Ephesians 5:25 KJV: *Husbands, love your wives, even as Christ also loved the church, and gave himself for it;*

Shifting from dating into a full relationship leading to marriage is often confusing and difficult for women of faith. The key is to learn how NOT to scare him off and at the same time put yourself in a position of NOT being replaceable in his mind. In other words, you are **maintaining your value** and building more attraction. Even though a man is praying for a wife, he is still a man, and attraction is extremely important. You must understand the attraction process.

I've discovered that how a man treats a woman in a marriage, as well as why he is turned off by a woman-of-interest, has a lot to do with her **losing value** to him. Men love women with standards because they are conditioned to value what they have earned. A man knows when he has NOT earned anything yet, and does not expect a reward. So, don't reward him if he hasn't earned it. That will help you to retain your value to him and be the woman he believes he cannot live without.

How to Maintain Your Value

Observing many women of faith shift from dating into a full relationship, I have been paying attention to which ones make it and which do not. Here is a list of do's and don'ts that worked for them:

➢ **Never give a man your entire schedule** and allow him to plug in at whatever times he wants. Make him earn your time. Ask yourself, "Has he earned the right to have the same amount of time as my family and friends?

➢ **Never sell the relationship or yourself.** Men just switch off when women are selling. He wants to buy, but not be sold. So stop bringing up all of your good points. Let him discover them. He will.

➢ **Are you fornicating?** Scripture tells us to *Flee fornication* and that fornicators will not inherit the kingdom of God (1 Corinthians 6:9, 18). Despite this prohibition, many of you who love God are still weak in this area. I understand that you are still fornicating, but will allow others to preach to you about how wrong it is. My job is to provide you with information. Because I love God's people, I want to help them all. Let me help those of you who are fornicating to understand what this is doing to your relationship.

➢ **If you are going to fornicate anyway,** please read the last section in this book called "Another Perspective on Fornication." It explains God's biological laws for attachment and how having sex outside of marriage can attach you to, or create a bond with, the wrong person. On top of this, if you do fornicate, please don't lose your value to a man by giving away **Free Sex without an agreement. Am I saying that premarital sex is OK when you have an agreement? No!** That would not be in alignment with Scripture. My point is simply that your agreement may save the day, because you may marry—eventually.

Curiously, unmarried men of God who are fornicating are very likely to be seriously seeking a wife because of this weakness and because that is what Scripture (Paul in Corinthians) advises, ***But if they cannot contain, let them marry*** . . . . (1 Corinthians 7:9 KJV).

Now, if you are sleeping with him during this time, he will NEVER marry you if he believes you will just give it away. And if you do not have an agreement, then he KNOWS you are giving it away.

> **Engagement**: Some women believe that an engagement ring is a license to have sex (C'mon, I know the game). Again, you should FLEE fornication. But at least you have a formal agreement to marry.

The bottom line for you women of God is this: If you are going to have premarital sex with such a man, make him feel that he is the only one who can break this barrier. Tell him that, if he does, then you want this relationship to lead to marriage. This is what I mean about an agreement. At least you are creating the condition that, if you have premarital sex, then he agrees to marry you "in the future." Most men in the church who are weak in this area, but really seeking a wife, will value this stand.

Remember: Don't give him all of the benefits of a married relationship before he is in one. BUT, if you must, then make sure it is in a relationship with a man who agrees that your relationship is leading to marriage. Again, I don't condone premarital sex.

If a man, any man, feels he can see you as he wants, have sex with you as he wants, he already has all of you. There is no incentive for marriage. Whereas, if a man of God feels this way, then he is associating you with his feelings of guilt and shame for going against Scripture. He will be looking for a woman of God who makes him feel aligned with Scripture.

> **What about you? Will this agreement benefit you, too?** I know from coaching them that women of God who are weak in this area have just as many concerns about performance in the bedroom and how they are treated, especially if she has something to compare it against. Are you "settling" out of eagerness to be married because you are burning? If not, and if you are sure you can LIVE with this agreement for the rest of your God-given life, you must be smart about it.

I've coached many people with status in the church that I uncovered were having premarital sex and struggling with guilt about it. They would say, "I'm so weak in this area." However, often I've noticed that they ended up marrying that person or someone else shortly after. Yes, its sin but it happens in today's church more than we like to believe. I can only help my clients get where they want to be and not drive them away for where they are now. Those acts are between them and God. Usually these individuals are seeking to get marry as quick as possible because they understand the following scripture.

1 Corinthians 6:18 (NLT): **_Run from sexual sin! No other sin so clearly affects the body as this one does. For sexual immorality is a sin against your own body._** Therefore, Scripture provides us instructions on what to do in this situation: 1 Corinthians 7:9 NLT: **_But if they can't control themselves, they should go ahead and marry. It's better to marry than to burn with lust._**

➤ **Have standards.** Have standards of what you will or won't accept and stick to them. If he does something you don't like, you can say, "I don't like that." A man likes women with standards. Remember you have to have tact and not come across as judgmental or fussy.

➤ **Do not change or lower your standards** because you like someone. When women really like someone and are trying to "catch" that man, you see them putting up with things. But later, when they relax, believing they've "caught" him, they start enforcing rules that were not set before. He will wonder, _This wasn't a problem before, so why now?_ It makes you lose value to him.

➤ **Make him live up to your standards.** A man will respect you more if he has to live up to standards. He will follow the restrictions you set for him—if he loves and respects you. So this can be a test to find out.

➤ **Do not allow him back too quickly.** Men sometimes get hot and cold. This frustrates women. Never worry about this, but take care about what you do next. Sometimes men get comfortable and lose the desire to chase and stop calling. This could happen especially if he feels that every time he comes back, you come back too. He loses the desire to work for you. Do not allow him to come back into your life quickly because he will make associations about you. He needs to be CHALLENGED so he can try to win you back.

➤ **Make him earn his way back in**. You are training this man to act according to your standards, so that he can make the right associations about you. This way he can appreciate his position because he had to fight back to get your approval; he will value it more.

➤ **Positive vs Negative**: There are always negative moments in healthy relationships. However there is a balancing theory to how much in all successful and lasting marriages. You must keep the positive to negative encounters at a five-to-one ratio (5:1). This means that there are five positive moments over each negative one. Keeping things more positive than negative should be a no-brainer; however it is important to share that there is a ratio to successful relationships. This is also the key to becoming the woman he cannot live without.

Following these guidelines will allow you to shift successfully from casual dating into a full relationship by establishing your value to him as a potential wife. Then he will want to integrate you into his life.

A full relationship leading to marriage includes inviting one another into the inner circle of your friends and family—within and outside of the church. This integration is essential to creating a lasting bond. Let's examine how you might do that.

Integrating into His Life

How do people of faith integrate into a relationship? Can I be honest? I really don't know because it is kind of a secret. You see, in the world, if this person is your girlfriend, or boyfriend, you usually have regular sex, go on trips and stay in the same hotel room. You may move in together, integrate your friends and family, and then get married.

In the church marriage is promoted, and many things are believed to be against Scripture. Since there are NOT direct guidelines for dating in the Bible, most keep their relationship a secret.

In some ministries it is OK to go to the movies, ballgames, concerts; others have more restrictions. Therefore, many couples hide their actions from other church members. Yes, we see them integrating friends and families, going out, but usually nothing else.

I've asked hundreds of Christian singles, "What do you do together?"

Sometimes I get total silence, or they may smile and say "Get out of my business!" Some will say, "We pray together, go out to eat, go to the movies." That's it!

I've asked "Do y'all kiss or hug?"

Most will say, "This is dangerous and would lead to other things, so we refrain from doing such things."

All I know is that I have not received complete answers.

Looking at these relationships from the outside, what do we

know? Well, we do know that church activities are integrated into their relationships because they are seen together at them. Shortly afterwards, they announce that they are getting married.

Depending on the ministry, some of these couples have regular relations, including sex, but are still faithful in the church. They just hide the sex part. Some of these couples date for years and have fully integrated their families and friends into the relationship. But again, what they do in their private time is totally unknown. There is NOT any research into this subject to fall back on, either.

So how do you successfully integrate into his life? Let's look at this subject from a practical approach. In order to integrate properly, you need to understand the process of relating, and for this you need to gain the necessary skills. Let me give you an overview.

First, understand that marital and dating relationships are often misrepresented on TV or in the media. Often they are sending messages that the relationships portrayed are fun and easy. However, at the first sign of trouble, they either dissolve the relationship or one of them runs away.

In reality, of course, it is better to pray, individually and together, seeking God's wisdom and guidance to discern whether you can have a future together. Most of the time Christian couples can be so ready for **marriage** that they rely on the butterflies in their stomachs and on their current overjoyed feelings.

Often this is when they say, "It is God's will for us to be together." They quickly get married and are in a dream-like state until they suddenly awaken to a nightmare and realize that the relationship is destructive to themselves and others.

Because these Christian couples often get married quickly, many of their marriages end in heartbreak. This could have been avoided if they had just slowed down and taken the time to sensibly and realistically evaluate how good a match they really are together and how well they can blend if kids are involved. The key is to get couple's coaching to gain the proper skills.

Integration Preparation Questions

As you begin to integrate into his family, take the point of view that you are conducting research, gathering information to discover whether this is REALLY the man God has for you. The one you want to marry. **Consider these questions:**

- First, do you really **like spending time** with this man?
- Are you comfortable with him? Can you **relax** around him?
- Do you often feel you must entertain him? If you have to entertain him to **keep his attention**, then it's hard to relax. He may not be a good fit for you.
- How about **dead time**? Can you just do nothing and still enjoy having him around? Or do you need for him to leave so that you can do other things, like work at home or read?
- If he gets bored because of dead time, then he may NOT integrate well into your life. How can one grow that way?

If you are a reader and he is not, if he can't find anything else to do with his time, while you do your thing, it's hard to integrate.

- What about **shared experiences**? Do you do things together and have shared stories with and about each other?

Make sure you are having shared experiences doing things that are NOT possible to be done alone.

- Can you **joke around** and be silly with each other?
- Do you feel comfortable enough with him to share what you like to do?

He may be trying to figure out how to **make you happy.** This can be stressful because men process things. (Yes! we men "worry" too, but we call it "processing.") E.g. we process about finding a great seat for you at an event, finding locations you will enjoy, making sure you are safe, among other things. A little direction from you about what makes you happy helps tremendously. It saves him from having to ascertain if you are happy or not. Then he can focus on the logistics of getting you there safely and other processes.

- Are you **comfortable including him** in all of your situations: "The rest of life's drama"?
- Can you handle integrating into his life, his family and friends, and tackling problems together, rather than independently?

The Integration Process

Here are some tips on how to make sure that the integration process gives you all of the information you will need to make a decision that you will not regret later. You can begin now, even before he starts integrating you into his world.

- Make sure to place the relationship in **different environments** so that you can gauge how he acts in different circumstances.
- To save time, structure a date at which he can be around your friends and family on the same day. This way you can **ascertain how he acts** with them and gauge quickly if he can integrate into your life.

Once you know this man, things are ready to integrate.

- Make sure you increase your connection with him by **having a curious perspective** about this man of interest.

Allow him to speak on subjects he feels you know NOTHING about. Men love sharing these types of stories. If he doesn't offer, then ask him to share such things with you, and really listen to him.

- **Men love sharing things you don't know.**

Even if you do know about something, do NOT talk about it. Let this be his realm of expertise. Show interest! If you reveal what you already know about the subject, or attempt to learn about it, you will lose connection.

- The key is to help him **create the association** that his world is becoming better because YOU are in it. He should be saying, "I've never done that before. It was great experiencing this with you."

Integrating with People in His World

Finally, he is ready to integrate you into his world. If you have been following my coaching suggestions above, then you are ready. Hopefully, by now, you know him well enough to know that you want to make the effort to fully integrate into his world. You are eager to meet his family and friends to confirm that it's a fit. This is the social and cultural piece that arranged marriages take care of first. Yes, and nowadays it is often last. Sadly, it can make or break the relationship.

Relax, even though this is very important. Just be yourself, knowing that this is who he loves and who he wants to introduce to his family and friends. You are not "there" yet! Not until you have the ring on your finger. So, learn what you can now, before it's too late. Make sure he really is the one. This is your opportunity to see how he fits into his world.

Here are some tips for you:

- You should know **what is important in his life**, e.g. his Family, Friends, and Hobbies. These are powerful. In order to successfully integrate, you must express an interest in knowing all about him. You should say: "Tell me about your family, your friends."

Remember the names of anyone he tells you about. It really connects you with what's important to him. Also, understand that he may not want you to meet his family because of how they are and because he's afraid that you may judge him. Just make him feel comfortable that you are totally interested in meeting them. Regardless!

- The key is to **become part of his world.** This will increase and deepen the connection you have with him.
- Make sure you express excitement to meet the people in his world.
- Most often, a man will assume that you are not interested in his world and won't say much. If you suggest to him that you want to meet the people in his world, he will think of things you can do around other parts of his life.
- If he keeps you separated from what's important to him, then you know he is NOT ready for a more serious relationship.
- When he does invite you to become part of his world, he will be wondering, *How well does she fit into my life?* He will watch closely to see how you operate in his environment. When he feels you have successfully integrated, it will be a major factor in his consideration of marriage.
- When you are in his world, make sure that you **separate from him** and talk to people away from him. Do NOT cling to him. Men love it when they don't have to babysit their woman. If he sees this, it will make him happy that you can find interactions anywhere he takes you. This is how you build connection.
- After he sees that you can hold your own in his environment, e.g. "working a room" away from him, he may come and get you at a certain point because he will want to have you all to himself. In other words, claim his woman so that everyone knows that you are with him! It can build an even deeper connection.

- When you walk away from that environment, you want the people in his world to see you as the person you are and NOT just the girl he is with. The way to do this is to make sure you are just being who you are, engaging in conversation with those around you in order to get to know them. Just own yourself. Then, people there will say, "Hey did you meet Tammy? She is really nice!"
- Look for the people important to him. Any relationship that is important to him should be important to you, too.
- Also, look for the people important to him because he will seek to gain their approval regarding you.
- Never try to separate him from the people important to him. Always look for the good in them.
- Make sure you handle difficult people in his world carefully. Look for the good in them, too. He knows they are difficult and will appreciate you for trying.
- Never act as if you don't like anyone in his world. Take the high road, even if someone seems obnoxious to you. Make sure you speak highly of him always, but especially in his world. Always compliment him around his family and friends.
- Make sure you are not standoffish, even if you feel left out. Try to engage the people important to him anyway. Make that effort.
- The way to be liked is to make sure they feel that you look after their loved one, meaning that his family and friends feel you have his back.
- And remember what I said about "Teasing a Man." Don't! Even if his family and friends have a standing way of joking about him, don't join in.
- Make sure you help out if around his family, e.g. doing dishes, setting the table, offering to help. Don't just sit

down doing nothing. If he tells you not to, make sure you know why he is asking you not to help, looking for a reasonable answer. It could be something within the family dynamic for guests not to help. Therefore, listen carefully. Just make it clear that you truly want to help. If you contribute to the family, it is a plus.

- Never join in with him in speaking badly about anyone in his world. Never jump on that bandwagon. Make sure you say nice things and give them the benefit of the doubt about their actions. For example, if he gets mad at his sister and says bad things, just say "She loves you and means well." Take the high road. This creates value for you, and he will see that you make him better.

- The key is for him to make the association that being with you makes him better.

These are some of the relationship skills that you will need when integrating into his life. They are actually good skills to use in any relationship, so you can begin watching yourself as you relate to those in your life right now. Do you find you already have these skills? Are there any you know you need to work on? Some of you may not have grown up in a nurturing environment where you would have learned these skills, so begin practicing them and see how you do. Consider personal coaching in this area. Make sure you have the skills by the time he begins inviting you into his life.

So, You Really Want to Be a Pastor's Wife?

As a pastor's son, I can say first-hand that the job of a pastor's wife is most difficult. To be honest, those women who want to be a pastor's wife usually don't know what is totally involved in the job. By observing my mother I've noticed that the number one concern is really having the ability to deal with the loneliness of not having true friends.

Mom found it helpful to get together with other pastors' wives or women leaders and even attended conventions with women from all over the world. I have also coached some of them. No matter the congregation, their experiences have similar themes.

So, you want to marry a pastor? Being his wife is a noble way to serve the Lord. Let me share with you some of the realities of life as a pastor's wife.

So, you are already married to a pastor? Compare my points below with your own reality and know you are not alone. The negative side of serving the Lord in this way is not personal. It comes with the job.

Pastors are human. As this book clarifies, a man, even a pastor, is still a man. He can and will make mistakes. He is NOT God.

Pastors' wives are human, too. You are a woman. You also make mistakes. People are just harsher with your mistakes.

No Privacy. As a pastor's wife, you live in a glass house. You are constantly being watched; your every action is judged. If you just run to the store and look a certain way, others will talk about your appearance. You have to always step out of the house looking your best. You represent the women at your church.

How to handle criticism. People will talk about you, your kids, and your husband. They will spread lies about you, too. Get ready for negative experiences and many conflicts. You have to pray that you prevent resentment from building.

People can be cruel. Some of the harshest words you will hear will be from people in the church. Yes, there are some cruel people there who do mean things, so don't be surprise.

Security is important. Jealousy can be a problem, and some may want to hurt you. You have to keep watch for those who wish to do physical harm to you and your family.

Set Boundaries. You have to put up a fence to avoid potential problems and to protect those in your guardianship. You have to be able to establish boundaries around people to make sure they are not privy to information they should not know.

The need for a confidant. You will have lots of surface friends, but may not have one who will be a heart friend. Some may want to get close to you for information. A friend has to be discreet, so you can share your true feelings with her without any fear that they will be repeated back to others.

Perception is reality. Many will believe you have it all: no money problems among other things. They may not invite you to outings simply because you are the pastor's wife. They can be standoffish with you, too. It will just be a perception, but not always the truth.

Be the best you. You can't please everyone and people-pleasing is the first step towards your complete break-down or destruction. There are many parts of you. The key is to try to be the best you, especially when you care about the results. Therefore let your hair down when you can. The glass house can be difficult, but YOU should not try to be someone else. Just be the part of you that is your core

Now that you have read this, begin paying attention to how the pastor's wife in your church is treated. What are people saying about her? Are you joining in? Do you really believe it will be different for you in her place?

Infatuation Guilt

> 1 Corinthians 13:4-7 NLT: *Love is patient and kind. Love is not jealous or boastful or proud or rude. It does not demand its own way. It is not irritable, and it keeps no record of being wronged. It does not rejoice about injustice but rejoices whenever the truth wins out. Love never gives up, never loses faith, is always hopeful, and endures through every circumstance.*

Infatuation guilt can explain why a man or a woman may leave a church because they have been embarrassed by an engagement that did not work out. It is a biological issue that actually applies to both men and women. I believe it is extremely important to include this subject here for your consideration.

Infatuation guilt develops when you meet someone and believe this is the person God has for you. The feelings are overwhelming. You cannot eat or sleep thinking about that man or woman. Often a couple will announce to the church that they may be getting married. However, after about two to three months, one or both will have lost that loving feeling.

Believe it or not, the reaction can be measured biologically within the brain by its secretion of the neurotransmitter **phenylethylamine (PEA).** Your body actually experiences this exhilarating feeling similar to that of cocaine or ecstasy. Yes, it can be a drug! But do you know why? It's a natural process that is designed to continue the species by reproducing. This is why so many say, "We had amazing chemistry." Although it feels like using drugs, it is a natural high.

What we all should know is that love does not create this type of high within itself. Yes, you can have chemistry with love, but love in itself is a strong connection between two souls.

The purpose of this section is to help you understand how one can become guilty for having such strong feelings of infatuation in the beginning, but no longer feeling the same way later. Guilt and loneliness are often the reasons why marriages in the church end in divorce. Most of us do not want to be alone, so we use the other person to pass the time away until we can find an upgrade in a man or woman.

This is why he/she cheats or spends time talking to other men or women. They are either seeking that feeling again, or just trying to find something better. Sorry, but they are seeking to no avail.

I hope you are not disappointed by what I'm about to say. Please understand the truth about all the novels you read and the movies you see that make you feel or say "Aweeee, that's so special!" It is usually not the case! They always show this perpetual high and love-at-first-sight romance in movies and books.

True love does not work this way at all. Yes, there is a connection at first, but the feeling of love requires time to develop. Also, true love usually grows and changes within the relationship. You do not have a steady, high-like infatuation. In fact, such feelings always fade eventually and never come back.

Stop feeling guilty and be straight. Let this person know how you really feel. If you are honest, maybe this can be a person you will grow to love via complementing values and understanding. Stop searching for that feeling of infatuation. Always evaluate the relationship instead of the person you are with. We always think we can do better and upgrade our current love affairs.

The question should be, "Are you doing better in this relationship than ever before?" If you evaluate the person, their skills and education, you may become confused as to whether or not it will work. Instead, you should know how this man makes you feel in the relationship.

Think of a relationship as a three-legged stool: first it's you, second your mate, and third the relationship. One leg cannot be supported without the others. So the relationship is a leg all by itself; you should judge this more than you are judging your mate.

Again, remove the guilt, be honest, and allow the chips to fall wherever they do. If you are not too attached to the outcome of the relationship, it could be the start of true, lasting love. You see, your soul mate could be that man you are looking at right now. You just don't know it yet. Think about it!

First-Date Attire

> 1 Timothy 2:9 NLT: *And I want women to be modest in their appearance. They should wear decent and appropriate clothing and not draw attention to themselves by the way they fix their hair or by wearing gold or pearls or expensive clothes.*

What to wear on your first date with a man of God? Does it really matter, so long as you follow Scripture and dress modestly? Well, yes, it does.

First, let's look at what Scripture says, e .g. the one above from Timothy: **be modest, wear decent and appropriate clothing....** Seems fairly straight forward, doesn't it?

Well, I've discovered that what "modest" means is subjective, with different individuals and different ministries interpreting it in their own way. Some ministries set rules; some actually have a formal dress code. You may already be following some general guidelines.

Within this context, I will give you some tips on dressing for a first date with a man of God. At the very least, following these tips will help to ensure that he asks you out again—if that's what you want. Applying them may also make you more attractive to him if you want to develop a relationship with him.

Just understand that, if you find a man who shares your values, but his ministry has a different dress code than yours, it is OK to adjust when you are with him.

Here is **one basic guideline** for you that will fit within any of the scriptural dress codes: Men respond on a subconscious level to soft fabrics that bring out the protector in him. If you appear soft and fragile, it's a plus because men are protectors by nature. Business suits and attire can make you appear competitive and physically strong, so watch out for that.

This is also the case in online dating based on the picture attached to your profile. (A picture is worth a thousand words.)

Each man also has basic categories for women based on their appearance, especially at first glance and even on the first date. It doesn't mean that you are like this, but it is his view of the way you look or dress. Yes, this is a mental thing, but deeply ingrained in each of us. You see, the mind's job is to seek patterns and put things in boxes. You've already caught his attention—something about you plucked at his heart strings. But now, on your first date, you have an opportunity to calm his mind by fitting into a category that will get its approval. Then you can begin growing a heart connection. (Of course, you'll be assessing him with your own categories.)

These categories are simply a reflection of what you are both accustomed to seeing in your family, your home church, and in your community. In other words, it is cultural. In this case, the old adage "opposites attract" can present you with a dilemma about what to wear on that first date. On that note, just know that when opposites attract, if you get together, it will eventually clash and could drive each of you crazy. This book will give you skills to keep things calm when you disagree because it will happen often. Learn to think and say: "We have different opinions but I still respect you."

But what if the "first date" is not the "first glance"? Well, if you've already met, or he's seen your picture online, he has a general impression, but something about you attracts him, so he wants to see how you will present yourself on a date with him as a potential love interest.

Here are the **male categories for women's appearance** that I hear from men the most often. As you read this, you will probably be wondering, *What category will he put me in?* Remember that how each man "sees" a woman in each of these categories is just as subjective as how he sees what is "modest."

You may also wonder *How will I know?* Basically, if you are not what he is looking for he will keep the first date short and will NOT call back. If he does call back, you will be able to tell if he's only interested in you for the right reasons or as someone he wants to introduce to his family and friends.

➢ **Classy:** Many men will find you are the type to take home to his mother or friends. This is where most women want to be, but you must speak, dress, and look the part to be in this category. *And how will you know?* He will treat you like a lady and be very gentlemanly. However, some men may prefer a woman who is Simple or a Plain Jane.

➢ **Standoffish:** He thinks that you appear to be uppity or arrogant, can't get your hands dirty, and may be difficult to deal with. He will also think that you are expensive.

And how will you know? You will hear critical comments about your personality or questions about your style. He will want to escape as soon as possible or, he will decide to play the role for a while to get what he can before he stops calling.

NOTE: Be alert to your own feelings. If you are feeling uncomfortable with him, he may take this as standoffish. Actually, it may be a signal to you that he is not the one.

➢ **High Maintenance:** *Can I afford her?* This is the question that will be in his head. He thinks that you appear to be all about status, money, and power. You will be considered financial trouble for most men. Sometimes you are heavy on the makeup. It can also be what you order on the first date.

And how will you know? He will make reference to how expensive your taste is and will be planning his escape. Some guys will also play the role to bring you down a notch. In this case, he may ask you out again just to take you to a place he feels you will not like and then will stop calling.

➢ **Overdone:** He thinks that you have too much of everything: makeup, hair extensions or weave, nails. It is over-powering and distracting.

And how will you know? He will treat you similarly to High Maintenance or be critical of other women. For example, he may make references to a reality show character to say how he doesn't like her altitude as a way for you to connect the dots.

➢ **Simple:** He thinks that you dress cute at times but look very simple in most cases. A higher version of Plain Jane. If he is not stylish himself, you may be what he is looking for.

And how will you know? If he is stylish, he may criticize your appearance or make some small suggestion about what you should wear. If he is embarrassed to be seen with you, he may actually plan his escape from this date. But if he likes you despite this, he may ask you out again, making some small suggestion about what you should wear. If he is NOT stylish, and he prefers your way of dress, he will treat you well and ask you out again.

➢ **Plain Jane:** He will think that you are not very stylish, but may be godly modest. Many women of faith fit into this category, because they are taught to be modest in their appearance, although how they actually dress will vary from ministry to ministry.

And how will you know? He will treat you the same way as Simple.

➢ **Ghetto:** No explanation needed. You know it when you see it. Yes, some Christian women look ghetto even in their church clothes. He can also determine this from your reactions when something happens.

And how will you know? He will just leave the first date as soon as possible and not ask you out again. If you are in the same church, he will be polite, but not seek you out.

➢ **Sister Temptation:** In his mind you dress a little too provocatively for a woman of God.

And how will you know? He will see you in a sexual manner and will NOT want to take someone like you home to mother. If he is weak, you may become a closet lover for him.

Is this reversible? In general, no! There is no way around this. You are simply categorized. However, after a great conversation, many men will change their minds more often about women who are **Standoffish** or **High Maintenance**. You may appear to be in one of those categories upon first sight, but can easily persuade him by your attitude that you are really a **classy/standard** type of lady.

First-Date Attire—My Recommendations

On the first date, just keep it simple and do not dress too provocatively. Please don't wear overpowering perfume, too much makeup, or those creative-type nails. I've tested this several times and much of this can place you in a non-positive category simply based on your appearance.

Another test shows that too much makeup can make you appear "high maintenance," and men do not want the hassle. If your make-up is flawless and you are dressed with lady-like tendencies, this is the best choice. Be very classy.

Ladies who do not wear lots of makeup, but put their lipstick on heavily create another issue to which men have an unfavorable response. It's okay to put on your lipstick, but do it lightly, just to add color, and do not make it overpowering. The interesting part about this is you do not look that much different. Lipstick alone does not make you appear more feminine, and it is very obvious. Again, use it for a little color; it must be very light to prevent a negative response.

Men of God like well-groomed women, including your hair and nails. Try French-tip or very soft colors on your finger and toenails; nothing overpowering or exotic. Men love this and, for some reason, look differently at women who wear them on the first date. I've tested this with hundreds of relationship-worthy men. Also if you are going plain on the hands and toes, this is great too, but be well-groomed. Why? Really, I don't know, because men can never explain why they have a different opinion of women regarding their nails. This is weird, but works on the first date.

Make sure that you dress properly for the occasion. If the event requires jeans and sneakers, wear that and not dress shoes. I know a lady who wears pumps to bowling alleys when invited. Her response? "This is who I am." Well, maybe so, but when meeting a man on the first date, or meeting his family for the first time, you do not want to do such a thing.

One more point for your consideration is the smell of your clothes. Ladies, know that what you wear smells like its environment. If your home or closet smells, or has a stale odor, so will your clothes; it will pierce through your perfume. I've heard countless men speak about a woman whose clothes smell, but not her body. I know that dry cleaning can be expensive, but not having fresh-smelling clothes could prevent you from getting to first base with your dream man, or he will just leave.

While we are discussing first dates, make sure you do the following:

- Have eye contact on the date.
- Touch him often on the hands and arm gently and smile.
- Compliment him, especially on his choices and other things.
- Tell him how much you are enjoying yourself.
- Always say, "Thank you."
- Be extremely interested in his conversation.
- Ask no pressure questions. Just have fun.

Try out these ideas on your next "First Date" and see if you get different results.

First-Date Environment

It is my belief that most sources providing questions-to-ask-on-the-first-date must have been written by concerned parents of marrying-age girls or by frightened women. ☺ Why you may ask? Well, these questions I see on the internet and in some books are all designed to get answers that provide certainty to those who are interested in a particular outcome.

This is what I observe often in women: asking questions instead of focusing on how well she can connect with a man. I've learned that women are so worried about getting the wrong guy that they focus on NOT wasting their time instead of on getting to know the guy naturally while building attraction. He may have been Mr. Right, but they will never know.

Here are some of these first-date questions often suggested by others:

"What do you do and where do you work?"

"What did you think of me before we met each other?"

"Are you a reader or are you more into video games?"

"If you ruled the world, what would you change?"

"Do you get up in the morning to pray?"

"Where do you see yourself in the next five to ten years?"

I know that you may think, "These are not bad questions," and you will be right to a point, BUT they are, when trying to build chemistry and attraction.

Actually, these are terrible first-date questions because a date is NOT an interview! It is an opportunity to connect with a man of God who is looking for a connection with a woman and wondering, *How well will she fit into my life?*

Why not give him a glimpse of how well you will fit by responding in such a way that shares your authenticity, playfulness, and concern for him, while also challenging him to be his best. I didn't say challenging his manhood, but challenging his instinctive desire to hunt and win.

To create the right dating environment, follow these steps:

- Smile often.
- Be excited to meet or see him.
- Be generous with your genuine compliments.
- Lean towards your date almost all throughout the date.
- Watch your body language: Don't fidget or rock your body backward and forward, and don't nod your head forever like you've got a spring for a neck.
- Watch your conversation and don't interrupt him. Don't speak over a minute about the same topic, unless he adds his point of view. Keep your sentences short, allowing him time to add his own point of view often.
- Make eye contact. Keep your eyes opened wide with excitement.

Just know that men like to be pampered and challenged to win something of value. But never pamper him like his mom, because he could place you in that category, and NO guy wants to be attracted to his mom. This is why putting things up for a challenge is the extra ingredient in building chemistry and attraction.

How to do this? I am going to send you directly to a YouTube video clip of a couple meeting for the first time. Although this is a movie, it really shows how a first-meeting environment should be. The movie is *The Adjustment Bureau* with Matt Damon as David and Emily Blunt as Elise. http://youtu.be/A8vp6AdjlY8

I usually share this video with women I coach because it gives them an example of how a man likes to feel in the presence of a woman he meets for the first time. It is also a way to build chemistry and attraction.

In this clip Elise and David meet in the men's bathroom where she is hiding out. What do you notice about her? Let me share what I observe: She is totally authentic, vulnerable, not putting on any airs. She does not bring attention to her shoes or what she is wearing; she makes great eye contact and they have something to talk about: Why is she in the men's bathroom? She also recognizes him because he is running for office. Her behavior and that interesting topic build attraction within themselves because a man can see himself taking care of this type and fixing a problem, such as saving her. It plays into the protective and provider instincts of a man.

There is playfulness as they exchange light questions and lots of eye contact. She expresses her concern for him by not wanting to violate his personal space. But notice what happens next: she challenges him at the same time, giving him a glimpse of how she will be in his life.

Here is the magic moment: She says, "My guy will know how to tie his own tie," while reaching out to touch and fix his tie. This challenges him to think or say to himself, *Yes, I can be your guy.*

Why? **Men like to win.** Therefore, it challenges him to respond by saying, "It's a clip-on," which suggests that, if it were a real one, *I would know how to tie it and therefore, can be your guy.*

Do you see how that worked?

She got him thinking about being her guy by challenging him with the comment that he couldn't be, because he didn't know how to tie a tie. He accepts the challenge, affirming, in essence, that he can be her guy because he can tie a real one, but this is just a clip on.

She also expresses herself in a way to say that she accepts him just as he is without negative judgment and can be an enhancement to his life and career. Can you see how David is processing these moments? His mouth is open with shock while he is thinking, *Who is this amazing woman?*

Then she asks him, "Is your campaign over?" with such delicate concern and sensitivity.

You see, guys always try to make things better than they appear, and he responds in that manner.

She pampers and challenges him again. Notice her body language that sends the signal: "You can be authentic with me because I accept you as you are and see the good in you."

After David says "I'm looking forward to having some time to myself," Elise has an excellent, soft, comeback: "I don't buy it, I think you love it," while touching him again. She was letting him know that "I accept what you do, I see you, and I am interested."

How does David respond? He asks her, *"Do I know you?"* Then every question and comeback is a challenge for him to learn more about her, to see her in his future, and in essence to chase her.

He says "Yeah, I guess I could have been more convincing." and she smiles and says, "OK, You don't have to worry about being convincing until the next election." This is her saying I'm convinced of your worthiness.

Then he asks, "Are you a registered New York voter?"

She responds softly by make eye contact and leaning forward, building more attraction, "Do I sound like I am?"

This is a challenge to learn more, and he cannot resist but to kiss her.

Now, your encounter, I'm sure, will be different and may be planned, but it should have the same feel. Notice that Elise asked David NO interview questions. There was only eye contact, authenticity, and care that built the chemistry and attraction between them.

This is how you should create the conditions in your dating

environment. I wanted to provide a glimpse by sharing this video clip so you can see firsthand how it can be done. In your presence a man should feel validated for his choices, challenged to be his best, and there should be enough playfulness for comfort. This should be your goal.

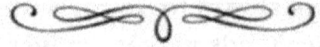

A New Normal: Women Breadwinners

Women earned more than men in almost a quarter of U.S. households in 2011, compared to only six percent in 1960, according to the Pew Research Center study, *Breadwinner Moms* (May 29, 2013). In the African-American community it is even higher. But if you factor in men who are divorced and/or pay child support, the numbers will explode.

What does this mean for men? Actually, Nothing! Maybe I should say that men NOW have more time to spend with their children than before when they were the top earners. This is a good thing.

What should change? How men and women perceive money in a relationship. All I can say is "wake up" because times have changed and women breadwinners and two-income households are here to stay.

This is the new normal in Christian men:

- Good: one with a job and can take care of himself.
- Rare: Can pay all the bills while you stay home.
- Normal: one with an income that can add to yours
- Still a good catch: A working, divorced man living with a roommate due to child support payments. .

If you are seeking a man who makes more than you, has more education, can take care of you financially (paying all of the bills), then you may be UNMARRIED for the rest of your life. HE is NOW pretty much obsolete, even in the church, and especially in the minority community. **What you will find is a man who can add to the household.** If the two of you can put your money together, you can build a quality life with such a man.

Another Point: Professionals are seeking to marry professionals (e.g. medical doctors). Yes, over ninety percent (90%) of Christian professional men are seeking to marry Christian women within the same profession. Why? Surprisingly, it's because of the high divorce rates (yes, even in the church). You see, if you are NOT a professional and have kids with him, he will have to pay you a lot more in alimony than if you also have a professional salary. Yes! A Christian man, looking for an "until-death-do-us-part" marriage, is still preparing for the possibility of divorce. So don't buy into those reality shows matching poor women with wealthy men. It rarely happens!

Don't let a quality Christian man with a job walk away simply because of his living arrangement. For example, he lives in an apartment and drives a pickup truck; you drive an Infinity vehicle and own a home. Don't say, "I know God wouldn't give me him because it's not the desire of my heart." That reasoning will keep you unmarried. Also, he may have less income, but still could be just the man God has for you to fit perfectly into your life. If you blink you will miss him **because of YOUR relationship with money!**

If you can learn to lose that relationship with money, your chance of picking up a quality man in the church jumps up almost one hundred percent. Don't get me wrong, money is important, but how much he earns should NOT factor into your decision. It should be more about how he manages what he has: values and his relationship with God.

Financial Struggles

Philippians 4:19 NLT: *And this same God who takes care of me will supply all your needs from his glorious riches, which have been given to us in Christ Jesus.*

As I've stated before, times have changed. To add to it, our global economic reset has created huge issues within the dating scene. So much more than you can imagine. We are coming out of it slowly, but have a ways to go. Here is a secret for you: many professionals are struggling too. They have huge student loans and many feel pressure to appear to live at a certain financial standard. For example, they must have the best seats at concerts, an acceptable home in a classy area, and a car that's appropriate to their title.

Those most affected by the economy are men. What does this mean? You have great men with character struggling financially. How does this affect dating? It is more about how men feel compared to others, and most of the time it is about money. Again, no man wants to be around a woman who creates an environment that makes him feel like a failure.

What should you do? You must be concerned about his wallet. Know that he is not a free loader. He has respect. He has character. He is just going through a financial setback and is not able to do some of the things he desires, such as taking you to special restaurants, going out every weekend, going to that concert. Also the higher gas prices could interrupt his frequent visits and outings.

Keep in mind that a man will be silent about his financial situation because he is proud and may be afraid of how you will view him. However, some will share this information outright. Become creative when you are dating. Let him know that it doesn't require a lot to have fun. The goal is to spend more time and enjoy each other while growing.

Do not complain about how often you see a man if he lives across town and is underemployed. Go see him or meet him in his area if possible. If you are accustomed to men doing all the spending, you may be in for a shock nowadays. This will definitely limit your dating options. Your complaining will run him away because it will make him feel as if he is not able to make you happy. Thus, he will feel like a failure, and all sense of attraction will be lost.

There has to be shared financial responsibility during this time. Those who understand this will win in the end. Remember, he is the cream of the crop in character and not a free loader, but just a man struggling financially at this point in his life. Just think where your relationship could go with your total support.

Text this man. Tell him how much you appreciate him. Let him know what he does to make you happy. Encourage him. Put a smile on his face. He will get over this situation and will be so thankful he had you.

A MAN OF GOD *is Still* A MAN

Grown Son Living at Home

1 Corinthians 13:11 NLT: *When I was a child, I spoke and thought and reasoned as a child. But when I grew up, I put away childish things.*

Another huge problem in relationships, and why some men of God will not marry a woman, is when she has her grown son living at home without any obvious reasons. This makes it very difficult to build or maintain the attraction between you. Bringing another man into the house usually causes testosterone clashes and disruptive problems in the house. The woman is placed in a position of not being able to have the love of her life while also pleasing her son. Times are tough and kids are having difficulties getting out of their parents' basement. Men also know this.

What I've noticed in my research is that women with a grown son(s) living at home are not able to secure a new relationship-worthy man, especially if that son is not doing anything with his life or has a troubled history. Don't get me wrong, you can get a man, but most of the time he may not fit your preferred standards. Also, in some cultures it's OK to have a grown son living with you if sharing expenses.

What I am saying is that more promising relationships have dissolved because of this situation—more than you think; it is at least a top-ten problem. It has always been a deal-breaker. Men in my research have always had a problem with this matter and usually will not marry a woman in this situation. He may go out with her a few times, but a lasting relationship never develops as long as there are grown children, especially men, living with her.

Here are my questions for you:
1. If you want a man in your life, how will you deal with your grown son?
2. Why is your grown son living with you anyway? Also, do you allow him to call the shots? Is he troubled?
3. What role do you want a new mate to have in your home with your grown son?
4. Do you make excuses for your son as to why he is getting into trouble, not working, or not contributing?
5. Is he going to school and contributing in other ways?

Women of faith, the only thing I can say is that in my research men overall just do not like this matter. This is why so many women with a grown, able-bodied, son living at home have difficulties getting a man of God to marry them.

Moms with Young Children

Moms with young children, let me say first, "NEVER see or think of your children as baggage!" Even if you are currently unattached, raising them independently, children will NOT weigh you down in your efforts to attract and keep a man of God.

I know men who actually seek a woman with children. They are motivated by many reasons. Some love motherhood and find it sexy, others prefer the freedom of being with a woman who has other responsibilities, and, of course, there are those who enjoy children but may not be able to have kids of their own. There are also men who have been hurt by women cheating on them and find that a mom with children is less likely to have various men coming in and out of her home. Whatever the reason, just know that, if it works for him and his lifestyle, he will want a woman with children.

On the other hand, I do not deny that young children can pose some issues for you. It destroys the attraction for some men, so they will not consider you for a relationship. Many will never explain why, but I will list the reasons here.

First, let me say that I have two names for these types of moms. You can be a "**single mom**" or a "**solo mom**." What's the difference? Well, a single mom will have the child's father in her life, while a solo mom will not. He could be a deadbeat, estranged, or maybe dead. Yes, it can make a difference to a man what type of mom category you fit into and how big of a headache he will encounter with them in your life.

Here are ten (10) reasons men leave or won't consider a woman with young children. You will be able to avoid some of them, but not others.

1. **"I Can't Find a Babysitter!"** Women will use this as an excuse to get out of a date with a man, or they may legitimately not be able to find a babysitter. In either case, it isn't the man's problem, and you shouldn't ask him to deal with it.

2. **Baby's Daddy.** When a man is dealing with a woman and getting to know her, he shouldn't have to deal with the baby's father. Some men can't get over the fact that their ex has moved on. Before he was an inattentive jerk and didn't care about her. Now that another man has entered the picture, he wants to be the ideal "Father-of-the-Year" nominee. Sometimes the man starts stalking her and wants to fight the new boyfriend.

Even if the woman and her ex are on good terms, the man feels as if he can always crash any gathering. He knows her. He knows what she wants to hear and what makes her happy. The next thing you know you are having this conversation, "I've decided to try and make it work with the baby's dad."

Therefore, some men feel that the best way to avoid this situation is to avoid single moms, as opposed to solo moms.

3. **Rent-a-Daddy.** "Can you be a father to my son?" Women with children are often searching for a role model for their sons. This is OK. A good man will be into that. Do you just want a man because of your son or daughter?

4. **The Kids Are Out of Control!** Men understand that a woman does not want to bring a man around her kids too fast, but there are times when she cannot go out, so she invites him over to her place. He arrives to find the kids are out of control and still up. He sees that she is not good at managing her kid's bedtime, which he translates into her NOT being a good manager of the home. This can make him lose interest.

5. **"You're NOT My Dad!"** A man starts seeing a woman

seriously. He notices that her children have behavior issues, throwing or breaking things and not being very respectful to adults. If he sees one of the kids doing something dangerous and attempts to protect him or her, a resentful child will shout, "You can't tell me what to do! You're not my dad!" A man will leave if you are not able to manage your children. It does NOT build attraction.

6. **Seducing: Trying to Get Pregnant!** Yes, unfortunately, women in the church do sometimes want to get pregnant, hoping to force marriage to prevent embarrassment. Some men believe that there are women in the church who will prey on men of God with status and attempt to make them weak by seducing them. If a man weakens, she will attempt to get pregnant by him in order to pay for her other children or to gain significance or status for herself.

This is bad thinking, because she never does gain any status. In some cases, if his money is earned via the church, she loses in the financial category, too, because it destroys his ministry, family, or status, too. This is sad, but happens more than you think.

7. **Bad Judge of Character?** If a woman got pregnant by a grossly irresponsible man who has been this all of his life, the new man in her life will leave. He can see that she is a bad judge of character and knows there could be issues in the future. He would rather that the father be irresponsible in the area of relationships, rather than in life (the ability to earn a living and be a good dad.

8. **Unnecessary Expenditures.** Eventually your potential will get to meet the kid(s). Soon those dates turn into family outings. Instead of paying for two people, he's paying for three or more. When this happens too fast, it becomes difficult to maintain the attraction and he will probably leave soon after.

9. **Tag! You're It.** There has been a lot of press about women in various states suing for child support from men who are NOT the child's biological parent. If she is applying for public assistance such as welfare and other financial programs, then the state may pursue whoever was supporting them most recently. If that is you, and the case goes to court, the key question from the court is often, "What

did you tell the child?"

Therefore, the best way to AVOID getting into this situation is to ALWAYS be honest with the child. Either you ARE the parent, or you are not. If this is a concern, I encourage you to consult a lawyer in your state. If researching on the internet, make sure you use professional legal sources. If you do tell the child you are its daddy, and the child has been calling you daddy, a court may find you liable for the child's support. You may find yourself paying the consequences.

10. **Birth Damage.** Keep in mind that you should never be ashamed of your body, because men hate this more. However, pregnancy can leave stretch marks, saggy breasts, and scars, what some men call "birth trauma." This is unavoidable and can be minimized by how you dress and groom yourself. It is more obvious in women who do not take care of themselves after birth. Just know that young men and older men who are into fitness may have issues with this. However, not everyone.

But I repeat: "NEVER see or think of your children as baggage!" Use the above list to help you recognize those you can avoid doing in your relationships and to distinguish which men are likely to marry a woman with young children and which are not.

Girlfriend Peer Pressure

Proverbs 13:20 NLT: *Walk with the wise and become wise; associate with fools and get in trouble.*

There is no denying the strength of women. Women are asked to be everything to everyone, but at the same time they face pressure from within their own sisterhood. The goal of this pressure is not the same for all women. In some communities it may be pressure to marry well and settle down; in others it is to excel in school and choose a professional occupation; and for some it is social—to be popular and fit in. Whatever the pressure, it is one reason why many women walk around depressed and do not know it.

"Girlfriend peer pressure," the stress that women put on each other, contributes greatly to the stress women feel and to the stress they can place on a man. Attraction cannot grow or be maintained when this happens, and a man of God will leave eventually or not pursue a relationship under such conditions.

Yes, your girlfriends can raise doubts and cause you to override your own intuition and beliefs in order to fit in with them and your home culture—whatever it is.

Let's say that you run with a group of girlfriends who want it all: fashionable clothes, big house, luxury cars, great man with status, and the whole works. The pressure coming from them is to find a man who can give you this. How can these friends cause a man-of-interest to leave you?

Your girlfriend will be watching out for you, making sure you get what she considers best for you. Right in front of him, she'll ask, "What did he give you for your birthday?"

You show her the watch he gave you, a thoughtful gift because you really like it; it's much better than the one you had.

Disapproving, she blurts out, "A watch? What else? What about some earrings or a trip? Is this all? Just the watch?"

If you don't straighten her out directly, and in front of him, he can become embarrassed and could leave you.

 Don't allow your girlfriends or family members to put uncomfortable pressure on you or your husband or love interest. Make him aware of any with such tendencies—before he meets them!

A MAN OF GOD *is* *Still* A MAN

Jealous Friends

I Corinthians 15:33 NLT: *Don't be fooled by those who say such things, for "bad company corrupts good character."*

The information to follow about jealous friends could make the difference between achieving that magical relationship or not. First I want to start off by telling you a quick story.

Steve from an upscale church in the city met this nice lady Kelly who was attractive, but somewhat of a plain Jodie—although it didn't matter to him because he loved her mind, love for God, and sincerity. He asked her out for lunch one day. It was a very nice date, and they both decided to see each other again.

The next date there was a dressy-casual function at which he got a chance to meet all of Kelly's girlfriends, a few family members, and many of her associates. Guess what? She changed right before his eyes. He was wondering what happened to this sincere woman of God who had piqued his interest.

Unbeknownst to him, a pack of four girlfriends and two female family members were asking her questions about him because he was so much higher in status than men she had gone out with before, and because he appeared better than the men with her friends. What was his type? He had a corporate look with a clean-cut style. Her friends were teasing hard, while suggesting that he was probably a church predator not living by the same Christian standards as they are. They spoke as if she did not deserve him and would be taken advantage of.

Steve noticed that Kelly started to make all types of demands on him and began asking crazy questions. She said things like, "Go get this for me. I need this. Aren't you going to do this or that? Are you a church playboy?" and "What do you want from me?"

It took him aback at first, but he realized what was happening. He pulled her aside and said, "What is the problem here?" Kelly said that she had received feedback from her friends. They thought that Steve was nice, but not her type, and that she would get hurt dealing with him. He asked her what she felt when they were out before and speaking on the phone. She replied, "Well, very special; and it was sooooo exciting."

So, Ladies, can you see what happened here? We had two people very interested in each other, and it all ended because of peers. She needed the approval of her friends, and it was over just like that.

Just think about this: She wanted an attentive, clean-cut-style man. She met a clean-cut-style man! But then she wanted the approval of her friends. Ladies, this may never happen.

You see, your friends and some family members may say they want the best for you, but if you bring home a man who they think is better in any way than what they currently have or don't have, it is possible that they will get jealous and attempt to sabotage your relationship.

Now let's talk about Steve's actions compared to her friends' men. By the way, three did not have one; the others had dates. Steve was a very attentive gentleman. He pulled her chair out for her, stood when she was leaving, helped her take off her coat, asked if she would like some refreshments, and did all the things that good men (relationship-worthy men) do. In contrast, the men with those ladies were not attentive at all.

Now, note this: the friends who were the most aggressive to Kelly about Steve did not have a date.

I can also tell you several stories regarding women who are very opinionated about men. They always make references to what they want or should get from a man instead of trying to be a good mate themselves. This is why most do not have a man and are always hanging around other women without men. You see, misery loves company.

When I share this story with women they often say, "I know females who are like this, but they are not the ones I hang out with." Here is my question: "Are you sure?"

My goal is to help you meet and keep a relationship-worthy, godly man. If you want a real relationship-type man, your friends, and—yes—some family, may not support you if they do not have the same. It is time to make a choice: him vs them. You will still love them and hang out, but girl, get your husband!

Just know that sometimes even your close sisters in the church, or family members, can be jealous of your relationship and unconsciously attempt to sabotage it.

PHILEMON

Jesus Is Not Your Boyfriend

John 13:35 NLT: *Your love for one another will prove to the world that you are my disciples."*

Do you know who says they are married to Christ? Nuns do. One nun actually made this statement: "It was so exciting, so romantic, to walk down the aisle in my white gown as a bride of Christ and come back as a nun."

How do men see nuns? One of the first prerequisites for becoming a Christian nun is to be unmarried. I discovered something really interesting. Unattached men of God often avoid women who say, "I'm dating Jesus." Or, they may use the phrase "Jesus is my man [or boyfriend or husband]."

You may hear these terms even across the pulpit by pastors who can get a good reaction by using them. However, on an unconscious level, some men who hear women say such things may think of nuns: someone who is married to the church and doesn't want a mate. Others may simply think these women will not make good wives.

I've asked several single men of God who had recently selected a wife about this. All had been seeking a virtuous, Christian or saved woman. I asked if they had considered a certain woman who seemed to match what they wanted, but who was using those phrases.

I said, "She is in love with Christ."

They responded, "Too in love. She acts as if she is dating Him and may be too far out there for my needs. She will be at prayer service when I may need her home."

They had each been seeking a wife, but did NOT want one who walks around with her head in the clouds romantically worshipping Jesus. One said, "It seems that this type of woman will bring Him into our bedroom by calling out his name in an intimate moment. How weird!"

Making statements like "I have a date with Jesus" or "Jesus is my man or boyfriend" are metaphors that could be hurting women of God who seek a romantic relationship with a man. These love songs to Christ, as if he is their romantic partner, are dangerous because Christ is not someone they are having a romantic relationship with.

He died to set ALL free, to remove our sins, to suffer our punishment, and to purchase our salvation. Saying he is your boyfriend, man, or husband, even if you are using this as a metaphor, misses the mark of what God designed marriage for.

Yes, these are just sayings, and you are using them until you get a man, but they could be getting in the way of your finding love. This is because it creates confusion. He wants to be your man, and for you both to follow Jesus' principles together. He is not interested in having his woman say that someone else, even Jesus, is her man and wouldn't want to risk getting involved with one who does say that.

Language is important and the words we use affect our lives. If you ever expect to get a husband, it is best that you stop saying that Jesus is your boyfriend.

Dating and Waiting?

1 Corinthians 6:18-20 NLT: *Run from sexual sin! No other sin so clearly affects the body as this one does. For sexual immorality is a sin against your own body. Don't you realize that your body is the temple of the Holy Spirit, who lives in you and was given to you by God? You do not belong to yourself, for God bought you with a high price. So you must honor God with your body.*

Let me ask, are you part of the dating and waiting for marriage movement? Part of a support group just for waiters? Scripture is clear: **Run from sexual sin!** (1 Corinthians 6:18 NLT) I am addressing this issue again in this chapter on love hints, because so many are NOT following Scripture and

NO ONE IS TALKING about it!

Often, I learn of research showing that married couples actually have better sex and divorce less often when they wait. But at the same time, people are marrying later and later, and research shows that many, who were waiting when younger, have actually had premarital sex by the time they do marry.

This is an explosive topic with lots of questions surrounding the subject. How many of us are openly discussing this? How many of us believe that couples really are waiting? Is it possible for researchers to get straight answers from them for research purposes? Think about this, and then listen for the gossip in your church about who's having sex with whom.

If you are asking what my take is, it is just an honest one: If a man or woman's goal is to stay connected to their faith, obeying the Word, they will refrain from having sex out of wedlock. But are men and women doing this? NO ONE KNOWS!!

First, as I often say: "Belief is powerful. Whatever we believe, our brain will seek to find evidence to support." That said, there are a host of **celibacy support groups** on social media encouraging people to wait on marriage before having sex and showing celebrity couples who did wait. I support these groups and their goal. But can I be honest about what I see? NO one has any true numbers on this subject. It is really a guessing game.

My Own Study: What did I do? I spoke personally, casually, with hundreds of men in many different church congregations. Overall, I found many married men who admitted to not having waited or to "slipping up" from time-to-time before they married. Among unmarried men currently telling people that they are waiting I found many who also admit to "slipping up" from time to time.

I asked these men what they do to control their natural, biological urges. Many said they are masturbating or using toys just to maintain testimony that they have not touched a woman since being saved. Just know that it is NOT everyone.

What does this tell us? People in the church are not waiting as some believe. Although against Scripture, it IS occurring and we have to be honest about that.

This section is not about pounding those having weakness in this area of their life. I know that they already suffer tremendously with guilt. Rather than preach to you about right or wrong, I will just provide some insights and suggestions for those of you who ARE truly waiting.

DO NOT HAVE ANY ATTACHMENTS TO MARRIAGE!

Does this surprise you? This means that if you are NOT having sex before marriage, maintain your standard. At the same time, detach yourself from the results of this stand. Do not look for support to provide you with evidence that others who waited did, eventually, get married. Stop going to websites searching for evidence and joining their support groups about how many waiters are now successfully married. This only makes you more attached to the outcome, which only leads to discouragement and depression.

Instead, remember 2 Timothy 2:22 NLT: **Run from anything that stimulates youthful lusts. Instead, pursue righteous living, faithfulness, love, and peace. Enjoy the companionship of those who call on the Lord with pure hearts.**

Perhaps you can find or create your own peer group that encourages you to maintain your walk with God and provides members with relationship skills while waiting.

I know women approaching forty who are still waiting to be married and have no kids. Many have friends who did NOT wait, but are now married with children. The question is, was it because they did not wait? I just don't know and am **NOT looking** for any evidence.

Many of the women in the church, who ask me for dating advice, desperately seeking help, are women in their late thirties or early forties. They have waited and waited and are now leaving the church discouraged, frustrated, resentful, and even angry because nothing is happening for them, while their friends—who they believe are NOT living right—are getting married.

Do you want to know my response to their situation and questions? Why where you waiting? To serve God's principle? Or do you falsely believe that you are entitled to a husband because you waited?

Waiting should be your standard. If you do get married, great! If you don't, it wasn't for you. It should be that simple without any frustrations or resentment. God did NOT let you down. You let yourself down by being attached to something that he never promised and by leaving it all up to Him.

This may NOT be what you wanted to hear, but it is honest: DO NOT GIVE UP! You women who are waiting CAN increase your chances of attracting a man. God wants to give you the desires of your heart, but He won't choose for you. You do the choosing. Therefore, you have to be prepared to make the right choice. Be proactive, developing skills to choose wisely and to create the relationship you desire. This book has all the tools you need to get started. Yes, at any age.

Another Perspective on Fornication

2 Timothy 2:22 NLT: *Run from anything that stimulates youthful lusts. Instead, pursue righteous living, faithfulness, love, and peace. Enjoy the companionship of those who call on the Lord with pure hearts.*

There are universal laws established by God that work the same way, every time, regardless of how one judges the outcome. For example, when a male's semen fertilizes a female's egg, she will become pregnant—even if she is 13 and was raped. This is a biological function. The same reaction occurs with individuals having sex within a marriage or via fornication. What happens on a biological level is known as **the Law of Attachment**.

This is what I share with young people, especially girls, about the principle of fornication, rather than piling on scriptures that will blow right over their heads. They can grasp this concept and it gives them something more to think about.

You see, if you have continuous sexual contact with a person, regardless of whether or NOT they are your husband or wife, and if you have an orgasm which intensifies the effect, biological hormones will kick in, and you can become attached to a person who is NOT right for you.

When such an attachment occurs with someone, even the wrong person, and the relationship comes to an end, the sense of loss can be overwhelming. You will have feelings of uncertainty, fear, and depression. This is why someone will continue to go back to a toxic relationship, even a physically abusive one.

For me, this explains the ultimate intent and the main purpose for why engaging in the act of fornication is defying the body.

1 Corinthians 6:18-20 NLT: **Run from sexual sin! No other sin so clearly affects the body as this one does. For sexual immorality is a sin against your own body. Don't you realize that your body is the temple of the Holy Spirit, who lives in you and was given to you by God? You do not belong to yourself, for God bought you with a high price. So you must honor God with your body.**

Fornicating is defying the body because you will be using God's biological laws for attachment to work against your best interest. These hormones are created in all of us and are called oxytocin and vasopressin.

You see, the way couples bond enough to have and raise children is instinctive, part of the human genetic code. Along with eating and sleeping, bonding is a basic human need. Without such bonding our species would not survive.

Oxytocin is a powerful hormone released by men and women during orgasm. It deepens the feelings of attachment and makes couples feel much closer to one another after they have had sex. The more sex a couple has, the deeper their bond becomes.

Oxytocin is also released during childbirth, bonding a mother to her newborn. This hormone has also been shown to increase in the bloodstream of people under stress, which encourages people, even people of God, to seek out physical contact with others.

Vasopressin is another important hormone released after sex. It works with your kidneys to control thirst, but has also been found to affect long-term commitment in a relationship. Its role in attachment was discovered when scientists looked at the prairie vole. Like humans, voles bond and form attachments. When male prairie voles were given a drug that suppresses the effect of vasopressin, the bond with their partner declined immediately and they lost their devotion and failed to protect their partner from new admirers.

To sum this up for you clearly, just know that sleeping around will weaken your ability to bond. You see, the chemicals that God created for bonding are like adhesive tape: their power is weakened when one has multiple sexual partners. Therefore, when it comes time to actually permanently bond in a marriage, the ability to do so is impaired. Your brain has learned not to accept that which is so important to a marriage: the ability to have a deep emotional connection. This is the primary reason why virgins are less likely to divorce than those who had premarital sex.

There is research to back this up. A long-term study by the Dunedin Multidisciplinary Health and Development Research Unit has been tracking over one thousand children for over forty years. Their findings are quite interesting. In both men and women, they discovered that the odds of developing substance dependence increased virtually in line with the number of sex partners they had. Yes, substance abuse, such as alcohol and drugs. Those in the study started drinking alcohol to cope with the feelings of loneliness and despair that paved the way for stronger drugs. The study concludes that casual sexual relationships present risk factors, inhibiting a person's ability to find emotional fulfillment.

I usually share this with women who tell me that they have the ability to have just casual sex with a guy and can break it off without incident. My own experience coaching these women supports the Dunedin research: most had difficulties in being fulfilled in any relationship and often made poor choices in selecting a partner for marriage.

Even women I know who claimed to love their husband and feel attached to him, but had an extramarital affair, were not virgins when married; many had had multiple sexual partners in their lifetime. Just know that casual sex presents risk factors.

Many of you reading this book are people who love God, but you still struggle in the area of fornication. You haven't managed to resist acting on the desire to have sex. Just know that the desire is natural, although against Scripture. Understanding the principle of attachment may be the leverage you need for restraint.

This section is here to provide knowledge about the body, not to create excuses. With this additional information, one will have the ability to make informed decisions.

PHILEMON

"I love you. You annoy me at times more than I ever thought possible. But I want to spend every irritating minute with you. I thank God for you!"

A MAN OF GOD *is* *Still* A MAN

Final Remarks

Love is patient and kind.
Love is not jealous or boastful or proud or rude.
It does not demand its own way.
It is not irritable, and it keeps
no record of being wronged.
It does not rejoice about injustice
but rejoices whenever the truth wins out.
Love never gives up,
never loses faith,
is always hopeful,
and endures through every circumstance.

1 Corinthians 13:4-7 NLT

Where Now?

You just read what a huge sampling of men of God have said about what they want in a relationship, why they picked one woman over another, and why they left a relationship.

Yes, some may believe this is too much for a woman to handle. Just remember, good treatment of your husband or future one should be by his standards, not yours.

Many of the topics within this book address issues that can destroy a marriage or relationship leading to marriage; however it is NOT just the issues themselves that will cause its destruction. Negative things will happen. Marriages and relationships are more likely to be destroyed when those negative things take up permanent residence within that marriage. It is about whether your mate can or cannot deal with your flaws. You see, if criticism, defensiveness, or disrespect is the norm in that marriage, these are predictors that a marriage will not last or will become an empty shell.

Here is something to consider. My goal throughout this book has been to help you feel safe enough in your relationship to become vulnerable because, without this, a man will not feel good in your presence. This is the key to a lasting relationship: the willingness to be vulnerable. Remember, those in a relationship are allies not opponents.

He will not want to waste his time being blamed for your past. As soon as you start that, he will move on fast. What you fear the most (being vulnerable) is actually the only way to find true love.

Women ask me all the time, "When is it safe to let down my guards?"

My response has always been the same: "When he says that you are the one, proposes marriage, and a date is set."

Just keep in mind that being too guarded can hurt extremely in the getting-to-know-you process. It's okay to be cautious, but also be fun and loving and spiritual. Remember that the un-guarded you may not be to his liking if you change suddenly. So remain consistent after dropping your guard.

Know that there are men living holy and faithful to God's Word, but this does NOT mean they are to be placed on a pedestal. They will make mistakes, often unknowingly or because they lack relationship skills. The mistakes they make will not be where these men of God live at their core. They are sincere and just want to do God's will and purpose for their lives. They love God and the life of living holy. I honor these men.

Please be aware that these men are still men, too. They react to the same issues in their marriages and relationships that face any other man in society. Their faith in God keeps them grounded, but it doesn't make them different from other men.

My goal in writing this book is to give you women of God a glimpse into what is actually occurring in the church today as men and women seek life-long, Christian, marital relationships. As a coach I have daily contact with men and women of God seeking advice, asking questions, and sharing what's going on in their personal relationships. Through them I see first-hand that the key to fulfilling their goal is to realize that a man of God *is still* a man. I want to share this insight with a broader audience, giving you a glimpse into the natural minds of men of God--only because this is what you as a woman will have to deal with in a relationship.

I have to admit that I found it confusing at first, seeing some of these relationships. How couples are openly living their lives NOT according to Scripture, but at the same time acting as if they do. For example, they attend church faithfully, pay tithes and give offerings, praise God openly, read their Bibles, post only spiritual messages on social media, spend lots of time at church, and seemingly live a sin-free life. However, they are privately living together or having sex regularly, even having kids together outside of wedlock, as if this is acceptable.

They will NOT go to spiritual counselors, but find a secular one to address issues in their relationship. It is as if the spiritual part of their lives should be ignored.

"What is your take when one is out of alignment with Scripture when it comes to a relationship?" is usually my first question to such couples to understand where they are now.

I will often get, "We know it is wrong, but we are NOT there yet. God knows our heart is to serve him. Plus we are planning to get married." These couples often do get married and seemingly have a great marriage.

Stating my beliefs and convictions would NOT have served them. As a coach I learned quickly that **my goal is to help them fill the gap from where they are to where they want to be in their relationship.**

This is why this book is so important. It is not condoning or judging those living out of alignment with God's Word. It is addressing issues for all types of relationships within the church, especially the private ones.

Homework?

What can you be doing now that you've finished reading *A Man of God Is Still a Man*? Here are some suggestions.

First, use the tips conveniently compiled at the back of the book for your review. Then, read and even re-read this book, discovering ways to apply what is offered here to your life and to your relationships. This book is also designed to be a reference tool for you to use from now on, as you seek, find, maintain, and/or improve your own marital relationship with a man of God.

Secondly, you may begin using the relationship evaluation forms that follow. The women I coach find them helpful for applying the knowledge given here to their specific situations. One is for looking within yourself; the other is for evaluating a current or potential love match with a man of God. Again, these are designed as long-term reference tools for you to use whenever your relationship does not seem to be going as well as you would like.

Thirdly, as you apply the information and the techniques provided here to your life, building more effective relationship skills, you will probably find you need help in relating it to your life situations and to go beyond what I have been able to include here.

For this, I encourage you to consider professional relationship coaching, either in person or from your home via phone. There are research-based principles you can learn that will prevent you from making destructive mistakes and may possibly rescue a struggling marriage or relationship. You will get to benefit greatly from those Christian couples who were not able to save their marriage and learned from their failures.

And finally, whatever you do, I hope and pray you are able to establish a great relationship and would love to hear your comments and feedback. If you are looking for personal coaching, I would love to assist in helping you create the love you deserve.

Just go to the website www.philemon.guru to communicate with me, read and participate in my blog, and to sign up for coaching or online workshops.

Intimate Relationships: How to Evaluate?

I am including two forms here for you to use in evaluating a current or potential marital relationship. Nowadays it is so easy for one to get in and out of marriages just because of uneasiness. You can simply say "I'm unhappy" and leave.

Even when you both love God, to establish a relationship you must have common interests too. You are God's child, but parents can raise kids the exact same way, and there will still be major differences between each one. Therefore, as a child of God, you may have a different viewpoint, different likes and dislikes, from a current or potential mate.

I find it disheartening when Christians accuse one another of NOT holding to God's standards when these clashes are actually about their differences. During disputes I often hear, "They are supposed to love God and are acting like this or that!" As I stated at the beginning of this book, wisdom is the ability to recognize differences, and it is essential within relationships.

Differences can be threatening to the relationship—if one allows them to be. I'm referring to the little annoying things that simply bug you. For a successful relationship learn how to be OK with differences. If you don't give your mate permission to be different, expect huge problems within your relationship.

Many try to resolve differences by compromising and I know this appears to work, but not in every area of a relationship. As I stated in "Compromising and Dysfunctional Needs" (Chapter Four), I've learned that, **if a compromise does not meet the needs** of an individual, even if one believes it is a fair agreement, the relationship is still doomed long term. Also, I've learned that compromising only works well when dealing with strategic issues within a relationship, like housework, but not really anywhere else. Evaluations are a valuable tool in to map out where you are in your relationship in order to make informed decisions.

Your Needs?

If in a relationship, how do you feel about it? If not, what are you seeking? Before making a move, evaluate where you are by looking within and asking yourself some basic questions. **As you recognize and acknowledge your needs, you create a pathway toward getting those needs met.**

Knowing what you need in a marital relationship doesn't ensure that you'll get those needs met. That takes good, effective, consistent communication and a partner willing to hear and be responsive to you. But it is still the first step in getting those needs met and thereby being happy in your relationship.

For example, if you have a need to be the most important part of your husband's life, then believing that he is giving more importance to anyone or anything else can create a huge loss of connection. You will find yourself feeling unloved and there will be a huge break in trust and respect between you. I've learned that this feeling is often a misconception. In this moment your husband is probably a victim of the demands in his life. The key is to communicate your feelings directly. But first, do your research, just like I do. The two forms at the end of this section will help you.

The Right Match?

If you know enough to complete the second form, "Is He the Right Match?" the answers to these questions will show how well-matched you are. Suppose you do NOT know enough about him yet to answer the questions about his needs? If you don't know, then the relationship is not far enough along for you to be evaluating it. No need to ask questions. It's time to do your research.

Begin by focusing on how you are together. Are you becoming friends? Do you enjoy one another's company? Pay attention to needs—become familiar with your needs and with basic human needs and see what you can figure out—without ever asking him. He probably doesn't have a clue anyway. He wouldn't know how to answer such questions. I find women are much more likely to be able to verbalize their needs.

This is why I ask you to figure out what you need and if he can provide or learn to provide that for you. Because if he can't, then **it won't matter what his needs are**. You will find a lot more tips throughout this book. The main way to "learn your man" is simply by taking an interest in him, by listening when he talks, and observing him with his friends and family. As you develop a friendship and integrate into his life, you will discover that he can meet your needs and that you are meeting his.

As I stated at the beginning, God never chooses your mate for you. He gives you complete responsibility, but He helps you. He has given you a powerful brain to make decisions, His word to regulate those decisions, the Holy Spirit to guide you, and His anointing for discernment.

Having a successful marriage is the result of applying knowledge. Notice I said "applying." Knowledge can empower you, but only becomes powerful when it is applied. This is how to evaluate and decide if a man of God is right for you.

Whenever you want to evaluate a current or potential marital relationship, use the following two forms: "My Relationship Needs?" and "Is He the Right Match for Me?"

Evaluation Forms:

How to Use These Forms?

Use these forms DISCRETELY!! Consider them like your secret, personal journal. In fact, many people who really want to understand themselves find that keeping a daily journal helps. Do not share these forms with him. And, most certainly, do not pull them out and begin interrogating him!

These forms can be your secret de-coder to discover what he REALLY wants in the woman he cannot live without.

My Relationship Needs?

1. What are my needs in a marital relationship?
2. Which of these needs are currently missing?
3. Is there a way for me to meet these needs within myself?
4. How important do I feel in this relationship?

To help you answer these questions, I am including a wonderful self-discovery tool adapted from Dr. Philip C. McGraw, *The Relationship Rescue Workbook* and from his website www.drphil.com.

I have these needs *(mark all that apply)*:

- ☐ To feel and be told that I am loved
- ☐ To feel I belong to and with him
- ☐ To feel respected as an individual
- ☐ To feel valued for more than tasks I perform
- ☐ To feel I am a priority in his life
- ☐ To feel special, more important than everything else in his life
- ☐ To feel he is proud to be with me
- ☐ To feel I am and will be forgiven for mistakes
- ☐ To feel accepted—flaws and all
- ☐ To feel we are close and trusted friends
- ☐ To feel desired
- ☐ To feel appreciated as I am and for what I do
- ☐ To feel passion between us
- ☐ To feel emotionally connected with him
- ☐ To be touched, caressed, held, or hugged
- ☐ To be kissed

A MAN OF GOD *is Still* A MAN

- ☐ To feel I am welcome in his personal space
- ☐ To be physically welcomed by him
- ☐ For tenderness
- ☐ For a satisfying and rewarding sexual life
- ☐ To feel that my spiritual values and needs are supported and respected
- ☐ To share a spiritual life
- ☐ To be remembered with calls and acknowledgments when apart
- ☐ To feel he will plan and structure his activities to include me
- ☐ For appropriate tenderness, politeness and support when interacting with the world
- ☐ To share fun, joy, and laughter
- ☐ To know that he will stand by me in times of distress and conflict
- ☐ To feel he will rally to my aid when needed
- ☐ To feel supported by him
- ☐ To know he is loyal and committed
- ☐ To know our relationship will not be put at risk because of any disagreements
- ☐ To know he is my soft place to land
- ☐ Anything else? _____

Does this make it easier to answer the questions at the top of this form? Can you add specific details?

Is He the Right Match for Me?

What do you really want in a marriage—in general?

Before evaluating a specific relationship, review what you learned about yourself in completing the self-discovery form, "My Relationship Needs?"

➢ What are the things I **must** and **should** have to be happy in a marriage?

_____
_____
_____
_____

➢ What are the things I **must NOT** have to be happy in a marriage?

_____
_____
_____
_____

What does he really want in a marriage?

What have you learned about him? **Do NOT ask him directly!** Read "Why He Stopped Calling" (Chapter Four) for tips on how to learn about him.

_____
_____
_____

➤ What are the things you believe he **must have** to be happy in a marriage?

_____
_____
_____

➤ What are the things you believe he **must NOT** have to be happy in a marriage?

_____
_____
_____

Who do you have to become in order to attract and keep this man of God?

It is easy to make a list of what everyone else should be, but you need to know how you should be. Are you working on yourself or sitting back and waiting on God to fix you?)

Are you that person right now, or do you have some work to do?

➤ Do you understand the needs of this potential man of God?

➤ Can you meet those needs? Without denying your own?

➤ Are your goals, interests and values mutually aligned or ?

If you are NOT sure about any of these things, review and apply what you learned in Chapters One and Two.

List of Tips

Why This Book?

 **Unmarried Women:** Be sure to read the parts for married women, too. The seeds of issues in marriages are present in dating relationships. Learn ways to recognize these issues now and avoid planting the seeds. (p. 11)

 **Married Women:** Be sure to read the parts for unmarried women, too, because the roots of issues in marriages are present in dating relationships. Many of the tips and techniques for them will help you to understand how you got to where you are now and how to understand your man, yourself, and your relationship better. (p. 11)

Relationship Changes in Today's Church

 There are men out there who are living holy and faithful to God's word. They are NOT to be placed on a pedestal, because they do make mistakes, although often unknowingly. It will not be where these men of God live at their core. (p. 25)

Happily Single?

 Requirements and deal breakers often go out the window when there is "chemistry" in a relationship. This is why attraction is emotional and not rational. (p. 40)

A MAN OF GOD *is Still* A MAN

Chapter One: Getting Started

 Most people repeat, react to or escape from the relationship patterns of their parents or others who had influence over them. Often all of their reactions to a relationship are actually still coming from these influences, more so than from their true self. (p. 43)

Want a Godly Man?

 Get clear about what you truly believe and are actually practicing, instead of pretending in order to please church peers and family. (p. 51)

Learn His Rules of Love

 When a man starts acting angry or disconnected, this is the time to be reassuring. Start praising him about his qualities. (p. 54)

Chapter Two: He's Still a Man

 Asking questions is great and necessary, but it cannot be excessive at any one time. He'll feel like it's a job interview instead of a connection. Relax and see if you can enjoy his company first. Observe, listen and get a feel for his personality.
Learn your man. (p. 59)

When He Leaves

 Understand this: quality men of faith have options and are usually wondering, *Do I want to marry her or her or her?* So take the pressure off him and yourself. (p. 108)

Chapter Three: Examining Yourself

 A man of God desires a woman who is praised by others for her great character and works. (p. 123)

PHILEMON

Good Person, Bad Mate?

Leave that strong, independent-lady speech behind. Men seek a soft landing, not competition. He likes to solve problems and fix things, so let him! This will make you a good mate for him *and* a good person. (p. 130)

Your "Just-in-Case" Man

To find the love of your life, you have to be ready and available totally. Stop running to that Just-in-Case Man! (p. 132)

To have a successful relationship: Give it your all! Stop running to that Just-in-Case Man! Stay and work it out.(p. 133)

If you have a breakup in your relationship, remain ready and available for a new person. (p. 133)

Honestly Sharing Too Much?

You should not irritate your mate with stuff you should simply keep to yourself. (p. 137)

Traditional Mental Boxes

Do NOT turn your back on a man because he is rushing things. The attraction may be lost and he will find someone else to marry. He is just ripe for marriage.(p. 140)

A MAN OF GOD *is* *Still* A MAN

Negative Thinking

 Our behavior on the outside is determined by the way we feel on the inside. (p. 148)

He Can't Read Your Mind

 No one can read your mind. Share with him what it takes to love you. If he won't do those things, then you will have a real answer about how he feels about you. (p. 150)

Are You a Plus-Size Woman?

 Total acceptance of yourself is the key. Don't' worry about being a plus-size woman. Just be a plus woman of faith. So many guys will love you just as you are now. Know that you are worthy. (p. 159)

Disrespecting Ex Dilemma

 Expecting a man of God to act on issues he cannot see does not work It's how he treats you personally that counts. However, he should recognize and acknowledge your feelings and have empathy for them.(p. 162)

Your World View

 Your husband or potential has his own approach to situations. When you stop making your opinions law, there can be a reconnection, an opportunity for you to form a stronger bond with your man of God. (p. 165)

This Man Is So Immature

 Learn to let some things go for another day. Enjoy yourself, your husband, your children, regardless of the circumstances or what you have to complete or accomplish. Laugh more. (p. 168)

PHILEMON

 A man of God, who is praised and appreciated by others, but NOT by his wife, can be placed in a weak and dangerous position. With these unmet needs, he is subject to great temptation to misbehave for being unfulfilled in his marriage. (P. 168)

 Praise and appreciate your man of God as much as other women, or he will turn to one of them to fulfill his unmet needs. (p. 168)

Chapter Four: Relationship Destroyers

 A man may not marry a woman for reasons that some may believe are insane, but they can be real to him. (p. 173)

The "Not-Me-Too" Syndrome

 Women of faith, if your current or future husband gets attention from other women, be a "ME MORE" type of woman. Give it up for him even MORE than they do. He really only cares when he hears it from you in the first place. (p. 186)

 If a man of God cheats, keep in mind, that this was his decision and NOT your fault. He has to be responsible for his own actions. Any excuse he provides is just that, an excuse. (p. 186)

When Things Go Bad

 **Forgiveness is the key when things go bad.** Let it go, work it out, and keep your husband.

The other option is to leave.

It should be just that simple. (p. 194)

A MAN OF GOD *is* *Still* A MAN

Teasing a Man

Teasing? Be careful. Your relationship may be in jeopardy. He may never discuss this matter with you, but will start acting up, even being cruel, because you bruised his ego. The attraction between you is gone and he will leave. (p. 196)

He Won't Lead

Leadership is not about doing it ALL. Nor has it anything to do with competency. The leader does not have to be smarter, more talented, or more spiritual than the followers. Leadership only requires having the ability to make a statement. (p. 205)

Giving Unsolicited Advice

Here is the key. Don't be so pressed to give advice. If he says, "I've got this" or "I can handle it," just let it go because he is not giving you his permission. He is step-ping up, being a man, and handling things himself.

And, do not take it personally. He's a man, and men like to solve their own problems.

You want him to take the lead? Let him! (p. 211)

Do Not Describe Your Ex

Do not describe other men to your husband or your intended. If you must, then talk about his character not his looks, or body, or his status. It could be the difference between your getting and keeping this man of God, or losing him in a hurry. (p. 214)

Your Characterizations

Keep in mind that people change, especially after awareness. Look at him with fresh eyes all the time. Notice and acknowledge his changes. (p. 217)

PHILEMON

He Is Not Your Girlfriend

Ladies, men are not wired to talk about what they are feeling right off. Most are just not good at talking about personal issues or comfortable talking about feelings, period. Men are just not good at it! (p. 225)

Vague Explanations

It is not about anything you may think that keeps your husband or future husband with you and happy. **It is about the way you make him feel, period.** (p. 232)

Why He Stopped Calling

Understand this: Just because you want to know doesn't mean that you will get an answer from a man that day. If you force it, the door could get shut permanently. (p. 244)

Cheating

The key to making the recovery process faster and possibly helping you get the marriage back on track, is this secret sauce: **Being Genuine**. Yes, sincerity! If your husband can feel your sincerity—that you are sincerely sorry for what you did, he will be more inclined to give you a second chance. Remember, he has to feel it, not you. (p. 249)

Chapter Five: The Bed Undefiled

Lack of sexual spontaneity is frustrating to men. You have to be able to sneak a quickie to take the edge off your husband from time to time or he can become frustrated, creating the conditions for weakness in this area. (p. 250)

A MAN OF GOD *is Still* A MAN

It Doesn't Fit

 One of the most interesting things in male psychology is that if you accuse a man of doing acts frequently, something primal inside of him can actually create the desire to do it or think about it strongly. Therefore, your jealousy can actually make him do or think about doing something he has never thought about before. (p. 2874)

Chapter Six: Love Hints

 If he says he is okay, believe him. Just because you are not okay, are feeling uneasy, is not relevant. He can be silent and happy. So stop asking. (p. 285)

Girlfriend Peer Pressure

 Don't allow your girlfriends or family members to put uncomfortable pressure on you or your husband or love interest. Make him aware of any with such tendencies—before he meets them! (p. 341)

www.ingramcontent.com/pod-product-compliance
Lightning Source LLC
LaVergne TN
LVHW041606070426
835507LV00008B/155